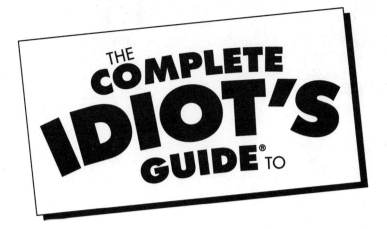

Jerusalem

D0572368

by H. Paul Jeffers

ALPHA

A member of Penguin Group (USA) Inc.

To Anton El Amma, a son of the Holy Land who found opportunities in the United States and had the wisdom to marry my niece Beverly and to become an American citizen.

International Standard Book Number: 1-59257-179-4
Library of Congress Catalog Card Number: 2003115288

06   05   04   8   7   6   5   4   3   2   1

Interpretation of the printing code: The rightmost number of the first series of numbers is the year of the book's printing; the rightmost number of the second series of numbers is the number of the book's printing. For example, a printing code of 04-1 shows that the first printing occurred in 2004.

Printed in the United States of America

Note: This publication contains the opinions and ideas of its author. It is intended to provide helpful and informative material on the subject matter covered. It is sold with the understanding that the author and publisher are not engaged in rendering professional services in the book. If the reader requires personal assistance or advice, a competent professional should be consulted.

The author and publisher specifically disclaim any responsibility for any liability, loss, or risk, personal or otherwise, which is incurred as a consequence, directly or indirectly, of the use and application of any of the contents of this book.

Most Alpha books are available at special quantity discounts for bulk purchases for sales promotions, premiums, fund-raising, or educational use. Special books, or book excerpts, can also be created to fit specific needs.

For details, write: Special Markets, Alpha Books, 375 Hudson Street, New York, NY 10014.

Publisher: *Marie Butler-Knight*
Product Manager: *Phil Kitchel*
Senior Managing Editor: *Jennifer Chisholm*
Acquisitions Editor: *Gary Goldstein*
Development Editor: *Jennifer Moore*
Production Editor: *Megan Douglass*
Copy Editor: *Keith Cline*
Illustrator: *Chris Eliopoulos*
Cover/Book Designer: *Trina Wurst*
Indexer: *Heather McNeil*
Layout/Proofreading: *Ayanna Lacey, Donna Martin*

Contents at a Glance

Appendixes

Contents

Foreword

"The thoughts Jerusalem suggests are full of poetry, sublimity, and, more than all, dignity."

—Mark Twain, *The Innocents Abroad*

Nothing in my life had prepared me for my first sight of Jerusalem when I visited in 1976. Even the beautiful approach to the city from the coastal plain, up into the Judacan hills, did not prepare me for how incredibly affected I would be when the "city on the hill" came into view, the golden dome of the Al-Aksa Mosque glistening in the fading sunlight. There is over the city an air of otherworldliness and spirituality that quite takes one's breath away.

For hundreds of years, pilgrims have made their way to Jerusalem to visit the sites they revere: Jews to the Western or Wailing Wall—all that remains of the Second Temple; Christians to the Church of the Holy Sepulchre; and Muslims to the Dome of the Rock.

I came to Jerusalem, not as a religious pilgrim but as a historian, eager to see the places I had been teaching about and studying. In my history courses at New York University I have tried to give my students an understanding of how a small, unlikely, provincial backwater became so central to Judaism, Christianity, and Islam and is now so central and so vital to the world's political interests. The story of Jerusalem is complex; its history tangled, diverse, and difficult to describe dispassionately.

The holy sites in and near Jerusalem, as well as the city itself, are, for Jews, Christians, and Muslims alike, familiar names on a spiritual landscape, all freighted with the greatest religious importance. But underneath is a city which the author of this book calls "the world's most treasured and embattled place."

It is this dual nature of Jerusalem that H. Paul Jeffers captures so beautifully in this fully rounded and fair-minded portrait. He takes the reader through the long history beginning in the Biblical era and, in clear and lucid prose, explains why Jews, Christians, and Muslims can each claim the city as their own. He takes his story to the present, describing the wars of the last century, the Intifada, and the continuing struggles to win control of the territory.

He also evokes the sights, sounds, and smells of the city—the tiny, winding streets paved with ancient stones, the markets, the food, and the religious holidays. He has eloquently evoked the richness of Jerusalem, past to present, and paints a lively picture of the modern town and the Israeli attempts to make it an international city.

Jeffers knows the city; its story is in his bones and he tells it with clarity and under-standing and, despite the sadness of the story, with humor and affection. This is alto-gether a valuable book, especially for all of us living through the current eruptions in the Holy City. I learned a great deal from it and I am grateful to Jeffers for writing it.

Jill N. Claster
New York City
October, 2003

Jill N. Claster is Professor Emerita of History at New York University. She is former director of the Center for Near Eastern Studies and former dean of the College of Arts and Science, both at New York University.

Introduction

In 1990, the Jewish mayor of Jerusalem, Teddy Kolleck, wrote, "No other city has played such a dominant role in the history, culture, religion, and consciousness of a people as has Jerusalem in the life of Jewry and Judaism."

Those words are also true for Christians and Muslims. "One prayer in Jerusalem," asserts an Islamic saying, "is worth 40,000 elsewhere." And the words of a Christian hymn proclaim there is "no city like Jerusalem." First-century Roman orator and statesman Pliny said that Jerusalem was by far the most distinguished city of the whole Orient. The Talmud describes a city "the fame of which has gone out from one end of the world to the other."

How one city came to be so important to so many people is the subject of this book. You'll read why Jews, Christians, and Muslims revere Jerusalem. It's where the Hebrew God dwelt in the temple's Holy of Holies, where Christ was crucified and resurrected, where Muhammad ascended to heaven to receive the word of Allah, and where people of all these faiths believe that evil will be defeated and the Kingdom of God will be established on Earth. To describe Jerusalem only as a site held holy by the world's three main religions and a magnet for millions of religious pilgrims doesn't do the city justice, however. It's also a city that attracts secular tourists with its historical, cultural, social, architectural, and archaeological treasures. And, of course, for the people who live there, it's home.

How This Book Is Organized

Part 1, "Heavenly Real Estate," explains the geography of a city that because of its history has become the shared symbol of Judaism, Christianity, and Islam. Each of these religions is associated with a distinct neighborhood of the city, and within those quarters are venerated sites and particular traditions and customs that have developed over thousands of years of shared—and often disputed—history.

Part 2, "Standing on God's Mountain," covers the history of Jerusalem from antiquity to 1948. Conquered and reconquered for more than 3,000 years, the city has been ruled by Canaanites, Assyrians, Babylonians, Greeks, Romans, Jews, and Muslims. It has seen and survived Christian Crusaders, Ottoman Turks, and the British imperialists. Today it is the capital of the state of Israel and focus of a half-century struggle between Muslims and Jews for its control.

Part 3, "Next Year in Jerusalem," details the impact that the British had on Jerusalem in the four decades following World War I. It also explores the role of Zionism in laying the foundation of a Jewish state and the significance of three wars (1948, 1967, and 1973) between Arabs and Jews.

Part 4, "Long and Twisting Road," traces the growing American involvement in Middle East politics, as several presidents seek peace between Arabs and Jews.

Part 5, "A Tale of Four Cities," looks at the lives of the people of Jerusalem's three religions as they coexist in a city that attracts tourists from all over the world.

Extras

Here and there as you go through this book, you'll find bits of information in little boxes offering the following:

Holy Facts!

Pertinent facts, dates, numbers, and trivia.

Reverent Remarks

Some reverent—and some not-so-reverent—quotations about Jerusalem.

What Does That Mean?

Definitions and explanations.

High and Mighty

Info about significant personalities.

Acknowledgments

I bow in gratitude to my Sunday school teachers, numerous authors of enlightening books on the subject of Jerusalem, and experts that I had the privilege to learn from during my visits to the city. Thanks go to my agent, Jake Elwell, and to Gary Goldstein for his confidence and assistance to me in writing my second book in *The Complete Idiot's Guide* series.

Special Thanks to the Technical Reviewer

The Complete Idiot's Guide to Jerusalem was reviewed by an expert who double-checked the accuracy of what you'll learn here, to help us ensure that this book gives you everything you need to know about Jerusalem and its history. Special thanks are extended to Doug Stein.

Trademarks

All terms mentioned in this book that are known to be or are suspected of being trademarks or service marks have been appropriately capitalized. Alpha Books and Penguin Group (USA) Inc. cannot attest to the accuracy of this information. Use of a term in this book should not be regarded as affecting the validity of any trademark or service mark.

Part 1

Heavenly Real Estate

In the following chapters, we'll explore the geography of a city whose history has made it the shared symbol of the world's three largest religions.

At the heart of a thoroughly modern Jerusalem, an ancient walled "Old City" is divided into "quarters" with different traditions, customs, and religions. They contain the most venerated sites and shrines of Judaism, Christianity and Islam. Beyond those walls is a vital, energetic, up-to-date, forward-looking, world-class city.

Chapter 1

Shining City on a Hill

In This Chapter

- An unlikely place for a city
- On the road to Jerusalem
- Some ups and downs in history
- Voice from the past
- What's old may be new

"The three rules when evaluating real estate" someone once famously said, "are location, location, location." Applying that maxim, it's hard to grasp what anyone saw of value in the land where Jerusalem sits. It had none of the things that you expect to find in a city. It had no seaport. Although a spring provided water, there was no river. It had no precious minerals to be mined. It was never part of a rich trade route and was of no militarily strategic value. It was also a very difficult place to get to.

Getting Grounded

As you can see on the following map, Jerusalem is located approximately in the middle of the country of Israel. You'll also note that the city is at the point of a bulge into a section labeled "West Bank." What this means—and it means a lot to the people who live there (Palestinians)—will be explained later.

On the eastern coast of the Mediterranean Sea (and with a short southern coastline on the Red Sea), Israel is bordered by the Arab nations of Lebanon, Syria, Jordan, and Egypt. Roughly 8,000 square miles in area, Israel is about the size of New Jersey. In a population of approximately 6 million, about 83 percent are Jews. Israel's largest city, Jerusalem sprawls over 48 square miles. Its population of approximately 650,000 is just under 70 percent Jewish. Israel has two official languages: Hebrew and Arabic.

Modern Israel.

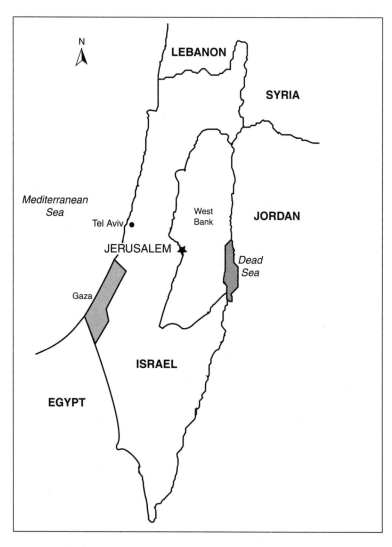

A Note About Time and Space

Although there is a Jewish calendar, Israel does business by the accepted global calendar that's based on a Christian division of time into A.D. (*Anno Domini*, meaning "Year of the Lord") and B.C. (Before Christ). While people who do not attribute divinity to Jesus refer to those eras as C.E. ("Common Era") and B.C.E. ("Before the Common Era"), this book marks time on the basis of the common calendar. For example, 300 years before the birth of Jesus will appear as "300 B.C.," but the "third century" refers to A.D.

To measure things, Israel uses the metric system, but in this book space will be noted in feet, yards, and miles.

With that groundwork out of the way, let's go to Jerusalem!

Reverent Remarks

Eternity means Jerusalem.
—Talmud: Berachot 58a

Ascending to the City of God

The 35-mile road to Jerusalem from the sunny Mediterranean beaches of Israel's second city, Tel Aviv, is all uphill. Heading south and east, it has cutoffs designated by signs marking locations of biblical events. Ashdod and Ashkelon were once cities of Phillistia, from which came the name Palestine (see Part 2). Gaza is the place where Samson trysted with a harlot while Gazites plotted to kill him. On the way to Rehovot are some of Israel's earliest settlements. Beersheba, the gateway to the Negev desert, has a history going back 6,000 years.

Head north from the Tel Aviv–Jerusalem highway and you'll enter the Jezreel Valley and eventually come to ruins of the fortress city of Megiddo, where Deborah defeated the Canaanite king Jabin, where Solomon built stables, and where, some biblical scholars believe, the final battle between the forces of good and evil will unfold in an apocalyptic showdown known as Armageddon.

Reverent Remarks

Ten measures of beauty descended to the world; nine were taken by Jerusalem.
—Talmud: Kiddushin 49b

Farther north stands Nazareth, childhood home of Jesus. Nearby is Cana, where Jesus, at his mother's request, kept festivities of a wedding celebration going with a miracle (his first). He changed water into wine.

As the road Tel Aviv nears Jerusalem, a left turn leads to Ramallah, the present-day headquarters of the Palestinian Authority, and the towns of Nablus and Jenin. Both are sites of large Palestinian refugee camps that have existed since the 1948 war between Arabs and Israelis (discussed in Part 3).

Relics of the battles that took place for control of the road to Jerusalem during 1948 can be found along the Jerusalem road. Hulks of wrecked armored vehicles stand as monuments to the convoys that, in the words of several commemorative markers, "forced their way through to Jerusalem" during the Israeli War of Independence.

As noted earlier, Jerusalem was never an easy place to get to.

The carcass of a wrecked Israeli army vehicle is a monument to the fighting for control of the road to Jerusalem in 1948.

(Author photo)

Behold, Jerusalem!

Suddenly, the steep walls of rose-tinted rock that border the twisting road from Tel Aviv part and ahead of you lies the Holy City of Jews, Christians, and Muslims. It's been there for more than 5,000 years and has always been a breathtaking vista.

The Jerusalem of old was built on a mountain named Moriah. It is separated from Mount Scopus to the northeast, Mount of Olives on the east, the Western Hill to the southwest, and by three prominent valleys.

Reverent Remarks

As the mountains surround Jerusalem, so the Lord surrounds His people from this time forth and forever.

—Psalm 125:2

Kidron Valley

Roughly 3 miles long and deep, the Kidron Valley runs between the eastern edge of the city and the Mount of Olives. Ending in the juncture of the other two valleys, it contained the original city's only water source, the spring of Gihon.

Tyropean Valley

Originally on the west edge of Jerusalem, the Tyropean Valley eventually became incorporated into the city. It's also known as the Central Valley.

Hinnom Valley

Beginning at the Western Hill and linking with the other valleys, the Hinnom Valley became ancient Jerusalem's dumping ground and a place where dead animals (and some humans) were thrown. Another name for it was Gehenna. Its burning piles of refuse came to symbolize the fires of hell.

In Terms of History, No Mountain Can Ever Top Moriah

Someone once said that history is dictated by geography. It's an axiom that certainly applies to the story of the habitation of the place that eventually got the name Jerusalem.

What we don't know for sure is who settled there first, or where they came from. A few bits of dug-up pottery are dated to 1200 B.C. The first time a place called *Rushalimum* is mentioned in any historical record is in the reign of Egypt's Pharaoh Sestris III (1878–1842 B.C.). It was on a list of 19 *Canaanite* cities that the ruler saw as enemies of Egypt. And the word "Rushalimum" was written on a vase that was made to be smashed in order to impose a curse.

The curse must not have worked: Despite the displeasure of Sestris and other Egyptian rulers, the Canaanites held sway over their land for a few thousand years. One group took up residence in a place they called Jebus. We know that spot on the map as Jerusalem. Called

What Does That Mean?

Experts on the period believe that **Rushalimum** translates to "Shalem has founded," meaning that the place had been started by Shalem. He was a Syrian god identified with the setting sun or evening star.

What Does That Mean?

According to the Bible, Canaan descended from Ham, a son of Noah of flood fame. Canaan's offspring included people who occupied much of the territory between the Mediterranean Sea and the Jordan River. This territory was logically called Canaan, and the people who lived there were **Canaanites**.

Jebusites in the Bible, they inhabited it until 1000 B.C. and the arrival of tough-minded outsiders called Hebrews.

Let's Make a Deal

In dealing with the Hebrew intruders who had crossed the Jordan with the intent of taking over the place on orders from their God, Jehovah, the Canaanites didn't stand much of a chance. Right away, they lost not only their prized city of Jericho, but their king, by the name of Adonizedek. Then the Jebusites were dislodged from their abode by a feisty Hebrew king who, as a young warrior, had shown a knack for using a slingshot with killing effect.

According to the Bible, David was directed by God to build an altar on the mount called Moriah on land that was owned by a Jebusite named Aranauh. David could have claimed the land by right of conquest, but the first book of Chronicles records that he chose to buy it from Aranauh for 600 gold shekels.

No Ordinary Rock

By the time David built the altar on Mount Moriah, the area already had a rich history. A multitude of centuries earlier, a man named Abram, later to be changed to Abraham, was told by God that if he left his home in a Chaldean city called Ur for a foreign land, God would make his children a great nation. Because Abraham had no offspring, this was quite a promise. But he eventually had two sons. Because first-born Ishmael was the child of Hagar, a concubine, and Isaac was born of Abram's wife Sarah, Isaac was Abram's legal heir. Ishmael's mother took that as a cue for her and her boy to pack up and leave.

To test Abram's fidelity, God now demanded a shocking thing. He told Abraham to go to a mountain called Moriah and build an altar on which he was to offer up Isaac as a "burnt offering." Abram proved that he was obedient. But as he took up a knife, an angel stopped him.

The saga had a happy ending. Both sons of Abraham would become patriarchs, with Jews stemming from Isaac and Arabs from Ishmael.

King David's Jerusalem

Having wrested Jerusalem from the Jebusites, King David decided to move his capital from the city of Hebron to Jerusalem. His reign lasted a total of 33 years. In that time, he changed the name to City of David and went about improving the place, including initiating a plan to construct a temple to house the venerated Ark of the Covenant and the Ten Commandments, which God had given to Moses on Mount Sinai. God, however, thwarted David's plans on the basis that the king had caused too much blood to be shed, and also because he'd done quite a lot of sinning. With David judged unworthy of launching the project, the building of the temple was delegated to his son, Solomon.

The King of Builders

Work began on the temple in the fourth year of Solomon's reign, but it wasn't his only building project. New cities went up all over his realm, as did numerous public works. In addition, workers dug quarries for the mining of gold, which was then traded with countries up and down the Red Sea.

This nineteenth century sketch of Solomon's Temple appeared as an illustration of the writings of Flavius Josephus.

For a word-picture of the glories of Solomon's Temple, we owe a debt of gratitude to a first-century historian, Flavius Josephus. In a massive volume titled *Antiquities of the Jews*, he recorded the following description:

Now, therefore, the king laid the foundations of the temple very deep in the ground, and the materials were strong stones, and such as would resist the force of time; these were to unite themselves with the earth, and become a basis and a sure foundation for that superstructure which was to be erected over it; they were to be so strong, in order to sustain with ease those vast superstructures and precious ornaments, whose own weight was to be not less than the other high and heavy buildings which the king designed to be very ornamental and magnificent.

The foundation stones served well. As you will read later, the building blocks of the base of the Western Wall are not only the lone remnant of the temple, but Judaism's most sacred artifact.

Solomon's Temple stood until 586 B.C., when it was destroyed, along with Jerusalem, by conquering soldiers of King Nebuchadnezzar of Babylon.

Eyewitness Descriptions

King Herod began building a second temple in 19 B.C. on the same site as Solomon's edifice, and it, too, was the center of Judaism. Once more, we have Josephus to thank for a description of Herod's Temple. But this time it's an eyewitness account, contained in *Wars of the Jews*:

> Now the outward face of the temple in its front wanted nothing that was likely to surprise either men's minds or their eyes; for it was covered all over with plates of gold of great weight, and, at the first rising of the sun, reflected back a very fiery splendor, and made those who forced themselves to look upon it to turn their eyes away, just as they would have done at the sun's own rays. But this temple appeared to strangers, when they were coming to it at a distance, like a mountain covered with snow; for as to those parts of it that were not gilt, they were exceeding white.

High and Mighty
Because Flavius Josephus was born in Jerusalem in 37 A.D. and died around the year 101, he was a witness to the destruction of the second temple and the beginning of Christianity. He was given the honor of Roman citizenship. His books were written in Greek and translated to Latin. Editions were published in English in the mid-nineteenth century.

Herod's Temple stood for eight decades. Set on fire during an attack on Jerusalem by Roman soldiers, it was looted and burned to the ground. Josephus was fatalistic:

Although anyone would justly lament the destruction of such a work as this, since it was the most admirable of all the works that have been seen or heard of, both for its curious structure and its magnitude, and also for the vast wealth bestowed upon it, as well as for the glorious reputation it had for its holiness; yet might such a one comfort himself with this thought, that it was fate that deemed it so to be, which is inevitable, both as to creatures, and as to works and places also.

A Timeless Place

Josephus calculated that between the laying of the foundation of the first temple in Solomon's time and the temple's destruction 1,130 years had passed. From the building of the second temple by Herod to its burning in 70 A.D., 639 years went by. Ever since, Jews have worshiped in synagogues around the world while anticipating building of a third temple in Jerusalem. According to biblical prophecy, that event will be the signal of the imminent arrival of the Messiah.

Until then, all that remains for Jews that tangibly signifies the promise of the God of Abraham that the Jews are "the chosen people" are massive foundation stones of the ancient temples in a section of Jerusalem known as the "Old City."

Reverent Remarks

Great is the Lord, and greatly to be praised in the city of our God, in His holy mountain. Beautiful in elevation, the joy of the whole earth is Mount Zion on the sides of the north, the city of our great King.

—Psalm 48:1–2

A city, the fame of which has gone out from one end of the world to the other.

—The Talmud

Thoughts on Visiting Jerusalem

In my letter at the beginning of this book, I noted that as I approached Jerusalem on my first visit to the city, my traveling partner said that he was never comfortable being there because he was "painfully aware of the presence of God." The plain truth is that if Jerusalem were not the Holy City of Jews, Christians, and Muslims, it would not rank at the top of a tourist's list of places to go. But even with its reputation as the Holy City, two very famous visitors came away disillusioned.

Mark Twain griped, "There will be no Second Coming [of Christ]. Jesus has been to Jerusalem once and he will not come again." Actually, Jesus had been to the city on several occasions, but even he looked upon the city with some misgivings. "O Jerusalem, Jerusalem," he says in the Gospel of Matthew 23:37, "thou that killest the prophets, and stonest them which are sent to thee." The playwright George Bernard Shaw, who found little to admire in anything or anyone except himself, wound up a tour of Jerusalem by advising, "Do not bother to stop here, it isn't genuine." Shaw had a point. What you see in Jerusalem isn't always what you might have been led to think it is. This is especially true for the Old City.

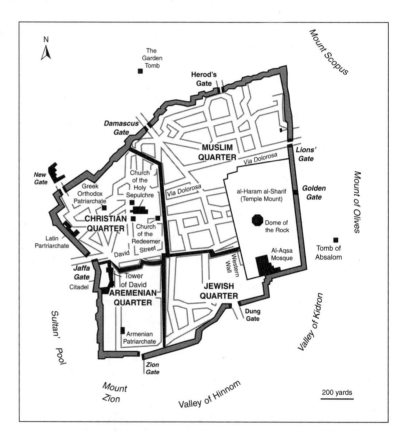

The Old City, showing walls, gates, and religious "quarters."

Most visitors to Jerusalem arrive with the mistaken impression that the walled section in the eastern part of the city is really the ancient biblical Jerusalem. The truth is that many spots that are represented as the actual places of biblical events can't be proved as such. For example, the walls and gates of the Old City date to between 1537 and 1540. They were constructed by one of the city's many conquerors, Suliman the Magnificent, and were built on the lines of Roman fortifications and Herodian ramparts (more on this in Part 2). So if you go to Jerusalem, don't expect that every site you look at was also seen by David, Solomon, Jesus, or Mohammad.

Gateways to God

The walls of the Old City have eight portals, or gateways, as follows:

- **Jaffa Gate.** In the western city wall, it is named for the road to the city of Jaffa, and its Arabic name is Bab-el-Khalil. Translated "Gate of the Friend," it refers to the meaning of Abraham's name, "friend of God," and also refers to the city of Hebron, a holy place for Muslims and site of David's first capital. This gate was known in Byzantine times as "David's Gate" because it stood near the Citadel of David, a fortress that was built long after his death. For a time, it was also given the Arab name Bab Mirhab Daudi ("Gate of the Prayerhouse of David").

- **New Gate.** North of Jaffa Gate in the west wall, it was opened in 1887 by Ottoman sultan Abdul Hamid to provide easier access to new suburbs.

- **Damascus Gate.** The easternmost of two gates in the north wall and the most elaborate of the eight gates, it is known in Arabic as Bab-el-Amud ("Gate of Columns"). From it began a road that led to the city of Damascus, on which the Christian-baiter Saul had a vision of Christ that resulted in a name change (to Paul), a life of converting Gentiles to Christianity, and sainthood.

- **Herod's Gate.** West of the Damascus gate in the north wall, it was named by Christian pilgrims of the sixteenth or seventeenth century. The Arab name is Bab-el-Zahr ("Flowered Gate").

- **Lion's Gate.** The northern gate of two in the eastern wall, named for lion emblems on each side, it's also known as St. Stephen's Gate. Suliman had called it Jordan Gate, taken from the Arab name Bab-el-Ghor. The gate is the start of the "The Way of the Cross" (Via Dolorosa), believed to be Jesus' route to the cross (discussed in Part 2).

- **Golden Gate.** Approximately in the middle of the eastern wall, it has two doors that have been sealed for more than a thousand years. If opened, they would provide an entrance to the Dome of the Rock, which you'll read about in Chapter 4. Muslim tradition holds that the gate was shut to keep a conqueror from entering the city and destroying it. Jews believe that opening of the doors will herald the arrival of the Hebrew Messiah. Arabic names for the gate are Bab-el-Yawba ("Gate of Repentance") and Bab-el-Rahma ("Gate of Mercy").

♦ **Dung Gate.** Toward the east end of the southern wall, the gate is an entrance into the Old City's Jewish Quarter (discussed in the next chapter). It got its unflattering name because it was used in ancient times for the removal of garbage and waste. It was also called Bab-el-Magarbeh ("Gate of the Moors") for North African immigrants who lived in the city in the sixteenth century.

♦ **Zion Gate.** The Bab Nabi Daud ("Gate of the Prophet David") is a portal to the Armenian Quarter (discussed in the next chapter). The name refers to the site where David founded his city, an area that lies to the immediate south of the gate and is called the City of David.

> **Reverent Remarks**
>
> If I forget you, O Jerusalem, let my right hand forget its skill! If I do not remember you, let my tongue cling to the roof of my mouth—if I do not exalt Jerusalem above my chief joy.
>
> —Psalm 137:5–6

Inside the Old City Walls

In the center of modern Jerusalem with its dazzling skyscrapers, noisy streets filled with gas-guzzling vehicles, and people sporting T-shirts, jeans, and sneakers, the Old City seems as out of place and time as a gem of great antiquity set in a gaudy, costume-jewelry necklace. If its ancient stones could speak, they would tell you about conquerors who came puffed up with their own importance but who now do their strutting only in words on the pages of history books.

Listen closely and you might catch the echo of footsteps of the city's past residents: Jebusites and Canaanites, the Hebrews of King David's time, Solomon, Babylonians who sacked the temple, Persians, Alexander the Great, Romans and Byzantines, Turks, and Crusaders from the Christian kingdoms of Europe. In modern times were the Ottomans, the British, and a new Exodus consisting of those who survived Nazidom's death camps and later fugitives from the gulags of the Soviet Union, all coming with hearts and minds set on creating a Jewish homeland named Israel. But you'll also hear an Arab counterpoint, as residents protested displacement as new Jewish settlements encroached upon their lands.

Under the weight of all that history, and in the din from outside and within, you may fear that encountering God, if that's what you've come for, is an exercise in futility. But suddenly you turn a corner and find yourself on the Via Dolorosa, glimpsing Jews praying at the Western Wall, or dazzled by the glint of sunlight on the gold of the Dome of the Rock.

In the following chapters, we'll venture into the Old City and explore the religious, historical, cultural, and other aspects of the unique and colorful Jewish, Christian, Armenian, and Muslim "quarters." We'll wrap up our touristy sightseeing excursion with a look at the modern parts of the wider city of Jerusalem.

The Least You Need to Know

- Jerusalem was a geographically unlikely spot to construct a city.
- The city was built on a mountain and was crisscrossed by several valleys.
- The Bible says that Mount Moriah was chosen by God to play an important role in the development of Judaism.
- A lot of what we know about the first and the second Jewish temples in Jerusalem and other areas of the city's earliest years came from a first-century historian named Flavius Josephus.
- The walls and gates of the Old City of Jerusalem are not as ancient as they appear.

2

The Old City of the Jews

In This Chapter

- ◆ The ins and outs of Jerusalem's Jews
- ◆ Picking up the pieces
- ◆ A wall with a direct line to God
- ◆ Getting in a little sightseeing
- ◆ You can't satisfy everyone

You probably assume from what you've read so far about King David making a deal for a chunk of hilltop ground from a Jebusite named Aranauh that Jews have held title to the land ever since. But the Bible and history books record that on a rather regular basis they were handed eviction notices. The polite word for those who were booted out was "Diaspora"—meaning displaced people. The cruder phrase was "wandering Jew." But all of that changed with the creation of the State of Israel in 1948, the retaking of the Old City and the rest of Jerusalem in 1967, and a massive job of reclamation around the most revered ground in Judaism.

They Left Their Hearts in Jerusalem

Despite a long story of rough treatment by one set of conquerors after another (which you'll read about in Part 2), Jews steadfastly believed in an inevitable glorious day when anyone of their faith who wanted to could go to Jerusalem and stay there. In their religion's writing called the Midrash, Israel is "the navel of the world, and Jerusalem is its center."

Although Jewish settlement in Jerusalem for much of the premodern period was "sparse and patchy," wrote historian Bernard Wasserstein in *Divided Jerusalem: The Struggle for the Holy City* (Second Edition; Yale University Press, 2002), "Jerusalem has nevertheless always been central to the thought and symbolism of Judaism: the resting place of the holy tabernacle, the site of its temple, the capital of its monarchy, the subject of lamentation down to our own time."

Today there are three Jerusalems: the modern West, which is mostly Jewish; the primarily Muslim East; and the one known as the Old City. For reasons that were strictly administrative and to keep law and order, the ancient city had been divided into quarters by the Romans when Jerusalem was the chief city of the area known as Palestine. Today, the "quarters" are "Christian," "Armenian," "Muslim," and "Jewish."

> **Reverent Remarks**
>
> Throughout centuries of exile, Jerusalem remained alive in the hearts of Jews everywhere as the focal point of Jewish history, the symbol of ancient glory, spiritual fulfillment, and modern renewal. This heart and soul of the Jewish people engenders the thought that if you want one simple word to symbolize all of Jewish history, that word would be "Jerusalem."
>
> —Jerusalem Mayor Teddy Kolek, 1990

As noted in the earlier description of the walls that surround the Old City, the doorway to the Jewish Quarter was the Dung Gate. Today the easiest way to reach it is through the Jaffa Gate. The quarter covers about 25 acres. It's bordered on the west by the Armenian Quarter. The Muslim Quarter on the east and north contains the area that Jews revere as the Temple Mount, so-named because it's where Solomon's Temple stood. It is also the site of two important Muslim landmarks, the Dome of the Rock and al-Aksa Mosque (see Chapter 4).

City of Revolving Doors

Because Jews, Christians, and Muslims trace their origins to the biblical patriarch Abraham, they are what today's sociologists would call an extended family. But as in all family trees, the passage of time can widen distances between the branches, often with disastrous results. No better evidence of this can be found than in what has transpired in the history of the Jews in Jerusalem, especially in the Old City.

Beginning with the Babylonian conquest in 586 B.C., the Jews found themselves run out of town again and again. The roster of new claimants, no matter how temporary their domination was, makes a daunting list. In came the Persians (539 B.C.), Alexander the Great (332 B.C.), Romans and Byzantines (63 B.C.–636 A.D.), and the Islamic Arabs. In 1099 it was Christian Crusaders. After about a century of restored Arab control, Crusaders returned and stayed until ousted by King Najim Eddin of Egypt in 1244. Next came the turn of Mameluke Muslims (1291–1516) and rule by the Ottomans.

When the British swept in (1917), Arabs formed 90 percent of the total population of Palestine and nearly half that of Jerusalem.

"Apart from the brief interlude of Crusader occupation," noted the distinguished historian of Israel, Karen Armstrong, in her 1996 book *Jerusalem: One City, Three Faiths* (Knopf, 1996), "Jerusalem had been an important Islamic city for nearly thirteen hundred years." It was also dear to the hearts of Jews. But they weren't alone in believing Jerusalem was Jewish. In *Descent to Suez: Diaries 1961–1956*, Winston Churchill went on the record with, "You ought to let the Jews have Jerusalem; it was they who made it famous."

The Longing of the Children of Zion

After seeing a mosque on land that once held the Jewish temples during a visit to Jerusalem in 1217, the Spanish poet Yehuda al-Harizi wrote, "What torment to see our holy courts converted into an alien temple. We tried to turn our faces away from this great and majestic church now raised on the site of the ancient tabernacle where once Providence had its dwelling."

More than 600 years later, a German Jew, Moses Hess, wrote a book titled *Rome and Jerusalem*. Citing the example of a nineteenth-century liberator of Rome, Giuseppi Mazzini, he urged the Jews of the Diaspora to do the same for Jerusalem. Hess is an important figure because he provided the theoretical foundation of a movement for return of the Jews to Israel known as Zionism.

Reverent Remarks

March forward, Jews of all lands! The ancient fatherland of yours is calling you.
—Moses Hess, *The Revival of Israel*, 1862

But it was a later Zionist, Theodore Herzl, who galvanized the members of the movement at a Zionist meeting in Switzerland by exclaiming the biblical vow, "If I forget thee, O Jerusalem, may my right hand wither."

After a visit to the city in 1898, Herzl had been appalled by "musty deposits of two thousand years of inhumanity, intolerance, and foulness." He went on to declare that if Jews reclaimed the city, "I would clear out everything that is not sacred," and retain "as much of the old architecture as possible," while building "an airy, comfortable, properly sewered, brand new city around the holy places."

How Herzl's dream of a Jewish state with Jerusalem as its capital became reality is described in Part 2.

High and Mighty

Born in Budapest, Hungary, in 1860, Theodore Herzl earned a law degree but gained fame as a writer, playwright (*The Ghetto*), and journalist. In 1896 he published *Der Judenstat* (The Jewish State) and in 1902 authored a novel, *Altnenland* (Old Newland), about a pluralist, advanced society that would be a "light unto nations." A phrase he coined ("If you will, it is no fairyland") became the motto of the Zionist movement. He died of pneumonia in 1904. His remains were reinterred in Jerusalem in 1949.

Gone but Not Forgotten

Since the second century B.C., Jews of the Diaspora were directed toward the site of the lost first and second temples. Taking to heart comforting words in the Midrash ("One empire cometh and another passeth away, but Israel abideth forever"), they made the remnant of the temple foundation the centerpiece of their hope and aspiration that one day it would again be theirs. But there was a stumbling block: Jerusalem was in the hands of the Muslims. When the issue of legal possession was investigated by a commission set up by the League of Nations in 1930, it agreed that Muslims had "absolute ownership" of the Wall, but that Jews had a right to worship there, as long as no one sounded a *shofar*.

What Does That Mean?

Shofar—A hollowed-out ram's horn blown by Jews on the High Holidays. Jews believe that the shofar will be blown by [the angel] Gabriel when the Messiah is about to arrive.

This arrangement continued, though not without periodic disputes, until December 1947. Because of some rather nasty clashes with Arabs, Jews were forbidden to even approach the Wall. Five months later, as a result of the 1948 conflict (discussed in Part 3), the Arabs got control of the Jewish Quarter of the Old City and Jews were prohibited from even gazing at the Wall from at a distance. This ban lasted until June 7, 1967. When Israeli troops took back the quarter, along with the rest of Jerusalem, nothing stood in the way of rebuilding the Jewish Quarter (as described later in this chapter).

Stones that Talk to God

Although the Western Wall is revered as all that's left to see of the temple that King Herod built on the site of Solomon's Temple, the stones of the Wall were not actually part of the temple. They were part of a huge buttress that held up the western side of the Temple Mount. The gigantic stones, a few of which are estimated to weigh 400 tons, were probably cut from a quarry that existed in biblical times near the Damascus Gate. That area is now the site of the Church of the Holy Sepulchre (discussed in the next chapter).

Better than Western Union or FedEx

Called *Beit HaMikdash* in Hebrew, the Holy Temple has always been considered the shortest route by which a prayer would reach God. The Hebrew name for the Western Wall is *Kotel HaMaaravi*. Because the Western Wall is the only part of the temple that remains visible, Jews who feel an urgent need to communicate with the Almighty use the Wall as a direct line, either in spoken prayers or by way of written pleas that they stick into crevices between the stones. The Hebrew word for such paper supplications is *tzetalach* or *tzetel*. Men pray at the left side of the Wall. Women and children pray on the right side, separated from the men by a fence.

A typical scene at the Western Wall.

(Author's photo)

The only visible remains of the Holy Temple, the Western Wall has been the Jewish focal point for prayer for more than 2,000 years. Jews pray there separately or in groups called *minyanim*.

A Troublesome Question

With the Western Wall taken back into Jewish hands in 1967, it was inevitable that someone would start asking aloud, "What might we find behind the Wall?" More remains of the first and second temples? Perhaps the Ark of the Covenant?

The trouble with this question is that to find out what's there requires digging under the Dome of the Rock. As you will read in Chapter 4, as a Muslim holy place it's surpassed only by Mecca and Medina in importance.

Just how Muslims feel about Jews trying to poke around inside the place Jews call the Temple Mount was made clear in September 1996 when Jews opened a 400-foot archaeological tunnel at the western edge of the site. The dig was approved by Israeli Prime Minister Benjamin Netanyahu and Jerusalem's mayor, Ehud Ohlmert. He called the daring move "a great present to humanity." Palestinians saw it as a great provocation. Violent protests throughout the West Bank and in the Gaza Strip resulted in 75 Palestinians being killed and the deaths of 15 Israeli soldiers.

Despite these tragedies, and in the face of Arab resistance to Jewish probing beneath the Dome of the Rock, the belief persists among many Jews that the Temple Mount contains precious relics of their heritage and that they have an obligation to find them and bring them into the light.

New Plan for an Old Quarter

After Jerusalem was reunified in 1967 (discussed in Part 2), the Israeli government put the city at the top of its list of priorities. The guiding principle was that historical sites be preserved, whether of religious significance or not. A ministerial committee headed by Prime Minister Levy Eshkol was set up for this purpose. Its first task was to define the borders of the Jewish Quarter. The reaction of almost all the Arab residents was to move out. As you will read later in Parts 3 and 4, this displacement, along with a later period of building Jewish "settlements" in other areas of the Arab territory known as the West Bank, has been at the core of the violence in the region for more than 40 years.

Wrecking Balls and Bulldozers

First to go were neglected and decrepit structures. Synagogues that had been turned into warehouses and stables by the former government (Jordan) because they'd been deemed "Jewish military positions" were leveled. Also falling to the wrecking ball was a neighborhood called Mograbi. Adjacent to the Western Wall, it was ordered cleared to make room for hordes of Jewish worshipers and tourists who were expected to descend on the city.

Although some planners advocated reproducing the quarter to how it had been prior to 1948, the plan adopted called for developing a new, modern neighborhood that preserved as much of the old as possible while creating an up-to-date area. The government ordered that all new structures be built of a pale-yellow local stone that had been used on buildings since 1917.

Travel writer Dorling Kinersely described the effect of the "Modern Eastern" style decreed by the post-1967 planners as deliberately asymmetrical to evoke haphazard historical development. Streets are also narrow and cobbled with many small courtyards and external staircases to upper levels.

In a recent book titled *Preserving the World's Great Cities* (Clarkson Potter, 2000), Historian Anthony M. Turg described the recent transformation of the Jewish Quarter as "a startling redefinition of the function of the historic city. The modern housing, designed by a number of different architects and all made of Jerusalem stone, is intimate and various in its interpretation of multicultural building traditions. Winding medieval passageways open up to public plazas, where ancient remains are juxtaposed with the structures of contemporary life. From out of a large depression, decoratively carved capitals of the columns of the old Roman marketplace (the cardo) suddenly rise up into view. At their base, one sees the ground plane of the Roman era, which then extends beneath the city into subterranean spaces where the vaulted Byzantine emporium has been restored, with modern shops inserted into centuries-old archways." He concluded, "In an era of continuing conflict, the essence of the Holy City has been reaffirmed: it is a place of unending search for self-knowledge. If ever the holiest city on earth achieves peace among its people, the restored Jewish Quarter provides a model for what the metropolis might become."

> **Reverent Remarks**
>
> O Jerusalem, builded as a city that is compact together.
> —Psalms 122:3

You Can't Satisfy Everyone

A Muslim critic of the changing character of Jerusalem's architecture wasn't so thrilled with the contrast between old and new styles. Commenting on the striking contrast between the usually blue sky and the light-colored local stone of which Jerusalem has always been built, and which has always reflected the bright sun, he wrote, "This contrast between stone and sky is a feature of the city which has been manifest for many centuries. We know that it has certainly been the case since the beginning of the Islamic era, and it was undoubtedly also the case before." But he found in the new Jerusalem a "troubling disjuncture" between the older structures of the Old City, surrounded by superb walls that were built in the sixteenth century, and newer, mainly Israeli, modern buildings which march along the hilltops. To many critics of the new structures, they seem to loom on the horizon, massive, bulky and square, filling space and covering land, often giving the impression of having been dropped there with no respect for the topography, but with attention paid to the need to be high up, defensible, and in a strategic position.

> **Reverent Remarks**
>
> And I will rejoice in Jerusalem and delight in her people; never again shall be heard there the sound of weeping and wailing. And they shall build houses, and inhabit them; and they shall build vineyards, and eat the fruit of them.
>
> —Isaiah 65:19,21.

In *Jerusalem: The Future of the Past* (Houghton Mifflin Co., 1989), architectural expert Moshe Safdie noted that one cannot build with indifference in Jerusalem. It requires either "arrogance" by building boldly as did Solomon and Herod, demolishing the old fabric and building anew as done by the Romans, or showing "humility" by absorbing the past, reflecting upon it, and respecting it with one's mind on the present and future.

The Israeli Government's Official Claim to the Old City

Having rebuilt the Jewish Quarter after the 1967 war, Israel's government made it clear that the changes were to be permanent. It stated, "History—both recent and ancient—has shown that, under an indigenous government, Jerusalem has flourished and its citizens have prospered. The future of the city—like its present and most recent past—must be that of a united city: a city in which all citizens are treated equally and whose Holy Places are accessible to all; a city where each community can preserve and develop its own culture and traditions; a city in which Jews and Arabs—who have lived together within its walls for centuries—can continue to work towards peaceful coexistence, and a better way of life for themselves and for future generations."

> **Holy Facts!**
>
> Residents of the Jewish Quarter have established their own website, titled "The Jewish Quarter of Jerusalem." You can find it at www.myrova.com. It expresses their pride of place and is intended boost tourism, provide a little history, and present a guide to the Quarter's attractions.

You will read in succeeding chapters that this policy has been disputed not only by Muslims, but by the United Nations.

What Would Caesar Say If He Could See This?

In the time of the Roman Empire, the main street of most Roman cities was called *Cardo Maximus*. It comes from the Latin *cardi*, meaning artery. With Jerusalem under control of Rome, this main stem cut through the city on a north-south axis, splitting the city in halves. Like main streets in American towns, the Cardo was lined on both sides by commercial enterprises and shops for the financially well-heeled.

When the government of Israel launched its renovations of the Old City, remains of the Cardo were unearthed. Recognizing a good thing, the renovators preserved it and turned the street into an upscale shopping arcade on Jewish Quarter Road.

Remembrances of Things Past

Not far from the Cardo in Hurva Square, you'll find a graceful arch. It marks the site of one of the most beautiful synagogues ever seen in Jerusalem. Built around 1860 by Ashkenazi Jews from Poland, it had a large dome supported by four arches. After being burned down by impatient creditors, it was reconstructed in 1864 in Neo-Byzantine style. It was one of the largest edifices in the Old City and stood in grandeur until 1948, when it was blasted to smithereens in the fighting that raged around it during the War of Israeli Independence. Rather than put up a new one, the planners of the new Old City chose to build a commemorative stone arch.

Another echo of the 1948 war is found in Batei Machaseh Square. In the southern corner of the Jewish Quarter, its name comes from a group of buildings that were put up between 1860 and 1890 as "a shelter for the needy." The money for the building was donated by European Jews. During the 1948 fighting, they were headquarters for the Jewish Quarter Fighters, a radio communication station, and a shelter for about half the population of the quarter. Here was also where the Jewish soldiers were forced to surrender. During the restoration of the battered landmark, the remains of the Byzantine "Nea (New) Basilica" were discovered. Built in 543 A.D. by Emperor Justinian, with its foundations measuring 328 feet by 171 feet, it was one of the largest basilicas in Palestine.

The House of Rothschild

Also in Batei Machaseh Square stands the Rothschild House. A gift of Baron Wilhelm Karl de Rothschild of Frankfurt, Germany, it's an arcaded structure on the western side of the square. In front of it are portions of Roman-era columns. When the British took over the city in 1917, they also took over the house.

Memorial to the Fallen

Just off Batei Machaseh Square lies a small memorial to Jewish soldiers. Killed in the 1948 War of Israeli Independence, their remains could not be recovered until Israel captured the city in 1967.

Remains of Homes of the Rich and Powerful

Spotting houses of rich people has always been easy, anywhere and at any time. Therefore, if you were a person of limited means walking the streets of the Old City when Herod the Great and his kin ruled the roost, you might have gazed with envy on domiciles that are now part of the Wohl Archaeological Museum. They stood in a section that in Herod's time was reserved for the rich and powerful that was called the "Upper City." Excavations between 1969 and 1983 revealed six houses that were close together on a hillside. Facing the Temple Mount, they proved that even way back then, when it comes to real estate the three rules were location, location, location.

These were places that appear to have been built by that era's Donald Trump. The biggest dwelling was probably that of the high priest of the temple. It had a balcony with a great view of the temple.

You'll recall that the Romans sacked Jerusalem in 70 A.D. Proof of this flagrant act of arson is a fallen, charred beam that was found in the ruins of one these palaces. But this bonfire of vanities didn't consume everything. Among discoveries made during the site's excavation were housewares that every early-first-century wealthy Jerusalemite might desire or require: good-quality tools, superb dinnerware, fancy cups, and jugs of imported wine. Some interior walls were decorated with lavish frescoes.

The Burnt House

Up a stairway and through a series of graceful arches from the Herodian mansions lie the charred ruins of what was probably another priest's home. Known as "The Burnt House," it's a large dwelling from the same period as those found in the Wohl Archeological Museum. Not all of it has been excavated because part of it lies under buildings that can't be torn down.

Evidently the owner of this house wasn't the most popular guy in town. He's identified as the "son of Kathras" in a stone carving. Kathras is the name of a priestly family that's described, along with others, in the Babylonian Talmud in very unflattering language. It reads:

Woe is me because of the House of Boesthus,
Woe is me because of their slaves.
Woe is me because of the House of Hanan,
Woe is me because of their incantations.
Woe is me because of the House of Kathras,
Woe is me because of their pens.
Woe is me because of the House of Ismael, son of Piabi,
Woe is me because of their fists.
For they arc high priests and their sons are treasurers, and their servants beat
the people with staves.

Obviously, they were not very nice neighbors.

The Broad Wall

West of the Wohl Archaeological Museum
on Tiferet Ysrael Street (one of the busiest in
the Jewish Quarter) are the remains of a massive stone wall (215 feet long, 25 feet thick)
that's believed to have been part of a fortification built by King Hezekiah in the eight century B.C. It was constructed to protect a new
part of the city that was built to accommodate
refugees from an invasion of Samaria by Syrians
in 722 B.C. But as in urban-renewal projects
today, existing houses had to be knocked down
to clear space for the wall.

Reverent Remarks

You'll find a reference to the
new wall built by Herod in the
Old Testament. The Book of
Isaiah (22:10) notes, "And ye
have numbered the houses of
Jerusalem, and the houses ye
have broken down to fortify the
wall."

A Church with a Terrific View

The post-1967 war plan also included restoring important non-Jewish places in the
Old City. In keeping with that plan, the remains of a Christian edifice have been preserved. Erected by German Crusader Knights of Hospitallers in the early twelfth century, St. Mary of the Germans was both a hospital and hospice for German-speaking
pilgrims. When the city fell to Islam in 1187, St. Mary's went out of business until the
return of Christian rule in 1229. When Christians were ejected again, the church was
partially destroyed and other structures were built over it. What remains of St. Mary's
on Misgav-la-Dakh Street is a set of impressively high walls that lack a roof. Next to
it is a modern stairway that provides a spectacular vista of the Western Wall Plaza,
Dome of the Rock, and the Mount of Olives.

You Can Never Have Too Many Synagogues

"Synagogue" is Greek for "convocation." It's also the equivalent in the Jewish world of a church building and a mosque. The history of synagogues in the Old City of Jerusalem is a saga of periodic destruction by invaders and hopeful rebuilding by Jews. A poignant example of this is found in a place you've read about earlier: Hurva Square.

Ramban Synagogue

The oldest synagogue in the Jewish Quarter, the Ramban Synagogue dates to 1267 A.D. When a famous scholar and commentator, Rabbi Moshe Ben Nachman, known as the Ramban, arrived in Jerusalem from Spain, he wrote his son that he found few Jews and no synagogue. "Much is deserted, destruction is everywhere, and one Holy Place is more desolate than the other," he wrote. A "ruined house with marble pillars and a dome" was converted into a synagogue. The only one in the city for almost three centuries, it was closed by order of the governor of Jerusalem in 1595 and subsequently became a flour mill, a place where cheese was made and raisins were dried, and a storage space for an adjacent mosque. Restored after 1967, it is again open for prayer.

The Sephardic Synagogues

Sephardim are Jews whose ancestors were expelled from Spain by Queen Isabella and King Ferdinand of Christopher Columbus fame. When the Sephardim built their first two synagogues in Jerusalem, they were the largest segment of the city's Jewish population. The Sephardim eventually built four temples: The Ben Zakka was built in 1610. The Prophet Elijah Synagogue dates to 1625 and got its name because the Old Testament figure was said to have taken a seat at one of the synagogue's Yom Kippur seders. The Central Synagogue dates in its present form to the 1830s. The Istambul was built in 1857. The synagogues, all on Ha Tupim Street, are below street level and reachable by stairs.

What Does That Mean?

Sephardim (also referred to as Sephardic Jews) had fled the Spanish Inquisition at the end of the fifteenth century. "Sephardi" is Hebrew for Spain.

Four Walls Do Not a City Make

There are plenty of other religious and historic sites beyond the walls of the Old City. Some are very close to the ancient walls, such as the City of David and a once-secret underground waterway named Hezekiah's Tunnel. Others are more distant (the Mount of Olives and the Tombs of the Prophets). Like the Old City, they're part of the modern, sprawling Jerusalem of Israeli government buildings and all the amenities of a twenty-first-century metropolis, which we'll explore in Chapter 5.

The Least You Need to Know

- When Jerusalem was taken by invaders, Jews were expelled.
- The present Old City of Jerusalem is cut into "quarters."
- A return of Jews to Jerusalem was the goal of Zionism.
- Restoration of the Jewish Quarter began in 1967.
- The holiest place for Jews is the Western Wall.

The Christian Old City

In This Chapter

- ◆ How the holy sites for Christians were found
- ◆ Walking in the footsteps of Jesus
- ◆ A church of many parts
- ◆ The Armenian Quarter
- ◆ A tomb in a garden

Jerusalem's second-oldest religion began with a small group of followers of Jesus of Nazareth. When they recovered from the double shocks of his crucifixion and their discovery, three days after his body had been sealed in a tomb, that he wasn't there, they were convinced that Jesus was the Messiah of ancient Hebrew prophecies. To spread the "good news" that believing in him was the route to the salvation of the soul, they set out to bring the world to Christ. A little more than 300 years later, a powerful convert in the person of the Roman emperor Constantine put Jerusalem on the map of Christian must-see places.

Cross in the Sky

The story goes that Constantine became a Christian after he had a vision of a cross in the sky and was promised by a heavenly voice that if he made the cross his emblem in an impending battle, he'd win the fight. He did both.

Making the eastern city of Byzantium his capital, he renamed it after himself (Constantinople) and decreed that his new-found religion was the empire's official faith. This decision proved to be the most significant event in Jerusalem's history since King David declared it Israel's capital.

To get all the ducks in a row concerning adoption of Christianity as the official religion of the former Roman Empire (which was now known as the Byzantine Empire), Constantine convened a meeting of religious leaders from all over. At that time, Jerusalem had a Roman name: Aelia Capitolina. Its bishop, Macarius, attended Constantine's meeting and spoke with sadness about the sorry condition of places in the city that should have been hallowed. He described sites where Jesus Christ had walked, preached, suffered and died on the cross, and was resurrected. He also reported that work was underway to demolish a second-century temple to Aphrodite that was believed to stand on the very spot—*Golgotha*—where Jesus had been crucified and interred in a nearby tomb.

> **What Does That Mean?**
>
> **Golgotha,** known today as Calvary, was a rocky hill outside the city walls where Romans crucified criminals. In the Gospel of Matthew (27:33) it's called "place of a skull" because that's what it looked like. Golgotha was also believed to be the burial place of Adam.

A Visit by the Queen Mother

Although Constantine would have liked to travel to Jerusalem to inspect the Christian sites, his schedule didn't permit it, so he sent his mother, Dowager Queen Helena. When she arrived, the demolition of the Roman temple was finished and excavation was well under way in the hope of finding Christ's tomb.

Whether Helena was on the scene for the discovery of the tomb is a debatable historical question. But it doesn't matter. She not only received credit for locating it, she claimed that she had found the actual cross on which Christ died, along with a wooden sign that had been ordered nailed above Jesus' head by Pilate that mockingly announced "The King of the Jews."

High and Mighty

Born around 255, Helena married General Constantius Chlorus, the emperor of the western portion of the Roman Empire (Britain, Gaul, and Spain). Although Constantius had divorced her, when he died in 306, their son Constantine took his place as western emperor. Constantine reunited the empire to rule it from his namesake city. One tradition holds that Helena was born in Colchester, England, and that her father was King Cole of "Old King Cole was a merry old soul" fame. It's more likely that she was born in Drepanum, now Helenopolis, in Asia Minor. Because Christianity had already been established there, she probably became a follower. For faith and works, Queen Helena was canonized. Her "saint day" is August 18.

The Martyrium

With what were believed to be Golgotha and the tomb revealed, the plan was to build a church over them (the "Martyrium"). Finished in 335, the basilica was dedicated in a lavish ceremony attended (on imperial order) by bishops of all the eastern dioceses, with Constantine picking up their travel expenses.

Like most of Jerusalem's early religious shrines, the Martyrium had a rough time of it. Burned and looted by Persians in 614, it was rebuilt, damaged by earthquakes (in 746, 808, 810, and 834), repaired, destroyed in 1009 by Muslims, and restored again in 1048. Rebuilt by Crusaders in 1144, it's known today as the Church of the Holy Sepulchre and covers an area that's only half that taken up by the original Byzantine church.

Before the Golgotha excavations, notes Holy Land historian Karen Armstrong in *Jerusalem: One City, Three Faiths*, there had been no Christian pilgrims to the city, but after the tomb had been found they poured in from all corners of the empire.

The Roman Empire is long gone, but there has been no end to the stream of Christians making their way to the Church of the Holy Sepulchre in the Christian Quarter. Believers trace Jesus' route to Golgotha on a street with the Latin name *Via Dolorosa*, meaning "Way of Sorrow."

What Does That Mean?

Via Dolorosa, meaning "Way of Sorrow," refers to an Old Testament description of the promised Jewish Messiah:

> He is despised and rejected of men; a man of sorrows, and acquainted with grief. (Isaiah 53:3)

Christians associate the description with Jesus on the way to the crucifixion.

In the Footsteps of Jesus (Possibly)

As with many of the religious sites in the Old City, there's a debate over whether the Via Dolorosa is the actual route Jesus took to meet his fate on Golgotha. Nonetheless, the Via Dolorosa has been accepted by countless millions of the faithful and tourists as truly the street that led to Skull Hill.

Via Dolorosa.

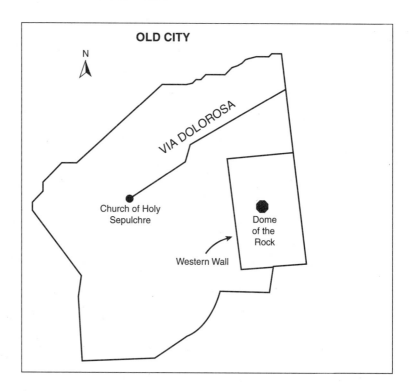

Stations of the Cross

The events that occurred during of Jesus' last hours are known as "stations of the cross." There are 14 of them, and many of them are thought to have happened along the Via Dolorosa, starting a few hundred yards west of Lion's Gate in the Muslim Quarter and ending inside the Church of the Holy Sepulchre.

Each of the following stations is marked with a sign:

◆ **Station 1.** Jesus is condemned. This is supposed to be the site of the Roman fortification (Antonia) where Pilate gave the order to crucify him. A little later you'll read about the Citadel. Not part of the Via Dolorosa, it's proposed as an alternative site for the place where Pilate condemned Jesus.

- **Station 2.** Jesus takes up the cross. It probably wasn't the whole cross, but the cross-beam. Nearby is a stone archway. It's known as the "Ecce Homo" arch because it's on the spot where Pilate is believed to have pointed at Jesus and declared to a bloodthirsty crowd of onlookers in Latin, "Ecce homo." ("Behold the man.") But the arch wasn't built by the Romans until 70 A.D. The nineteenth-century archaeologist who named the arch, Edward Robinson, also found what was left of an archway that was part of the second temple. You'll read about Robinson and two other important men who explored Christian sites later.

- **Station 3.** The place where, says the New Testament, Jesus fell.

- **Station 4.** Jesus looked up and saw his mother, Mary.

- **Station 5.** When Jesus falls again, a Cyrenian named Simon is told to pick up the cross and carry it the rest of the way.

- **Station 6.** A woman, who by tradition is honored as St. Veronica, wipes sweat from Jesus' face with a handkerchief that, tradition says, was imprinted with an image of his face.

- **Station 7.** Tradition holds that it's here on a wall of the city gate that the official death-sentence notice was posted.

- **Station 8.** Where Jesus said to a group of wailing women not to weep for him, but for themselves and their children.

- **Station 9.** Jesus falls a third time. This station is in front of the Church of the Holy Sepulchre.

Stations 10, 11, 12, 13, and 14 are within the Church of the Holy Sepulchre.

A Little Shopping Along the Way

Streets leading to and surrounding the church are jammed with shops, stores, and stalls that purvey postcards, souvenirs, and myriad memorabilia. You can buy items for yourself or as gifts for folks at home along the Via Dolorosa, Christian Quarter Road, King David Street, and Souk el-Dabbagha, which leads directly to the plaza that's the entrance to the church.

Whose Church Is It?

Since the Crusades, parts of the Church of the Holy Sepulchre in and around the building have been shared by the Roman Catholic, Greek Orthodox, Armenian

Orthodox, Egyptian Coptic, Ethiopian Orthodox, and Syrian Orthodox churches. Rights and privileges are protected by the "Status Quo of the Holy Places" and guaranteed in Article LXII of the Treaty of Berlin (1878). To make sure that none of them can be locked out, the key to the entrance to the church has been in the keeping of a Muslim family since 1187. To the left of the main entrance as you enter the church is a bench where the Muslim doorman sat. Until 1967, Jews were banned from entering the church.

Believer or Not, It's Impressive

No matter what your religious beliefs are, you can't enter the Church of the Holy Sepulchre without feeling the full weight of history. In sights, sounds, and smells, it's all around you. If your only interest is history, it's a Crusader structure that was built over the fourth-century Byzantine church that was built on the site of a Roman temple. If you believe in the God of Jews, Christians, and Muslims, it's a holy place because Adam was said to have been buried here. Whether it's true about Adam, and whether it's really where Jesus Christ was crucified, buried, and resurrected, is debatable.

Standing on Calvary

A few steps to the right of the southern entrance to the church, a stairway leads to the tenth, eleventh, twelfth, and thirteenth stations of the cross. Enshrined beneath your feet at the top is the Bible's Golgotha, Christianity's Calvary—it's where Gospels say that Jesus was stripped and Roman soldiers who'd nailed him to the cross between a pair of thieves gambled for his robe. Here, too, after Jesus was declared dead, his mother is said to have held him in her arms for the last time. You can touch the top of the rock through a hole in the floor. Part of the stone can be seen through a window at the foot of the stairs of the Chapel of Adam.

The Tomb of Christ

According to the Gospels of Matthew, Mark, Luke, and John, Jesus was laid in a tomb that had been cut out of rock for the eventual repose of a well-to-do and highly placed member of the temple hierarchy named Joseph of Arimathea. The tomb was found beneath the Temple of Aphrodite in the fourth century, possibly with Queen Helena looking on.

Paces away from Golgotha/Calvary, the tomb is within a chapel that dates to 1810. This is the last station of the cross. You have to stoop to get through a very low doorway. The space is so tiny that only a few people can fit in at a time. A marble slab against the north wall is where Jesus is believed to have lain until rising from the dead on the day that Christian's celebrate as Easter. If you like crowds, try visiting the Via Dolorosa and the Church of the Holy Sepulchre at Easter.

Other Things to See

Over your head in the rotunda of the Church of the Holy Sepulchre soars a dome that has been repaired, restored, and rebuilt often. What you see today is the result of a plan that was approved in 1959 and completed in 1997. Twelve golden rays represent Jesus' original apostles. Each ray consists of three streams of light, signifying the Holy Trinity of Father, Son, and Holy Spirit.

In the back wall of the rotunda is a Syrian Chapel. To the north is the Chapel of St. Mary. It memorializes Christ appearing to Mary after the Resurrection. Opposite the tomb to the east is the eleventh-century Arch of the Emperor (Justinian). It was built as a roof support. Beyond it is the "Catholicon" (Greek Orthodox), from which steep steps go down to the Armenian Chapel of Helena. More stairs go down to the "Inventio Crucis" ("Finding of the Cross"), where Helena is said to have discovered the true cross.

The Mauristan

Immediately south of the Church of the Holy Sepulchre, the area called Mauristan (Persian for hospital or hospice) is a jumble of unnamed little streets, churches, and a busy Greek bazaar, Souk Aftimos, that's full of touristy shops. Founded in the early ninth century by Charlemagne, the section also had its ups and down at the hands of intruders. It was home base in Jerusalem for the merry band of Crusader Knights of St. John of Jerusalem (the previously mentioned Hospitallers). This is where you'll find the churches of St. John the Baptist, St. Mary Major, and Church of the Redeemer (a Lutheran church). The latter was consecrated in 1898 in the presence of Germany's Emperor William II and the Empress Augusta Victoria, daughter of England's Queen Victoria.

Opposite the Church of the Redeemer is the Alexander Hospice of the Russian Orthodox community. It contains St. Alexander's Chapel. There are also remnants of a triumphal arch from the time of the Roman emperor Hadrian. Nearby stands the Omar Mosque. Notable for a square minaret, it commemorates the caliph Omar. He prevented the Church of the Holy Sepulchre from falling into Muslim control in 638. The mosque was built in 1193 by Apldal Ali, the son of Saladin.

Tucked into the Mauristan are covered markets that make up the main bazaar of Jerusalem. It's a souvenir-hunter's paradise in which the unwary visitor who doesn't know how to haggle over prices is almost certainly going to be overcharged. One guide book noted, "Daunting in their dimness and size and in the massed quantity of goods in small shops, they epitomize the market of an oriental town." These quaint attractions are squeezed into three parallel streets connected by a warren of alleys. Once upon a time, they were Crusader streets. Before that they were trod by troops of the Roman and Byzantine empires. Although all this is no doubt exotic to the outsider, for the locals the souk, or marketplace, is the equivalent of a combined American shopping mall and supermarket. (More on souks in the next chapter).

The Citadel

What some scholars propose as an alternative location of Christ's trial and condemnation, the Citadel is an imposing fortification. Towering above the Jaffa Gate, it dates to the fourteenth century. It's also called the Tower of David, but that's misleading. David had nothing to do with it. It's believed by some to have been the site of Herod the Great's palace and that it served as the residence of Pontius Pilate when he had to leave his permanent abode on the Mediterranean coast at Caesarea to attend to official business in Jerusalem. It was on such a visit that he found himself facing the problem of what to do with an alleged troublemaker from Nazareth named Jesus.

The Citadel's more recent role in history unfolded in 1917 when British General Sir Edmund Allenby chose to accept the surrender of Ottoman Empire troops in front of its triple-arched gateway. The British remained in control of Jerusalem until 1947 (more on that in Part 3). Now the Tower of David Museum of the History of Jerusalem, it's a recommended starting point for a tour of the Old City.

The Armenian Quarter

East and south of the Citadel, and bordered on the east by the Jewish Quarter, the Armenian Quarter stretches to the southern wall of the Old City. It's divided by the Armenian Patriarchate Road. The jurisdiction of the Armenian patriarchate of Jerusalem covers Israel, the Palestinian West Bank, and Jordan. With about 5,000 Armenian residents, it shares custody of the Church of the Holy Sepulchre and of the Church of the Nativity in Bethlehem.

In part of what is now Turkey, Armenia was the first nation to embrace Christianity (301 A.D.). Consequently, Armenians were among Jerusalem's earliest Christian pilgrims. Archaeological evidence shows the existence of numerous Armenian

monasteries within and around Jerusalem in the
sixth century, and Crusader maps depicted a
well-defined Armenian Quarter (1099–1187).
When the Crusaders were driven from the Holy
Land, there were about a thousand Armenians
in the region. Today there are about 5,000. The
patriarchate is run by the Brotherhood of St.
James, named for an apostle of Jesus.

St. James Cathedral also venerates a second
James. Known as "the brother of Jesus," he was
the first bishop of the early Christian community in Jerusalem and was stoned to death in

> ### High and Mighty
>
> James (the son of Zebedee) was
> beheaded in 44 A.D. on the
> order of King Herod Antipas dur-
> ing a period of persecution of
> Christians. The Cathedral of St.
> James the Great in the heart of
> the Armenian Quarter contains a
> chapel that's believed to be the
> site of the execution. It reputedly
> contains James's head.

62 A.D. A recently discovered stone ossuary (a box containing bones) was found to be
inscribed (in Aramaic, the language of Jesus' time) "James the brother of Jesus." If the
ossuary had been what it appeared to be, it would have been proof that the Jesus of
the Bible really existed, and, according to archaeologists, would have served as the
most important find of all time. But in June 2003, the Israeli Antiquities Authority
determined that the inscription was a forgery.

Also in the Armenian Quarter is the Syrian Church of St. Mark. It stands on the traditional site of the "House of Mark." Believed to have been the home of the author of
the Gospel of Mark, it's also said to have been where the Virgin Mary was baptized,
the place of the Pentecost, and where the Last Supper was held. A second purported
location of Jesus' final meal is the Hall of the Last Supper. Located outside the Old
City in an area called Mount Zion (see Chapter 5), it's on the first floor of a Gothic-
style building that was once the location of a Crusader church devoted to Mary, a
Franciscan monastery, and an Ottoman mosque.

Three Men Who Did Some Important Poking Around

You'll recall that when you were reading about the Via Dolorosa the name Edward
Robinson came up in connection with the Ecce Homo Arch. Esteemed as a pioneer-
ing Holy Land archaeologist, he was an American Protestant clergyman who believed
that he could prove the truth of biblical stories by poking around in ancient ruins.
Examining the Western Wall in 1852, he found what was left of an arch that supported steps leading to an entrance to the second temple that was described by
Flavius Josephus.

Fifteen years after Robinson discerned the remnants of the arch, an Englishman,
Lieutenant Charles Warren of the Royal Engineers, did some digging south of the

Temple Mount of the Jews, which had become Islam's sacred Haram al-Sharif, site of the al-Aksa mosque and Dome of the Rock (more on that in Chapter 4). His discovery was that Herod's Temple had been constructed on rubble that throughout centuries had filled the Tyropean Valley. He also found a Jebusite water system that was promptly named "Warren's Shaft." But that's not what made Warren a significant name in the history of his homeland. Twenty-one years after his Jerusalem digging, he was back in London and given the dubious distinction of being put in charge of catching Jack the Ripper. Failing to do so, and having stupidly destroyed what may have been vital evidence, he felt compelled to resign.

No such ignominy attached to the name of another military figure connected to the history of Christian Jerusalem. Charles George Gordon was known as "Chinese Gordon" because he'd been commander of the "Ever Victorious Army" that had suppressed a rebellion in China in 1871. Twelve years later, while exploring an area north of the Damascus Gate, he gazed in astonishment at a formation of rock that resembled a human skull overlooking a delightful little garden. Knowing the Gospels, he recalled John 19:41. "Now in the place where he was crucified," wrote John, "there was a garden; and in the garden a new sepulchre, wherein was never a man yet laid." With his Protestant heart racing, Gordon believed he'd discovered that the actual site of the crucifixion and the tomb of the Risen Christ was not within the Catholic section of the Holy Sepulchre, but in a lovely garden. Despite evidence that the tombs in the area have been dated to before the time of Christ (9 B.C. to 7 B.C.) the "Garden Tomb" has been a shrine for Protestants ever since. It's also called "Gordon's Calvary."

High and Mighty

Born in southeast London in 1833, "Chinese" Gordon ranks high on the roster of England's heroes. Two years after he'd found the Garden Tomb, he was governor of the Sudan. When its capital city, Khartoum, was stormed by a Muslim force after a 10-month siege, he was killed. His body was found by a British relief force that arrived two days later. Gordon was so famous that when Arthur Conan Doyle wrote his Sherlock Holmes stories, he adorned a wall of Holmes's sitting room at 221-B Baker Street with a portrait of Chinese Gordon.

Christian Shrines Outside the Old City Walls

Although not within the confines of the Christian Quarter of the Old City, the Mount of Olives and its Garden of Gethsemane are an essential stop on the itinerary of all Christian visitors to the city of Jerusalem. The Mount of Olives is also an important location for Jews and Muslims. It has served as a cemetery for Jews and Muslims and is the site of the Tombs of the Prophets, in which three Old Testament sages are said to be buried.

Named the Mount of Olives because it was an olive grove with an olive press, the hill provides a spectacular panoramic view of the Old City. Between the Old City and the Mount of Olives is the Valley of Jehoshaphat ("Yahweh judges") where the King of Judah, Jehoshaphat (ninth century B.C.) is said to be buried. This is the Kidron Valley from which the dead are to be resurrected on the Day of Judgment. Among the myriad tombs and graves is the traditional burial place of King David's rebellious son, Absalom.

Other key Christian shrines in the area include the …

◆ **Garden of Gethsemane.** It's here that the New Testament records that Jesus passed the night before his crucifixion. After praying alone while Peter and the other disciples snoozed, he was met by men who'd come with orders to arrest him. According to the Gospels, Judas betrayed him by kissing him.

> **Reverent Remarks**
>
> Then cometh Jesus with them unto a place called Gethsemane, and saith unto the disciples, "Sit ye here while I go and pray yonder."
>
> —Matthew 26:36

◆ **Tomb of the Virgin Mary.** An underground tomb in the Valley of Jehoshaphat that is believed to be where Jesus' disciples buried his mother, Mary.

◆ **Church of the Paternoster.** Meaning church of "Our Father," it's so named because tradition holds that it's here that Jesus told his followers how they should pray (the Lord's Prayer).

◆ **Church of All Nations.** Built in 1924 with money contributed by 12 nations, it stands on the site of a Crusader church that had been built to replace a fourth-century edifice that had been ruined in an earthquake. Said to stand over a rock where Jesus prayed on the night before his death, it's decorated with 12 domes and the coats of arms of each nation. It's also known as the Church of the Agony, a reference to Jesus' dread of being crucified. On its pediment is a mosaic of Jesus as he prayed, "O my Father, if it be possible, let this cup pass from me."

◆ **Mosque of the Ascension.** A medieval chapel that's now part of a mosque, this is where tradition attributes Christ ascending to heaven after promising his disciples that he would come back in clouds of glory to establish the Kingdom of God on earth.

Caught in the Middle

You'll read in detail later that Christians are not only a small part of Jerusalem's total population, but that they are even a minority in the Christian Quarter. As a result, they worry about what their status might be should a settlement be reached between Jews and Muslims over political control of the Holy City.

The Least You Need to Know

- ◆ The Holy Sepulchre church was built over Jesus' tomb.
- ◆ The Via Dolorosa is said to be Jesus' route to Calvary.
- ◆ There are 14 "stations of the cross" on the Via Dolorosa.
- ◆ Armenian Christians have been in Jerusalem since 301 A.D.
- ◆ British war hero "Chinese" Gordon found the "Garden Tomb."

Chapter 4

The Jerusalem of Islam

In This Chapter

◆ The Muslim Quarter is the Old City's largest

◆ Why Jerusalem is a Muslim holy city

◆ Dome of the Rock

◆ Al-Aqsa Mosque

◆ Shopping and bargaining in the souk

The Muslim Quarter extends from the north wall of the Old City to the southeast corner. It's the biggest, busiest, most densely populated, and poorest area. A fascinating tangle of winding streets and narrow alleyways make it the most Middle Eastern in look and cultural style. Looming over it in gleaming gold is the Dome of the Rock.

Defining the Terms

By now you've read the words "Muslim" and "Islam" quite a lot. Because you're about to find them used a great deal more, this is a good place to define them. "Islam" is the name of the religion practiced by Muslims.

It is an Arabic word that means "surrender." It's derived from the Arabic "aslama" and comes from the same linguistic root as "salam," meaning "peace." Surrendering in Islam is done to Allah (God). The religion of Islam has three fundamental beliefs: oneness of Allah, prophethood, and life after death. Muslims are people who accept the Islamic way of life and practice it. Islam is considered to be one of the three great monotheistic faiths, along with Judaism and Christianity.

Although the majority of Arabs are Muslim, the majority of Muslims are not Arab—Islam is a worldwide religion. The faith's three holiest places are in Saudi Arabia (the Ka'bah in Mecca and the Mosque of Mohammad in Medina) and in the Old City of Jerusalem (Haram al-Sharif).

The Arabs

You've read that Abraham had two sons. Isaac, the firstborn of Abraham's wife, Sarah, was Abraham's legal heir. Ishmael, born before Isaac but the child of Abraham's concubine Hagar, was sent away along with his mother. But just as God promised to Abraham that the children of Isaac would become a great nation, God told Hagar that He would also make Ishmael a great nation.

Although the Bible makes clear that the descendants of Isaac are the Jews, it provides few details about Ishmael's fate, except to say that "he grew, and dwelt in the wilderness," was an archer, "took him a wife out of the land of Egypt," and "dwelt in the wilderness of Paran." Everybody agrees that the people who stem from Ishmael are the Arabs.

Spread across what is now the Arabian Peninsula, Syria, Lebanon, Iraq, the Sudan, and countries of North Africa, Arabs were once mostly desert wanderers united only by their language (Arabic). Those who lived in settlements were called fellahin or hadar. The nomadic Arabs were (and still are) called Bedouin.

The Palestinians

The name "Palestinians" is derived from the Roman Empire's name for their homeland (Philistia). The "Philistines" of the Bible were probably Greek-speaking "sea people" from the Aegean who invaded the land of Canaan around 1000 B.C. Greek historian Herodotus called the land of Israel "the Philistine Syria." It was eventually shortened to "Palaistinei." This was transformed to "Palestine" and "Palestinians."

Prophet of "The One True God"

Century after century, the religion of Arabs and Palestinians was the faith of whatever group happened to be their rulers. But in the seventh century A.D. along came Mohammad, prophet of a new religion named Islam.

Born in Mecca in 570 A.D. and orphaned young, Mohammad was raised by a grandfather and an uncle and grew up in Medina. He traced his ancestry to Abraham's second-born son, who's known in Arabic as Ismail. Under the guardianship of the uncle (Abu Talib), Mohammad earned a living as a businessman and trader. His work earned him a reputation for unimpeachable character and a title, "al-Amcen," defined as "the Honest, the Reliable, and the Trustworthy."

At age 40 (610 A.D.), during one of many retreats to meditate on Mount Hira, he received a revelation from archangel Gabriel. He would experience many more over the next 23 years and recite them annually in the order that Gabriel gave them. Written down, they became the Qur'an (often referred to as the *Koran* in English), the Muslim holy book. Gabriel also presented Mohammad with a mission to restore the worship of the One True God, the creator, as taught by Abraham and all other prophets, and to demonstrate and obey moral, ethical, and legal laws.

Muslims believe that in 621 A.D., following years of persecution because of his faith, Mohammad was transported during the night to Jerusalem to meet Abraham, Moses, Jesus, and other biblical prophets. After leading them in prayer, he was taken to heaven. Having been given five daily prayers to be observed by members of the faith, he was returned to Mecca. All of this came about on the same night. Although he met resistance from established powers in the region, and had to lead armies in defense of Islam, he persisted in his mission. By 630 A.D., almost all of Arabia had been converted to Islam.

After receiving a last revelation during a pilgrimage in 632 A.D., the Prophet fell ill and died in Medina (June 8, 632 A.D.) and was buried there. Within 90 years, Islam had spread through North Africa and into Spain, extended eastward to India and China, flowered among Arabs, and took root in Jerusalem. Sixty years after the death of Mohammad, Islam's presence was unmistakable in the shape of a giant dome marking the stone where Abraham was ready to sacrifice Isaac, and from which Mohammad had ascended to heaven.

Reverent Remarks

Glory be to He
Who carried His servant by night,
from the Holy Mosque,
the precincts of which
We have been blessed
so that We might show him
some of Our signs.
Surely He is the All-Hearing,
the All-Seeing.

—Qur'an 17:1

Dome of the Rock

Called Qubbat al-Sakhra in Arabic, the Old City's most majestic landmark is the first major sanctuary built by Islam. It has survived basically as it was built on a hill the Jews called the Temple Mount but that Muslims named the "Noble Sanctuary" (Haram al-Sharif). Constructed by Ommayad Caliph Abdul Malik bin Marwan (from here on out referred to as Caliph Abdul Malik) between 688 A.D. and 691 A.D., the dimensions of the Dome of the Rock are based on mathematical dimensions related to a circle drawn around the "Noble Rock" from which Mohammad ascended. In Jewish tradition, the rock is the foundation stone and the symbolic base on which the world was created, and over which were raised the temples of Solomon and Herod.

Cleaning Up One Unholy Mess

Muslims took control of Jerusalem from Christian (Byzantine) defenders in February 638 A.D. Following the defeat, the city's patriarch, Sophronius, rode out to meet the victorious Muslim leader, Caliph 'Umar, to escort him into the city. Sophronius invited 'Umar to pray at the tomb of Christ (the Martyrium), but 'Umar explained that if he went in, his very act of entering would convert the church into a mosque. A no doubt grateful Sophronius then led 'Umar to a place 'Umar and his men very much wanted to see: the Noble Sanctuary or Haram al-Sharif, the site where they believed Mohammad ascended to heaven—and also the site of the first and second Jewish temples, called the Temple Mount.

Although Jews had continued to worship on the Temple Mount after its destruction by Babylonians and the Jewish return following the conquest of Babylon by Syria, 'Umar was shocked to discover that Christians who'd come to the city later had been using the Temple Mount as a garbage dump. According to a Muslim historian, Mujir al-Din, the visitors found that refuse and debris "came out into the streets in which the gate opened, and it had accumulated so greatly as almost to reach up to the ceiling of the gateway." To get onto the Temple Mount, the visitors had to crawl on hands and knees.

Deciding that the Temple Mount should be the site of a great mosque, 'Umar built a wooden structure. A later Christian pilgrim wrote of seeing "a four-sided house of prayer, which they have built rudely, constructing it by raising boards and great beams upon some remains of ruins." Although modest in appearance, the mosque had room to accommodate 3,000 worshipers. It stood at the south end of the mount where Herod had a palace. The first mosque is now the location of the Mosque of al-Aqsa, which you'll soon learn about.

Sending a Message in Stone

Fifty years after 'Umar chose the Temple Mount for a mosque, the modest structure was almost embarrassing in comparison to the magnificence of the city's Christian shrines. To correct this, Caliph Abdul Malik decreed that a structure be built that would have a dome that surpassed the Christian domes and with a grandeur that asserted Islam as the true faith. And it would stand on the site of the Jews' destroyed temple, where Mohammad was believed to have ascended to heaven. An inscription over the arches of the inner arcade would say to the "Followers of the Gospel" of the New Testament that "Christ Jesus, son of Mary, was but God's apostle" and "a soul created by Him"; and that God is not "a trinity." It went on to warn Christians to "desist" from saying so for their "own good"; and that "God is but one God: utterly remote is He in his glory from having a son."

The Dome of the Rock has become as identified with Jerusalem as the dome of St. Peter's is to Rome, St. Paul's dome is to London, and the dome of the Capitol is to Washington, D.C. Originally of copper, the Dome of the Rock is now covered with gold leaf, a project that was financed by the late King Hussein of Jordan. A supporting wall (drum) has been decorated with tiles and verses from the Qur'an that tell of Mohammad's night journey. The dome's interior cupola has elaborate floral decorations and inscriptions that commemorate Saladin for sponsoring later restorations.

A covered walkway between inner and outer arcades is meant to recall a ritual circular movement of pilgrims at Mecca. At the center is the "Noble Rock" of Abraham and the Prophet Mohammad's night journey. It's also said to be the location of the Holy of Holies of Solomon's Temple.

 Reverent Remarks

The dedicatory inscription of the Dome of the Rock reads, "This dome was built by the servant of God Abd al-Malik bin Marwan, emir of the faithful, in the year seventy-two" (of the Muslim calendar).

Holy Facts!

The Temple Mount/Haram al-Sharif covers 35 acres. The gold Dome of the Rock stretches about 20 yards across the Noble Rock and soars about 35 yards above it.

Built between 688 A.D. and 691 A.D., the Dome of the Rock was the first major sanctuary built by Islam and is the religion's third holiest place.

(New York Public Library)

The Muslim Quarter takes up the eastern half of the Old City. At its heart are the Dome of the Rock and the al-Aqsa Mosque.

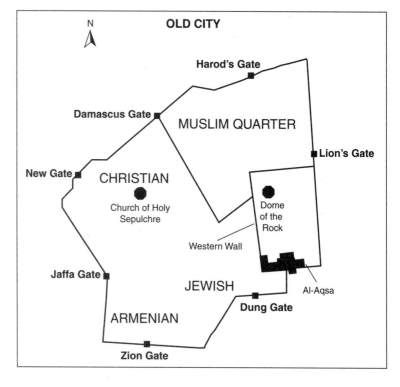

Al-Aqsa Mosque

With the completion of the Dome of the Rock, construction began for a mosque to replace the modest one built by 'Umar. Work was completed by Abdul Malik ibn Marwan's son, al-Walid, in 705. It was called Majidal-Aqsa Mosque. It was largely reconstructed in 1033 by the Khalif al-Hdahir and has been modified several times since then.

Some of the changes in the mosque were made by Crusaders—among them was the addition of a porch. The Knights Templar used the building as their headquarters. The twentieth-century Italian dictator Benito Mussolini donated marble columns. The late Egyptian king Farouk paid to have the ceiling painted.

A fully functioning place of worship that accommodates thousands of Muslims during Friday prayers, the mosque stands directly over the Western Wall. You'll read in Part 4 that the proximity of the two religious sites has resulted in violent clashes between Jews praying at the Western Wall and Muslims leaving Friday prayers.

Holy Facts!

While Jews still call the area surrounding the Dome of the Rock and al-Aqsa Mosque the Temple Mount, to Muslims it's al-Haram al-Sharif, meaning "The Noble Sanctuary," or Haram for short. Because it's elevated, it is has numerous stairway entrances. They're named the Gate of the Prophet, Gate of Repentance, Gate of Mercy, Gate of the Tribes, the Gate of the Divine Presence, Gate of David, and the Gate of Remission.

Four Smaller Domes

Dome of the Chain, directly east of Dome of the Rock, was also built by Abdul Malik ibn Marwan. It marks the exact center of the Noble Sanctuary. It may have been a treasury, hence the need for a chain to control entry. There's also a legend that anyone who told a lie while holding the chain would be struck dead by lightning. Dome of the Miraj commemorates the Prophet's ascension. He is also recalled by the Dome of the Prophet. Others are the Dome of al-Nahawiah, built in 1207 as a school of literature, and the Dome of Hebronite, erected in the nineteenth century.

Solomon's Stables

Subterranean halls under the southeastern corner of the Temple Mount/Haram al-Sharif may or may not have been stables for King Solomon's horses. They certainly were used by Crusaders for that purpose. Since that time, the space has been used for storage. But recent work to convert the area into a mosque led to alarm on the part of the government of Israel concerning a bulge in the wall that seemed to threaten structural integrity of that section of the Old City wall. In 2002, Jerusalem mayor Ehud Olmert warned, "It could collapse." Dismissing this concern, the director of the Islamic religious authority that oversees the Mount/Haram, Adnan Husseini, replied, "This bulge is under our monitoring since the 1970s and has neither grown nor shifted in 30 years."

A Plan that Might Have Started a Third World War

Following the takeover of all of Jerusalem by Israel in the Six-Day War of 1967 and Israel's victory in the Yom Kippur War of 1973 (discussed in Part 3), some Jews believed that the promised Messiah was about to arrive and that the third temple would soon be built. Convinced that all that stood in the way of these prophesied events was the Dome of the Rock, a few zealots decided to take the matter into their own hands and hasten the Messiah's coming by blowing it up. Masterminds of the plot were Yehuda Etzion and explosives expert Menachem Livini. But when they were ready to act in 1982, they were unable to find a rabbi who was willing to give a blessing to the plot, so they called it off. Students of a Cold War—in which the United States backed Israel and the Soviet Union supported the Palestinians—agree that if the bomb plot had succeeded, the result could have been World War III.

Holy Facts!

On the night of April 17, 1910, an English explorer named Montagu Brownlow Parker decided to check out a rumor that a treasure was buried in vaults beneath the Noble Rock. As he began digging, the noise woke a Muslim attendant. Rushing to investigate, he found Parker flailing at the stone with a pickax. Infuriated Muslims expressed their outrage by rioting for four days.

Museum of Islamic Art

Occupying a Crusader-era refectory of the Knights Templar, the Museum of Islamic Art is west of the al-Aqsa Mosque and to the right of a stairway that flanks the Western Wall. Its collection is largely from the Middle Ages. It includes textiles, ceramics, weaponry, and many old copies of the Qur'an in Islamic calligraphy. The museum also contains fifteenth-century doors from the Dome of the Rock and part of an eighth-century carved-cedar ceiling of the al-Aqsa.

Time Out from Religion and Politics to Do Some Shopping

The main entrance to the Muslim Quarter is the Damascus Gate in the north wall of the Old City (Bab al-Amud in Arabic and Sha'ar Shekhem in Hebrew). The biggest, most lavishly decorated, and once the most heavily fortified of the city's gates, it's also the one that's been most closely examined by archaeologists. A recent travel guide described the Damascus Gate entrance as a place where the city's eastern half seems to converge in a melee of pilgrims, shoppers, and tourists steaming in and out of the Old City past assorted beggars, street traders, and moneychangers. There are also a number of cafés for watching these comings and goings. On Fridays and Saturdays, and on Jewish and Muslims holidays, this gateway is jammed with worshipers on their way to either the Western Wall or al-Aqsa via Tariq al-Wad, meaning "road that leads to a wad" (valley). In this case it's the Tyropean Valley, running to the southeast through the heart of the city.

About halfway to the Western Wall/al-Aqsa Mosque, the street intersects the Via Dolorosa. To the consternation of Muslims, it's an area into which Israelis—most notably Ariel Sharon—began moving and establishing homes. A former defense minister who became the prime minister in 2001, Sharon settled into an apartment in the heart of the Muslim Quarter in December 1987. He did so in keeping with a new and controversial Israeli policy of establishing "settlements" in Muslim areas that you'll read more about in Part 4. You'll also see how Sharon purposely infuriated Muslims by entering the Noble Sanctuary to demonstrate Israel's claim to all of Jerusalem.

But for now, as the headline of this section notes, we're setting aside politics and religion to do a little shopping in an age-old institution in Jerusalem and in every town and city of the whole Arab world. If you've seen the movie *Casablanca* (if you have not, where have you been all your life?), the scene where an Arab is trying to sell Ilsa a lace tablecloth is just such a place. In a region where almost everything and every place usually has two ways of being spelled, it's the "souq" or, the one that we'll use, "souk," meaning "marketplace."

The Central Souk

Despite a disappointingly unromantic name, Central Souk looks as though it were built as a set for an Indiana Jones movie. It consists of three parallel, covered, narrow streets and has been a market since Roman and Byzantine times, when it was part of the Cardo. At the intersection of David and Chain streets, it offers mostly clothing and souvenirs. You'll also find Palestinian Arabs selling posters and pictures of PLO leader Yasser Arafat and other Arab leaders.

A Souk for Every Desire

Souk al-Attarin was originally a perfume market, but it now offers mostly clothing. To the west is a meat market (Souk al-Lakhamin). If your recipe calls for a sheep's head, this is where to go. The market was restored in the 1970s.

Souk Khan al-Zeit, separating the Muslim and Christian quarters, is the Old City's busiest shopping street. If you have a sweet tooth, this bakery-filled souk is for you, but you can also pick up whatever you need for the main course. And if cooking's not your thing, there are lots of restaurants. Farther along the market you can buy clothing, shoes, tools, electrical supplies, audio and video tapes, kitchen utensils, and the ever-present souvenirs.

Souk al-Qattanin (Cotton Merchant's Market) connects al-Wad Road and dates to the fourteenth century, when Jerusalem was under the control of Mamelukes. Built on orders of Sultan al-Nasir Muhammad on the site of an old Crusader marketplace, it catered to textile traders from the east. The sultan also ordered a new gate to the Haram, Bab al-Qattanin. Many of the shops have living quarters above them.

Other Places to Part with Money

David Street Market is devoted almost wholly to tourists. Located on the way to the Via Dolorosa and the Church of the Holy Sepulchre, it is where Christians can buy olive-wood nativity scenes and statues of Jesus carrying the cross. Jews can go home with a menorah of any size. Dome of the Rock trinkets also proliferate.

Christian Quarter Road is yet another venue for souvenirs, as well as for Palestinian handicrafts—from carpets to pillows, Hebron glass, and leather goods. The road runs along the western side of the Holy Sepulchre and borders the Muristan, another shopping section.

The Art of Haggling

With few exceptions, such as buying a new car or wheeling-and-dealing at a flea market, bargaining is not an American custom. In the souk, it's the only way. Bargaining is traditionally a highly ritualized affair in which haggling means more than getting a cheap price.

As part of the ritual, a shop owner may invite you to have a cup of tea or coffee. You may be in a hurry, but you should not appear to be in a rush to close a deal. Patience generally results in both parties being happy. And although an offer of a lower price may seem to have insulted the merchant, rest assured that it hasn't. Finally, don't concern yourself with what currency to pay with. No one's going to refuse to take the almighty American dollar. In fact, offering bucks may get you a nice discount.

Reading, Writing, and Religion: The Madrasas

You'll find Islamic schools or colleges, called madrasas ("places for learning"), wherever there's a Muslim community. Like Roman Catholic parochial schools and the yeshivas of Jews, they combine basics of reading, writing, arithmetic, and other worldly subjects with religious instruction. In the present period of tensions between the Judaic-Christian West and the Islamic world, some critics of madrasas allege that they are used to inflame students against the West, particularly against the United States, and that madrasas have become schools for terrorists.

> **Holy Facts!**
>
> Madrasas trace their origins to Mohammad, who said "it is the duty of every Muslim man and woman to seek education." Under his influence, Arabs were encouraged to pursue knowledge for its own sake. Among the early elementary educational institutions were mosque schools founded by the Prophet. He taught in the mosque surrounded by a haiqa (circle) of listeners and sent teachers to the various tribes to instruct members in the Qur'an.

Most of the buildings at the edges of the Old City are madrasas. They include the Ashrafyya, built in 1482; the Uthmantyya; the triple-domed Isardiyya and adjacent Malekiyya; and the Omariyya, entered from the Via Dolorosa.

Numerous madrasas also line streets leading to the Old City. One that runs east from the center of the Old City, called Bab al-Silsila, goes directly to the main gate (Chain Gate) of the Haram/Temple Mount and borders the Western Wall. If your interest is architecture, Bab al-Silsila Street is notable for examples of the Mameluke style, but most buildings are not open to the public. Many of the buildings around the Wall have been taken over by the Israeli government for use as lookout posts by the army. The Madrasa al-Baladiya was built in 1380 as a mausoleum and houses the al-Aqsa library. Madras al-Tankizya dates to 1329 and was used in the fifteenth century for tribunals. It's also an Israeli army observation post.

The Madrasa al-Arghuniya in Bab al-Hadid Street was built in 1358 and holds tombs of its founder (Argun al-Kanili) and Sharif Hussein bin Ali, leader of an Arab revolt against Turks in World War I. Others in this street are Madrasa al-Muzhariya (built in 1480), Madrasa al-Khatuniya, and Madrasa al-Jawhariya (now occupied by the Department of Islamic Archaeology).

The African Quarter

Not really an Old City "quarter," what's referred to as the African Quarter is really a section of Ala al-Din Street, also called Bab al-Habs Street (Prison Gate Street). The name of the quarter refers to groups of African Muslims who emigrated to Jerusalem when the city was under Jordanian rule. One of the buildings, the Ribat Ala al-Din al-Basir, was used as a prison by Turks until 1914. Cells around the inner courtyard divided the inmates into those who were sentenced to death and those who weren't.

What's in a Name?

You've no doubt noticed that almost everything and every place in the Muslim Quarter of the Old City has at least two names. This goes for the Muslim Quarter's other two gates. The main one, you'll recall, is the Damascus Gate. East of it is the Gate of Flowers, known as such in both Arabic (Bab al-Zahra) and Hebrew (Shaar ha-Prahim). Previously called Herod's Gate, it gets its present name from a rosette above its arch.

In the eastern wall is Lion's Gate, which leads to the Via Dolorosa. This portal actually has three other names. To Christians, it's St. Stephen's Gate and Gate of Our Lady (the Virgin Mary is said to have born in a house just inside in). For Arabs, it's the Jordan Valley Gate (Bab al-Ghor). This is the entrance to the Old City for people coming from the direction of the Mount of Olives. (As previously noted, the fourth gate to the Muslim Quarter—which if opened would provide entry to the Haram/ Temple Mount and called Mercy Gate and Golden Gate—has been sealed because it's the gate where the Jews expect their Messiah to enter the city.)

It's not the Coming of a Jewish Messiah that Worries Muslims

Because the Muslim Quarter of the Old City has been controlled by Israel since 1967, its Islamic residents have feared that they will be driven out of the area to clear the way for Jews. (This policy of "displacement" and "settlements" is discussed in detail in later chapters.) One Muslim observer gloomily predicted that under Israeli rule the Muslim Quarter was "quite likely to see the clearance of areas of Palestinian residence, leaving only the major historical sites, museums and schools."

Others have envisioned commercial areas of the bazaar and markets turned into tourist attractions while Christian sites along the Via Dolorosa will be retained "so as not to alarm the Western church hierarchies." There are fears that Israeli settlement will increase in the Muslim Quarter, with the main emphasis being the restoration of synagogues and Jewish historical sites. Should the Israeli occupation of the Old City continue, feared one resident of the Muslim Quarter, "by the end of the century we are likely to see an Old City 'Disneyworld' of variously-clad religious men and women and a sprinkling of Palestinian shopkeepers providing an exotic biblical backdrop for sightseers."

When you exit the Old City by way of the available gates, you are leaving behind a Jerusalem of the Bible and many centuries of conquests and reconquests that shaped it. You now find yourself outside the city walls of Jerusalem, in the modern city that's the subject of the next chapter.

The Least You Need to Know

- Muslims regard Jerusalem as a Holy City because they believe the Prophet Mohammad ascended from it to heaven.

- The Dome of the Rock is the first Islamic sanctuary that has survived as it was built in the seventh century.

- Islam's Noble Sanctuary is the Jews' Temple Mount.

- The Muslim Quarter covers the eastern half of the Old City.

- Markets of the Muslim Quarter are called souks.

Chapter 5

The Secular City

In This Chapter

◆ Jerusalem has steadily grown in area and population

◆ New Jerusalem, capital of Israel

◆ Jaffa and Ben Yehuda streets

◆ The Shrine of the Book

◆ Yad Vashem: Everlasting Memorial to the Holocaust

Today's Jerusalem has a significance that goes far beyond its geographical boundaries. It is at the same time the center of Judaism, of spiritual and cultural importance to Christians and Muslims, caretaker of archaeological treasures, a modern secular international city, and political capital of the nation of Israel.

A Little More Biblical History

When King David first made Jerusalem a Jewish capital (1000 B.C.), the area he chose was not the Old City that you've been reading about. It was a section of the southern slope of Mount Moriah and was never in the Old City walls.

Now called the City of David and Mount Zion, the settlement is believed to have covered about 15 acres with a population of around 2,000. Within it are the "Tomb of David" (although he's not buried there) and the "Hall of the Last Supper." (Despite serious doubts as to its authenticity, tradition holds that it's the "upper room" where Jesus conducted a Passover meal with his disciples before he was crucified.)

If you want to see stones that Jesus would have walked on, visit the Ophel Archaeological Garden. Excavations in the 1970s near the Dung Gate are dated to the second temple period. There are stone steps that Jews of Herod's time would have climbed to enter the Temple Mount, including Jesus on the day he barged into the temple's outer courtyard to drive out the moneychangers.

Moving On Up

It was David's son, Solomon, who expanded the city onto the top of Mount Moriah in order to build the first temple. To do so, he had to fill in a lateral valley between David's city and the hilltop. A later king, Hezekiah, widened Solomon's city into the area of the Old City containing the present Jewish and Armenian quarters.

To ensure a water supply, and to deny drinks to soldiers of the Assyrian Empire (701 B.C.), Hezekiah had a tunnel built from the city's spring (Gihon) outside the walls to a huge cistern within the city (Siloam).

A Boring but Important Job

The 581-yard tunnel was an amazing feat of engineering. Two teams of diggers worked from opposite ends with no way of knowing if they were in line with each other. When they thought they were close, they started shouting and dug toward the voices. Breaking through where they were supposed to be, they recorded the success with a bit of bragging. They engraved into a rock wall that "the hewers hacked each toward the other, ax against ax, and the water flowed." The spring, pool, and tunnel are popular tourist sites. You can walk through the tunnel. The inscription was removed, so if you want to see it, you'll have to go to the Istanbul Museum.

Spreading Out

Because Jerusalem remained pretty much the same size and shape for thousands of years, you won't find the phenomenon of "urban sprawl" in the Bible. Although a few venturesome souls settled on the far sides of the walls, expansion beyond the Old City borders didn't get rolling until the mid-nineteenth century. The man who started it was an English Jew, Sir Moses Montefiore.

High and Mighty
Born in Leghorn, England, in 1784 and raised in London, Moses Montefiore married into the Rothschild banking family and became rich enough to retire in 1824 and fight against the oppression of Jews in Russia, Romania, and Morocco. A strict observer of Jewish religious rituals and customs who believed that Jerusalem would be restored only with the coming of the Messiah, he used his wealth to acquire land in Palestine to help its Jewish population develop agricultural communities. In recognition of his humanitarian work on behalf of Jews, he was knighted in 1846 by Queen Victoria. His 100th birthday (1884) was declared a public holiday in Jewish communities.

Given permission in 1857 to buy a plot of land opposite Mount Zion to build a hospital, Montefiore changed his mind. He turned the project into a row of houses for impoverished Jews living in the Old City. Named Mishkenot Shaananim, the suburb (a word that didn't exist at that time) included a windmill in which the settlers would be able to grind grain and make flour. Unfortunately, on most days the breezes were insufficient to turn the sails. Still there, the windmill is a unique and unexpected Jerusalem landmark. Montefiore's houses now serve as a government guest house for artists and writers. Among its temporary tenants were novelist Saul Bellow and artist Marc Chagall. Chagall designed and decorated the State Hall of the Knesset (Israeli parliament) that you'll explore a little later.

Sparked by Montefiore's experiment in suburban living, Old City Jews who could afford to pick up and move out did so happily. By 1880 there were nine new settlements. One of them, Mea Shearim, meaning "Hundred Gates," sprouted half a mile from Jaffa Gate. Started as a colony of eastern European Ashkenazi, it was built according to rules of the Torah and had its own synagogue, schools (yeshivas), and markets.

What's Good for Jews Has to Be Good for Arabs

With Jewish suburbs sprouting almost every year, Arabs of the Old City also looked past the walls and saw no reason why they ought not create settlements that would be less crowded, healthier, and all-in-all more pleasant. By 1874 they'd built five. To the north were Karim al-Sheikh and Bab al-Zahreb. Muersa was a few hundred yards northeast of the Damascus Gate. A mile from the Jaffa Gate was Katamon. Abu Tor stood overlooking Kidron and Hinnom valleys.

A Growth of Christian Enclaves

Due in large measure to the mid-nineteenth-century discoveries in and around the Old City by Christian explorers Edward Robinson, Chinese Gordon, and Charles

Holy Facts!

The Russian Compound served Russian pilgrims until the Communist revolution, when the Soviet government ban on religion put an end to such journeys. After 1917, a hostel that had been built in 1889 was used as a British police headquarters and prison. When the Israeli government purchased it in 1955, it was again put to use as a police facility.

Warren, the Holy City experienced an influx of European pilgrims. Christians who lived in the Old City were insignificant in number and mostly connected to Christian holy sites. They were also involved in charitable and educational work. One of these groups, the Swiss German Brotherhood, opened an Arab orphanage in fields outside Jaffa Gate in 1860. Eleven years later, German Protestants from Wurttemberg built the German Colony south of the city. In the next decade, an American family started a Protestant mission north of Damascus Gate that became the American Colony. Roman Catholics set up institutions beyond the walls. The Russian Compound took care of Russian pilgrims.

Time Out to Count Heads

Eight years before Edward Robinson's 1852 discovery of the stubby remains of an interesting archway that proved to have supported a grand stairway to the Temple Mount, the population of the Old City consisted of around 7,000 Jews, about 5,000 Muslims, and a little more than 3,000 Christians.

In 1896, the estimated population of the Old City combined with the new areas was 28,000 Jews, 7,500 Muslims, and 3,400 Christians.

The following table shows population growth in the twentieth century.

Jerusalem's Growing Jewish, Muslim, and Christian Populations

Year	Jews	Muslims	Christians	Total
1922	33,971	13,411	4,699	52,081
1931	51,222	19,894	19,335	90,451
1948*	100,000	40,000	25,000	165,000
1967**	195,000	54,963	12,646	263,307
1987	340,000	121,000	14,646	485,000
1990	378,200	131,000	14,400	524,000
1999+	433,000	180,000	20,000	633,000

This was the year of Israel's War of Independence
**The year of the Six-Day War, when Israel took over the city.*
+ Estimated totals

Before the 1967 war, Israeli West Jerusalem covered 23.5 square miles. Arab East Jerusalem, including the Old City (ruled by Jordan) consisted of 3.7 square miles. Following the war, the territory of Jerusalem claimed by Israel almost doubled in size. This was the result of annexations of land "exclusively for the benefit of the Jewish population," which we'll discuss in Parts 3 and 4. In 2000, the total population of 646,000 was about 31 percent Arab, with that share growing because of a greater Arab birthrate. In the Old City population, Jews made up about 9 percent.

The following table from the Israel Central Bureau of Statistics shows population distribution in the Old City by quarter in the year 2000.

Old City Population Distribution by Quarter

Quarter	Jews	Muslims	Christian	Total
Christian	200	1,200	3,900	5,300
Armenian	700	500	1,200	2,400
Jewish	1,800	500	0	2,300
Muslim	400	21,900	1,400	23,700
Total	3,000	24,100	6,500	33,700

 Holy Facts!

According to a July 26, 1999, report by the Jerusalem Institute for Israeli Studies, the Jewish population in the previous year (433,000) had grown by 1 percent, compared to a 3 percent increase among the city's Arab residents. Since unification in the aftermath of the 1967 war, the Jewish population went up by 199 percent and that of the Arabs rose 186 percent. The birthrate of Arabs was 32.5 per thousand and that of Jews was 25.2 per thousand.

How Do Jerusalemites Earn Their Living?

As the capital of Israel, Jerusalem's economy is built on government and public services. But in the northern part of the city, factories make shoes, textiles, metal products, printed materials, and pharmaceuticals. Because of the religious, political, and ideological division of the city into East (Arab Old City) and West Jerusalem (Jewish) following the 1967 war, there have been two economies, with that of the Arab section subordinated to the larger Jewish area (more on this in Part 5).

As a holy city of the world's three main religions, the major portion of the city's annual revenues comes from tourists. Because Jerusalem doesn't have an international airport, most visitors arrive at Ben Gurion Airport near Tel Aviv and take a car or bus to Jerusalem. Recently, the Gaza International Airport went into operation. In Gaza City, it's a symbol of pride for Palestinians.

Some sojourners from Italy, Greece, Turkey, and Cyprus come by ship and arrive at the northern port of Haifa. It's possible to enter Israel by land from Egypt (through Gaza) and from Jordan.

Israel's official currency is the New Israeli Shekel, available in 200, 100, 50, and 10 paper notes. The equivalent of the cent is the agorot, available as coins of 10, 5, and 1. But as noted earlier, no one refuses U.S. dollars. In Arab East Jerusalem, the Jordanian dinar is also readily accepted. (Jordan's connection to Jerusalem is explained in Part 3.)

What Might Solomon, Jesus, and Mohammad Think About All This?

Forgetting about modernities such as electricity and what people are wearing when you meander through the streets and alleys of the Old City, it's easy to exert a little imagination and expect that around the next corner you could bump into King Solomon on his way to supervise construction of the temple, or encounter a determined-looking Jesus, with his disciples trailing him and wondering why he'd picked them. You might also ponder what the Prophet Mohammad would make of what's become of the third Holy City of Islam.

But once you leave the Old City by way of the Jaffa Gate, you leave behind a Jerusalem built on faith and enter the world of materialism, which Judaism, Christianity, and Islam warn us not to embrace, lest we imperil our immortal souls. Suddenly, you are in a city of governmental institutions, business, cars, and worldly enticements undreamed-of by the founders of the Old City. No wonder, then, that the city you're about to explore is known as "New Jerusalem."

On and Around Jaffa Road

If you leave the Old City by the Jaffa Gate, you find yourself on Jaffa Road. Running northwesterly and cutting through the heart of the modern city, it's one of three main streets. (The others are King David and Ben Yehuda.) As it name indicates, it goes to the port city of Jaffa. Although it was first developed when the city was under the

Ottoman Empire, it was during the British era (1917–1947) that public buildings were constructed, including the Anglo-Palestine Bank and the Central Post Office. Buildings are only two and three stories high and are distinguished by red tile roofs and carved stone ornamentation.

The first landmark you'll see is New City Hall. Just outside the Old City walls, on the cusp of East and West Jerusalem, it was completed in 1993. Nearby is the old City Hall, with its rounded facade scarred by bullets fired during fierce battles in 1948 and 1967, when it served as an Israeli army post.

The Russian Compound

The Russian Compound is north of Jaffa Road and contains the Russian Cathedral, a municipality information office, law courts, and police headquarters. An old quarry in front of the police building contains a large column that was unearthed in 1871. Evidently it cracked when it was cut and was abandoned where it lay. It may have been intended as part of the Royal Portico of Herod's temple.

The Hall of Heroism is also in this area. In a former British prison, it commemorates Jews who were considered terrorists by the Brits as they fought to drive the British army out of Jerusalem/Palestine after World War II (see Part 3).

North of the police headquarters on the opposite side of Jaffa Road, on the site of what was the Russian Palestine Society Hospice, is the Agriculture Museum. Displays include ancient farming tools and old olive presses.

Mea Shearim Quarter

Meaning "100 Gates," Mea Shearim is home to ultra-orthodox Jews and presents a living model of Jewish life in eastern Europe in the eighteenth century. Like the Montefiore housing development, the homes were built in a row, forming an unbroken facade and enclosing courtyards with communal kitchen and toilet facilities. Once the city's largest private building project, Mea Shearim is, in the description of a travel guide, possibly the "most unusual district in all Jerusalem." Well into the twentieth century, the narrow streets were blocked at night by gates.

Men wear traditional long black coats, knee-high black stockings, and flat-brimmed and fur-bordered black hats. Women keep their hair covered. Known as "haredim," they reject all aspects of modern life: no cars, no TVs, and no photographs. The use of Hebrew is reserved for prayer and religious studies; in ordinary discourse, Yiddish is the language of choice. Observing Judaic law and studying the Torah, they hold that only the Messiah can establish Israel. Therefore, they refuse to recognize the government.

The Knesset

In a city of stupendous religious buildings with majestic domes, the low, flat-roofed house of Israel's parliament, the Knesset, stands in sharp contrast. It combines classical architectural elements that were inspired by the Parthenon in Athens with echoes of Solomon's Temple. Designed by Joseph Karwin and inaugurated in 1966, it became the symbol of the only democracy in the Middle East.

Holy Facts!

The Knesset is divided into several factions which can submit a motion of no confidence in the government (meaning the prime minister), requiring a vote at the first meeting during the week following the motion. As a result of this factionalism, the most successful candidates for prime minister are often those without a clear majority of votes but who can forge coalitions.

Its name recalls the Knesset Hagedolah (Great Assembly) that was convened as a representative council by Ezra and Nehemiah in the fifth century B.C. It had 120 members, as does the modern Knesset. They are elected every four years and choose the prime minister, but the Knesset is free to dissolve itself, or be disbanded by the prime minister, at any time during its term, in anticipation of calling for a new election.

Like the U.S. Congress and the British Parliament, the Knesset conducts much of its work in committees. Unlike the U.S. House of Representatives and the Senate, but very much like the British House of Commons, debates in the unicameral Knesset are often boisterous.

The Chagall State Hall

In recognition that the Knesset is the legislature of a people who believe that their country was promised to them by God, the formal reception hall of the Knesset building was designed and decorated to proclaim Jewish faith and history by renowned Jewish artist Marc Chagall.

His work consists of 13 mosaics (12 floors and a wall) and tapestries in the form of a triptych. They depict Moses on Mount Sinai, the offering of Isaac as a sacrifice to God, the Exodus, the Diaspora, David playing a harp, Jerusalem as the focus of Jewish history, and the priest Aaron facing a seven-branch candelabrum (menorah).

High and Mighty

Born in 1887 in Vitebsk, Belorussia, Chagall attracted attention of German expressionists in 1914 at a Berlin exhibition. Stranded in Russia during World War I and the Communist revolution, he was a commissar for art, but quit the position when his ambitions ran afoul of the local academy and museum. He painted murals and designed settings for Moscow's Yiddish theater into the 1940s. After spending most of the years of World War II in the United States, he went to France to create lithographs, sculpture, and ceramics. Among his other works in the 1960s were the ceilings of the Paris Opéra and New York City's Metropolitan Opera. In addition to the works for the Knesset, he created stained glass "Chagall Windows" (1962) for the Hadassah Hospital in Jerusalem. After a lifetime of commitment to visual portrayals of his Jewish heritage, he died in 1985.

The Knesset Menorah

A giant menorah sits in a park in front of the Knesset building. It is the work of Benno Elkan, a German-born Jew who fled to England in 1933 to escape the Holocaust. A gift of members of the British Parliament in 1956, it stands as a symbol of the nation of Israel and the "continuity and eternity" of the Jewish people. Carved on it are representations of influential people and important events in Jewish history. You'll find out more about the significance of the menorah to Jews and Jerusalem in Part 2.

Israel Museum

South of the Knesset, the Israel Museum was opened in 1948. Its collections include archaeological exhibits and antiquities of Israel and neighboring cultures, period rooms, and Judaica. Its wings also display pre-Colombian and modern art. The Billy Rose Art Garden has sculptures by Pablo Picasso and Henry Moore. The Youth Wing houses a children's museum.

The Samuel Bronfman Biblical and Archaeological Museum

The largest section of the Israel Museum, named for the Canadian businessman Samuel Bronfman, offers exhibits relating to earliest traces of humans in Israel. Other displays offer artifacts dating from 15,000 B.C. to the Roman era, including a life-size head from a statue of Emperor Hadrian.

The Bezalel National Art Museum

Displaying a permanent collection of works by Israeli artists, the Bezalel Nationl Art Museum, also part of the Israel Museum, features paintings by international painters, too, including Cezanne, van Gogh, Gauguin, Chagall, and Picasso.

Shrine of the Book Museum

Containing the Dead Sea Scrolls (first-century manuscripts that were discovered in caves at Cumran on the Dead Sea between 1947 and 1956), the Shrine of the Book museum is below ground level and ranks as one of Jerusalem's most-visited museums. Its central exhibit is in a circular case on the upper level of the shrine, which contains a copy of "The Great Isaiah Scroll." Written around 100 B.C., the original dates to a thousand years before the oldest biblical manuscript. Because the scrolls were found stored in earthen vessels with conical lids, the roof of the shrine replicates that form. (An irreverent visitor might see the shape of a Hershey's Kiss.)

Near the entrance to the shrine, a black granite wall, designed to contrast with the white stone of the dome, signifies the theme of the scrolls. They anticipate a decisive battle between the Children of Darkness and the Children of Light that will precede the arrival of the Messiah.

Bible Lands and Rockefeller Museums

Opposite the Israel Museum, the Bible Lands Museum is a smaller archaeological museum but is not restricted to exhibits of Judaica. Artifacts cover more than 6,000 years, from the Neolithic period to the Byzantine Empire. Geographically, it spans from Nubia (the Sudan) and Egypt to Syria and Afghanistan. Displays are in chronological order.

The Rockefeller Museum used to be the museum of the Department of Antiquities of Palestine. But in 1920 it was renamed the Department of Antiquities of the British Mandate (the Mandate is discussed in Part 3). It got its present name when philanthropist John D. Rockefeller funded the Palestinian Archaeological Museum in 1927. After the 1948 war, it was administered by an international committee of trustees. That lasted until 1966, when the government of Jordan claimed it. A year later, Israel took charge and turned it over to the Israel Antiquities Authority.

Ancient Jerusalem in Miniature

For a look at what Jerusalem looked like in 66 A.D., but in small scale, you need only visit the gardens of the Holyland Hotel of West Jerusalem. The "Model of Ancient Jerusalem" is about 65 feet across. Each of the 1:50-scale buildings is made of the same type of stone and other materials that went into building the original by King Herod. Dominating the panorama is the second temple, as described by Josephus. Movie and documentary makers with a desire to avoid building expensive re-creations of the Old City have filmed it. Others have taken advantage of stock footage that was shot against a background of flames that sent billows of smoke across the tiny buildings to simulate the fire that Romans set to destroy the city in 70 A.D.

Landmarks to Jewish Sacrifices and Struggles

Reminders of Jerusalem's recent history of violence and suffering are found in all parts of the city. One of the most dramatic of these tragic events involved the city's most illustrious hotel, the King David. On July 22, 1948, its south wing was blown up by members of a Jewish independence group (Irgun) that was fighting British occupation. The hotel became a target because it was the headquarters of the British army. The casualty toll was 91 dead and 45 injured, including 15 Jews. You'll find out more about it when you read Part 3. Still in business after more than 70 years (it opened in 1931), the pink sandstone building has hosted kings, queens, princes, deposed potentates, presidents, prime ministers, movie stars, and rock bands.

A memorial to U.S. President John F. Kennedy is found in the Jerusalem Forest park. It's a building that resembles the stump of a tree that was cut down in its prime. Fifty-one columns represent the states and the District of Columbia. There's a bust of Kennedy and an eternal flame. Another honor to the United States, and a symbol of U.S. support for Israel, is a replica of the Liberty Bell in Liberty Bell Park, just south of the Montefiore windmill near the Old City.

Mount Herzl (National Memorial Park), honors Theodore Herzl, the founder of modern Zionism (whom you met in Chapter 2). His simple grave is at the summit. Also here are the graves of former prime ministers that you'll soon read about: Golda Meir, Levi Eshkol, and Yitzhak Rabin. Israel's principal military cemetery, it's the equivalent of the U.S. military cemetery in Arlington, Virginia.

A little way beyond Mount Herzl is a place that is dedicated to a vow expressed by Jews following the Holocaust: "Never again."

An Everlasting Memorial

Created by an act of the Knesset in 1953, Yad Vashem, meaning "an everlasting memorial," is the world's primary memorial and museum to the murder of 6 million Jews in Europe by Nazis and their collaborators before and during World War II. Archives preserve 60 million pages of documents and nearly 263,000 photographs.

This sculpture at Yad Vashem represents victims of the Holocaust.

(Author photo)

Holy Facts!

A principal mission of Yad Vashem is education. Its International School for Holocaust Studies has held courses for over 100,000 students, 50,000 soldiers, and thousands of educators. Courses for teachers are offered in seven languages in addition to Hebrew, and the school also sends its professional staff abroad to further education about the Holocaust.

The floor of a dimly-lit Hall of Remembrance is a mosaic with the names of 21 concentration camps around an eternal flame. Non-Jews who saved Jews from the Nazis are honored in the Hall of Remembrance. More than 16,000 names have been memorialized. Its approach is lined with trees planted to recall men and women known as the "Righteous Among the Nations."

Yad Vashem records the history of the Holocaust through photographs, artifacts, and documents. The chronological presentation shows the progression of Nazi anti-Jewish policies from persecution and ghettoes to systematic mass murder. Displays also present the history of Jewish resistance to the Holocaust, including the heroism of Jewish partisans. Jewish children who perished in the Holocaust (about 1.5 million) are remembered in the Children's Memorial, an underground cavern flickering in the light cast by memorial candles.

The Least You Need to Know

◆ Jerusalem began expanding in the mid-19th century.

◆ The population today is more than 10 times that of 1922.

◆ Israel's parliament is the Knesset.

◆ The Shrine of the Book contains the Dead Sea Scrolls.

◆ Victims of the Holocaust are memorialized at Yad Vashem.

Part 2

Standing on God's Mountain

With such a religious magnetism that it has been cherished as God's mountain and his earthly dwelling place by three faiths, Jerusalem has been the scene of fierce battles over the right of possession for more than 8,000 years. The following chapters cover Jerusalem's history from the Bronze Age to the end of World War I.

Chapter 6

The Promised Land

In This Chapter

- ◆ Jerusalem before the arrival of the Jews
- ◆ What happened when the Jews got there
- ◆ Conquests by Babylon and Persia
- ◆ How Jerusalem became a Greek city named Antiochia
- ◆ King Herod goes on a building spree

Fasten your seat belt, it's going to be bumpy and bloody chapter. It has combat, conquests, brutal enslavement, power grabbing, looting and pillaging, family fights, and a cast of truly nasty characters. In this saga of thousands of years of fighting for military and political supremacy, and on behalf of various gods, the people of Jerusalem suffered invasions, endured blasts of warfare, and saw the desecration and destruction of its holiest places countless times.

God's Special Place

The first mention in the Bible of the lofty ridge that became the site of the city that we know as Jerusalem is found in Chapter 14 of Genesis. Verses 18 and 19 refer to Melchizedek, king of Salem, which can also be spelled Shalim (You'll recall from Chapter 1 that Rushalimum, the early name for Jerusalem, translates to "Shalem has founded.") In Genesis 22:2, God tells Abraham to take his son, Isaac, and go to "one of the mountains which I will tell thee of," in the "land of Moriah."

When Jerusalem appears in the fifth chapter of the second book of Samuel, King David is dispatched by God to "Jerusalem unto the Jebusites" to take their land.

> **Reverent Remarks**
>
> For out of Zion shall go forth the law, and the word of the Lord from Jerusalem.
>
> —Isaiah 2:3

Naturally in no mood to hand the place over, the Jebusites shut the gates and introduced into the history of warfare a device that the world would witness in the 1992 and 2003 Iraq wars: "human shields." The Jebusites put "the blind and the lame" on the walls in expectation that David wouldn't dare attack the defenseless. Instead, David chose to start a siege. When he felt the time was right, he took on the Jebusites in their citadel, beat them, and called the place the City of David (also known as Zion).

As noted earlier, David's tussle with the Jebusites took place in 1000 B.C. But people had been living in the area long before then. The earliest walled town that we know of stood on the eastern slope of Mount Moriah around 1800 B.C.

Feeling threatened by David's presence in Jerusalem, where he called himself king of Israel, neighboring Philistines marched into the valley of Rephaim (Valley of the Giants) in a manner so alarming to David that he asked a prophet whose side God would be on if he launched a preemptive strike. According to the Bible, God instructed David to "Go up, for I will doubtless deliver the Philistines into thine hand."

A Description of the First Arab-Israeli War

According to the Bible, God did more than give David the green light. He handed him a battle plan. David and his men were to get behind the enemy and hide among some mulberry trees and wait for the sound of a gong, "for then shall the Lord go out before thee, to smite the most of the Philistines." The Bible reports only that "David did so." But the Philistines rallied to fight again.

The Jewish historian Josephus depicted a second battle that was far more than a clash between the Jews and Philistines. To use a term applied to twentieth-century Arab-Israeli conflicts, it was "a regional war." According to Josephus's account, "all of Syria and Phoenicia, with many other nations besides them, and those warlike nations also, came to their assistance, and had a share in this war." This time David faced an army that was "three times as numerous as before."

On this occasion the Lord provided a different plan. David was advised to conceal his army among trees known as the Groves of Weeping, but he was not to make a move until "the trees of the grove should be in motion without the wind's blowing." He was then to go out and "gain what was an already prepared and evident victory." Doing what he was told, David led his men in a pursuit of the retreating force to the city of Gaza." Josephus reports that he "spoiled their camp, in which he found great riches; and he destroyed their gods."

First Capital City of Israel

David's choice of Jerusalem as a religious and political capital made sense geographically. It was midway between the northern and southern Israelite tribal territories, as well as on a militarily strategic route running north and south. But, as noted earlier, it was David's son Solomon who built the temple and made the city so important to generations of Jews, whether they lived there or in foreign cities of the Diaspora. Josephus calculated that the temple was built approximately 590 years after Moses led the Jews out of Egypt, 1,020 years after Abraham left Mesopotamia to go to Canaan, 440 years after Noah's Ark and the great flood, and 3,102 years after God created Adam and Eve.

> **Holy Facts!** _____
>
> Historians refer to the era that began with Solomon as the "first temple period." It lasted from David's conquest of Jerusalem until soldiers of King Nebuchadnezzar swept down on the city from Babylon in 586 B.C.

Good Times and Hard Times in God's Mountain City

After Solomon's death (circa 928 B.C.), the Israel that David had unified fell apart. The nation was divided into Israel, in the north, and Judah in the south. The break was in large measure because Solomon wasn't much of an administrator and spent a good deal of time romancing women. As a result, Jerusalem fell into hard times, both economically and politically. (It was now only the capital of Judah.) Because breakaway tribes of the northern half of the country (Israel) had established rival cults, Jerusalem also lost its place as the religious center of the region. All of this left it vulnerable to attack. Remember Hezekiah's water tunnel from Chapter 5? It was during one of these numerous assaults that he had it built. (Details on this post-Solomon period are related in 1 Kings and 2 Kings of the Old Testament.)

The Marauding Host Out of Babylon

Here's a scary scene at the opening of Chapter 25, 2 Kings:

> And it came to pass in the ninth year of his reign, in the tenth month, in the tenth day of the month, that Nebuchadnezzar, king of Babylon came, he and all his host, against Jerusalem, and pitched against it; and they built forts against it round about.

In 597, the Jewish king, Jeholachin, his mother, and the city's leading citizens had been exiled and the city plundered by Babylonians. Then, only nine years later, Jews again found Babylonians at the gates. Our historian, Josephus, put a brave face on Jews who confronted the situation in 586. He wrote that "those who were within bore the siege with courage and alacrity, for they were not discouraged, either by famine, or by the pestilential distemper, but were of cheerful minds in the prosecution of the war, although those miseries within oppressed them also, and they did not suffer themselves to be terrified." Maybe they weren't, but with Babylonian soldiers all around them it was just a matter of time until they'd have no recourse but to give in and give up. They did so after a year and a half. The ruler at the time, Zedekiah, fled and was captured. After being forced to watch as his sons were beheaded, he was blinded and hauled off in chains to die in Babylon. Then the Babylonians commenced burning the city down, including Solomon's Temple.

> **Reverent Remarks**
>
> And they burnt the house of God, and brake down the wall of Jerusalem, and burnt all the palaces thereof with fire, and destroyed the godly vessels thereof.
>
> —2 Chronicles 36:19

Without a temple to worship in, the Jews who were taken away to Babylon had to make do with what they still had—faith and hope for a return to Jerusalem. Liberation came when Babylon fell to the army of Cyrus, king of Persia. Probably to the amazement of the Jews, he declared that the Lord God of Heaven had charged him with rebuilding the house of the Lord God at Jerusalem. The task was given to a descendant of David named Zerubbabel, along with the high priest, Joshua. The work was completed and the temple dedicated "with joy" in 515 B.C. in the seventh year of the reign of a new Persian king, Darius.

Beware of Greeks Bearing Weapons

Even people who don't give a hoot about history are likely to have heard of Alexander the Great and that he conquered the known world by the age of 33. Born in 356 B.C.

in Macedonia, the son of King Philip grew up surrounded by soldiers and had the benefit of learning at the feet of the age's greatest teacher, Aristotle, who taught him philosophy, ethics, politics, and literature.

When Philip died under mysterious circumstances in 336 B.C., suspicions centered on Alexander. As soon as he was king, he informed everyone that he was to be addressed as Alexander the Great. To show that the title was more than self-flattery, he led his army in crushing a revolt in the city of Thebes, taking 30,000 Egyptian slaves.

Three years later (332 B.C., at age 24), he crushed Persia. With a desire to add to his conquests, he set out through Arabia toward India. Along the way, his men captured Jerusalem (313 B.C.). Violent, destructive, and arrogant, they did their best to impose their ways, and their gods, on a city that was populated by Jews who didn't take kindly to the worship of pagan deities. But there was little they could do about it.

An Act that Jews Found Revolting

When Alexander died in 323 B.C. without having named a successor, his empire disintegrated. Part of it was claimed by a series of Egyptian rulers (the Ptolemies). They held sway for 144 years. Then came the Seleucids of Mesopotamia. The most memorable act of their period of control over the city occurred in 169 A.D. It was perpetrated by a greedy king named Antiochus IV Epiphanes. When he heard that the Jewish temple had a golden altar and many other valuable furnishings and ornaments, he raided it and stripped it bare. To make matters worse, he banned the Jews from worshiping in the temple and profaned it with a burnt offering of a pig on the altar. Decreeing that the temple was now to be called the Temple of Jupiter Hellenius, he renamed the city Antiochia.

The Hammer of Jerusalem

The desecration of the temple by Antiochius (remembered by Jews as "the abomination of desolation") triggered a revolt led by an outraged member of the Hasmonean family. One of five sons of an aging priest named Mattathias, Judas was nicknamed "Maccabeus," meaning "the hammer." (Some translate it as "hammer-headed.") He'd earned the moniker because of his superb fighting skills.

Arrayed against Judas and his men were 40,000 foot soldiers and 7,000 cavalry. "And when Judas saw their camp," Josephus tells us, "and how numerous their enemies were," he persuaded his own soldiers to be of good courage, and exhorted them to place their hopes of victory in God, and to pray wearing sackcloth.

At dawn the next day, he led a surprise attack against one of the camps at the nearby town of Emmaus. "So he commanded trumpeters to sound for battle," Josephus wrote, "and by thus falling upon the enemies when they did not expect it, and thereby astonishing and disturbing their minds, he slew many of those that resisted him." When the rest of the enemy's forces fled, the Maccabeans could claim that they'd won history's first successful rebellion for religious freedom.

Judas then turned his attention to purification of the temple. He found it deserted, the gates burned, and the area surrounding it overgrown with weeds. Determined to restore it, he brought in new religious vessels, candlesticks, and stones to make a new altar. When the work was done, he led a celebration that lasted eight days. The event is still celebrated with a "Festival of Lights" called Chanukah (Hanukkah). It's why the giant menorah stands in front of the Knesset as the symbol of Israel.

Be Careful What You Ask For, You May Get It

The next task for Judas was rebuilding the city walls and putting up lookout towers. For the first time in centuries, Jerusalem was free of paganism. But as with most revolutions in the name of one cause or another, the rebels eventually forgot why they'd fought. Historian Karen Armstrong notes in *Jerusalem: One City, Three Faiths* that the Hasmoneans "had become imperialists who were insensitive to the religious traditions of their subjects." The Hasmoneans learned that the trouble with winning a revolution is that the victors have to govern. That's a hard enough job for anyone. In this case the job was complicated by the fact that the winners were brothers. To say that there was a raging outbreak of sibling rivalry is an understatement. Claims and counterclaims to power led to factionalism that lasted until each side came up with the idea of getting help from a superpower.

One of the first acts of Judas the Maccabee was to enter into a kind of defensive treaty with the Roman Empire. But following his death and the demise of the mother of the Hasmonean family, one of the brothers, Aristobulous, declared himself high priest. This didn't go down well with another sibling, John Hyrcanus. By 67 B.C. there was a full-scale civil war. Looking for an ally, John sent out a call for help from Rome.

The Road to Rome Was a Two-Way Street

In 64 B.C., the Roman general Pompey chose sides in the Hasmonean family squabble by backing John. He entered the drama with an army that pitched tents north of the Temple Mount. The battle for the Temple Mount lasted three months. The fighting, wrote the indispensable Josephus, "was full of slaughter," with "some of the Jews being slain by the Romans, and some by one another." Josephus put the death toll at 12,000 Jews and that of the Romans "very few." When the battle was over, Pompey held Jerusalem, and along with it the entire nation of Judea.

High and Mighty

Born in 106 B.C., Pompey (full name: Cneius Pompeius Magnus) won glory as a commander by helping crush a slave revolt led by an ex-gladiator named Spartacus. A friend and ally of Julius Caesar until they had a falling out, he was given a commission to find and destroy pirates in the Mediterranean Sea (67 B.C.). This feat opened up a career as a conqueror that included annexing Syria and Palestine and paved the way for capturing Jerusalem. After Caesar crossed the Rubicon and sparked a Roman civil war, Pompey was on the wrong side. Losing a major battle, he fled to Egypt, where he was assassinated in 48 B.C.

Pompey Does a Little Sightseeing

Even in 63 B.C., everyone who visited Jerusalem was eager to see the famous and beautiful temple of the Jews. Even pagans found it impossible to ignore a building that loomed majestically over the city. But the honor of actually entering the temple was reserved for the priests, unless your name was Pompey. Flush with his victory, he strode into the temple and saw, in the words of Josephus, "all that which was unlawful for any other men to see but only for the high priests."

In a word, Pompey was dumbstruck. "There were in that temple," Josephus reported, "the golden table, the holy candlestick, and the pouring vessels; and besides these there were among the treasures two thousand talents of sacred money." Pompey could have taken all of it, but because he was a pious man with respect for the religions of others, he "acted in a manner that was worthy of his virtue." Rather than ordering the temple sacked, he ordered that it be cleaned and appropriate offerings given.

Pax Romana with a Little Help from a Jew

With the Hasmoneans ousted, Pompey installed an imperial Roman government that would rule Jerusalem for 600 years. Julius Caesar selected the man who would run both the city and the rest of Judea. He chose a cunning convert to Judaism named Herod. Herod was well known in the city the Romans called "Eternal" and therefore was a logical pick by Caesar to run Judea and Jerusalem with the title King of the Jews.

With Pompey assassinated while in exile in Egypt, and after Caesar was also assassinated, a civil war raged for control of the empire between Mark Antony and Octavian. It ended with Octavian winning and taking the name Augustus. Firmly in control of the empire in a world pretty much at peace (Pax Romana), Augustus saw no reason why Herod shouldn't remain King of the Jews.

Herod's dominion stretched from Gaza to Masada in southern Israel to north of Nazareth (the town where Jesus would grow up) and east to the Golan Heights. You'll learn more about the importance of these strategic hills in the story of modern Israel later.

It Was Good Being King of the Jews (Most of the Time)

When Augustus declared that he was divine, Herod wasted no time in building a city that he named Caesarea in his honor. On the shore of the Mediterranean Sea (it's now a Roman ruin and tourist attraction), it had a fine harbor that was made even better by dredging, a huge amphitheater, and everything to be expected in a Roman city, including temples to Roman deities. Herod was not a man to let the fact that he was a Jewish king get in the way of politics. It is not a stretch to look back on Herod as an expert at political correctness.

Keenly aware of Jerusalem's history as a vulnerable target of people with their minds set on conquest, he began (in 35 B.C.) to build a fortress on the northern edge of the Temple Mount. Since Mark Antony had yet to meet his fate at the hands of Octavian before he became Augustus, Herod named the fort the Antonia. (In the unlikely event that you've never seen the movie extravaganza *Cleopatra*, starring Elizabeth Taylor in the title role and Richard Burton as Antony, see it to get a reasonable depiction of what was going on at that time.)

Holy Facts!

During the reign of Herod the Great (37–4 B.C.), the population of Jerusalem was around 120,000. But during religious festivals the number swelled to between 300,000 and 500,000 as pilgrims came from all over Palestine.

Twelve years after work started on the Antonia, Herod began an ambitious building program, including a palace suitable for the King of the Jews in the western part of the city. Although he had a genuine desire to make civic improvements, such as expanding the city and laying out new streets in a grid, the projects also filled an important socioeconomic need by providing work for people at a time when they were suffering from a disastrous drought.

A Demonstration of Kingly Spin

In the eighteenth year of his reign, King Herod gave a speech on the subject of the new Temple that proved he was as consummate at what we call "spin" as any present-day politician. Beginning by saying that he need not speak of all he had done "to bring more security to you than glory to myself," he went on to assert that with "God's assistance" he'd "advanced the nation of the Jews to a degree of happiness which they never had before."

Although the temple that had been built by Zerubbabel after the return from the Babylonian exile was splendid, he said, it was less than the one built by Solomon. "Since I am now, by God's will, your governor," he reminded the Jews, "and have had a peace a long time, and have gained great riches and large revenues, and what is the principal thing of all, I am at amity with and well regarded by the Romans," he intended to re-do God's temple.

Writing about the speech many years later, Josephus cut through the spin by noting that Herod's new temple "would be sufficient for an everlasting memorial" to Herod.

Bigger and Better by Every Measure

Herod did more than replace Zerubbabel's temple. He expanded the Temple Mount and strengthened its foundation with massive walls. (As you've read, the "Western Wall" that's the focus of Jewish reverence today is one section of the Herodian retaining walls.) Ten thousand skilled workers were employed to widen the mount and erect various buildings and dig a tunnel between the Antonia and the temple so that Herod could go from one to the other without worrying about a problem that monarchs have always had to face—personal safety.

When it was time to build the temple itself, the work was done by priests who had to be taught how to cut stones and do carpentry. They obviously were good students and hard workers—the temple was finished in eighteen months. Then came the celebration. The people, Josephus wrote, "were full of joy; and presently they returned thanks, in the first place, to God; and in the next place, for the alacrity the king had showed."

Saying Good-Bye to Herod the Great

The temple would dominate the city of Jerusalem long after King Herod took his last breath. He died in 4 B.C. in Jericho, another city that he'd rebuilt to the east of Jerusalem. He left three sons, Archelaus, Philip, and Antipas. (You'll meet them in the next chapter.) He'd actually fathered six boys, but he'd ordered three of them killed just before his death on the suspicion that they were plotting against him. He was right. He'd also killed his wife, Mariamne, in 29 B.C., for the same reason.

In his last months, Herod had also committed a crime that to Jews of the city surpassed the sin of murder. In a gesture to his Roman bosses, he'd installed a golden eagle, a symbol of Jupiter and the ensign of Rome, over a temple gate. When word reached the city that he was dying, three young Jews lowered themselves from the portico on ropes and hacked the eagle from its roost with axes. Not dead yet, Herod heard about the act and had the three men and their teachers executed. When he died in agony a few days later, Jews regarded his suffering as a just punishment.

A Trio of Curious Visitors from the East

According to the New Testament, about a year before Herod died in his "Winter Palace" in Jericho, he'd been surprised to learn that three men claimed to have followed a new star that they believed to be a sign that a king had been born in Israel. Because Herod hadn't fathered any new children, he was naturally curious. After the three men said that such a royal birth had been prophesied, Herod questioned a religious adviser and was told that there was a prediction concerning a king who would be born in the nearby town of Bethlehem. Herod told the three men that when they found the child, they were to report back to him where the child was so that he could offer his respects.

> **Reverent Remarks**
>
> And he sent them to Bethlehem, and said, "Go and search diligently for the young child; and when ye have found him, bring me word again, that I may come and worship him also."
>
> —Matthew 3:8

As everyone familiar with the story of the birth of Jesus knows, the three men found the child, but were told by an angel not to report back to the king and to return home "another way."

To say that Herod was furious is an understatement. Worried that he was facing a future contender for his throne, he did what came naturally. He sent soldiers with orders to kill every male child in Bethlehem, and "all the coasts thereof," that were two years old and under. Their killing rampage is known as the "slaughter of the innocents."

But the New Testament records that Herod failed in his objective. Alerted to the danger by an angel, Joseph rushed Jesus and his mother, Mary, out of town and took them to the safe haven of Egypt. Informed of Herod's death and learning that he had been succeeded by his son Archelaus, Joseph and his family made their way to

Nazareth, well north of Jerusalem and out of reach of Archelaus, in the province of Galilee.

That little boy would one day be crucified in Jerusalem, but a religion would be founded in his name that would spread from the Holy City and convert a Roman Emperor, who would then make Jerusalem the heart of that faith.

Holy Facts! _____

A Jerusalem chronology (all dates B.C.):

1000	King David captures Jerusalem.
964	Solomon begins building the temple.
586	Nebuchadnezzar of Babylon destroys the temple and city.
539	King Cyrus lets Jews return and rebuild the temple.
332	Alexander the Great conquers Jerusalem.
313	Ptolemy takes the city.
169	Antiochus of Syria desecrates the temple, leading to the revolt of the Hasmoneans.
63	Pompey claims the city for the Roman Empire.
37	Herod the Great begins his rule.
19	Construction of the second temple begins (actually the third).
4	Herod the Great dies.

The Least You Need to Know

- David's conquest of Jerusalem was the first Arab-Israeli war.

- Solomon's Temple was destroyed by Babylonians.

- Jerusalem was conquered by Alexander the Great and Syria.

- After a revolt led by Judas the Maccabee, the Roman Empire ruled Jerusalem for 600 years.

- The second temple was built by Herod the Great.

Chapter 7

Birthplace of Christianity

In This Chapter

◆ A rebellious city is governed by a Roman procurator

◆ History's most famous and significant trial

◆ The beginning of a new religion

◆ A revolt by Jews ends in the destruction of the temple

◆ Jerusalem becomes the centerpiece of Christianity

Approximately 30 years after the death of Herod the Great, an itinerant preacher from the town of Nazareth arrived in Jerusalem and caused such a ruckus that he was crucified. Believing that the preacher was the Son of God and had risen from the dead, a group of his followers founded a religion in his name. Once it became the official faith of the Roman/ Byzantine Empire and sites associated with the preacher were certified and sanctified, pilgrims were attracted to the city for most of the next 300 years.

You Can't Tell the Players Without a Program

You'll recall that in the civil war that followed the death of Julius Caesar, the man who defeated Mark Antony was Octavian, and that he took the name Augustus and claimed the title "Caesar." One of his first acts was to slap a tax on everybody in the empire. Needing to know exactly how many taxpayers there were, he ordered history's second census. (The first had been decreed by Cyrenius, governor of Syria.) Augustus's tally required subjects of the empire to register at the places where they were born. According to the New Testament, this was why a carpenter named Joseph had to leave Nazareth in Galilee and go with his pregnant wife, Mary, to the southern town of Bethlehem.

Shortly after the birth of their son, Jesus, the proud parents took him to the temple in Jerusalem to "present him to the Lord." As he grew up, the family returned to the city from time to time for religious festivals. On one of these occasions, Jesus disappeared for three days. When his distraught parents found him, he was seated in the temple having a spirited conversation with the learned men, "hearing them, and asking them questions." He had everyone "astonished at his understanding and answers." Luke's gospel says this was in the fifteenth year of the reign of Augustus's successor, a really nasty emperor named Tiberias.

With Herod the Great long gone, the power that he'd wielded had been divvied up among his three sons. Herod Archelaus was given Samaria, Idumea, and Judea with his capital in Jerusalem, but he was fired after 10 years and replaced by a Roman governor, called a procurator. Philip got Iturea, Gaulanitis, and Trachonitis. Antipas was put in charge of Perea and the province where Jesus lived and did much of his preaching (Galilee). This fact meant that Antipas would find himself tricked into playing a part in the drama that surrounded a trial and crucifixion that would result in Jerusalem becoming the holy city of a new religion founded in Jesus' name.

Jerusalem Gives the Romans a Colossal Headache

If you know your New Testament or have seen movies and TV shows dealing with the crucifixion of Jesus, you've heard that the procurator of Judea (a subprovince of Roman-ruled Syria) and its main city, Jerusalem, was Pontius Pilate. Ruling from the city of Caesarea that Herod the Great built on the Mediterranean coast, he commanded the province's Roman legion and had the official responsibility for collecting taxes.

By all accounts, Pilate was not what you would call a culturally sensitive guy. Contemporary Roman writer and philosopher Philo said that he earned a record of ruling by "venality, violence, robbery, ill treatment, insult, careless executions without trial, and by irrational and terrible cruelty."

Chalk One Up for the Jews

Unlike previous Roman officials who were careful not to offend the Jews by letting troops enter Jerusalem carrying "graven images" of eagles and depictions of Caesar, Pilate saw nothing wrong in it. Our ever-reliable historian Josephus tells us in chapter three of his *Antiquities of the Jews* that Pilate "set them [graven images] up there" in the dead of night. This sent the Jews into a such a tizzy that they "came in multitudes" to the capital of Caesarea and interceded with Pilate for "many days that he would remove the images."

After putting up with the pestering for six days, Pilate warned the Jews that if they didn't go away he'd have the troops slaughter them. When the Jews fell to the ground and "laid their necks bare, and said they would take their death very willingly," rather than let the laws of their religion "be transgressed," Pilate caved. Orders were sent out to Jerusalem for the offensive symbols to be removed.

Pilate Raids the Temple Treasury

Everywhere the Roman Empire extended its reach, things got built, from roads, amphitheaters, and temples to huge aqueducts. Because Jerusalem's main source of water was inadequate pools that had been in use since the era of the Jebusites and King David, Pilate decided to build a conduit that would bring water from a stream a long, long way from the city. Reasoning that this was for the benefit of the Jews, he saw no reason why they shouldn't foot the cost from the wealth they had stored in their temple. Back then, this was the equivalent of the U.S. Interior Department helping itself to the Social Security fund.

The Jews were outraged. They once again gathered, as Josephus noted, in the "tens of thousands" and "made a clamor." When the protesters got personal "and abused the man," Pilate called out "a great number" of troops armed with "daggers under their garments." Unable to get the Jews to leave, he signaled an attack. Because the people figured Pilate would give in as before, they were unprepared and unarmed. "And thus," Josephus reported, "an end was put to this sedition."

A Hotbed of Radicals, Zealots, and Messiahs

A legacy of the Maccabean revolt that was discussed in the previous chapter was a rise in militancy on the part of Jews looking for the arrival of the Messiah in the expectation that he would overthrow the Romans and establish God's kingdom on earth. One of the most hot-headed of these Messianic groups was the Zealots. Pioneers of what we call guerilla warfare, they carried out assassinations, murder, and terrorism. One element of these revolutionaries was the Sicarii (dagger bearers). Josephus described the Zealots as opportunistic bandits. Among the leaders were Simon Zelotes and a thug named Barabbas (more on him shortly). Some students of the era believe that Judas Iscariot was a Zealot.

The group drew its greatest strength in the Galilean hills, but they were also a presence in Jerusalem, much to the chagrin of Pontius Pilate and the Jewish religious establishment. Centered in the temple, the priestly class (Sadducees) believed that the Messiah would make his appearance on his schedule, and certainly not in response to the dirty work of the Zealots.

High Priest, Top Religious Authority, and Pilate's Main Man

In the time of Jesus, the high priest—a hereditary position—was Joseph Caiaphas. In addition to ceremonial duties in the temple, Caiaphas controlled the temple treasury, managed the temple's workers, including a police force, and served as president of a council and religious court known as the Sanhedrin. He was also a liaison between the Jews and the Roman procurator. Men with power, the priests were committed to maintaining a status quo that they knew could easily explode. This was especially true when the city's population was swollen by outsiders who'd poured into the city for Passover. Pilate was so concerned about the possibility of trouble that he'd traveled from Caesarea at Passover time with more than his usual contingent of troops.

A Week of Disturbing Occurrences

Having a job that Jews respected and Pilate saw as vital in the task of keeping the Jews under control, Caiaphas enjoyed a lot of perks. Among them was a palace in the classy Upper City with a splendid view of the temple. Whether Caiaphas was at home on the day that Jesus of Nazareth rode into the city on a donkey isn't known. Having heard about Jesus' activities in Galilee, he must have been told that Jesus' arrival in the city had been greeted by cheering crowds that strewed the road with palm leaves while shouting "Hosanna!" and yelling "Save us, Son of David." The word from Galilee was that Jesus had been going around preaching to increasingly large crowds, and that a lot of people had gotten the idea from what he said that he was the long-awaited Messiah. This was dangerous stuff in itself, but Zealots were reportedly nurturing a hope that Jesus would emerge as a rallying point for outright revolution.

The high priest's natural alertness to the potential for trouble escalated to alarm with reports that this Jesus had barged into the Court of the Gentiles on the Temple

Mount and launched an attack against the legitimate moneychangers and those who sold sacrificial pigeons. Lashing them with a whip cord, Jesus had shouted, "Does not scripture say: My house will be called a house of prayer? You have turned it into a robber's den." Another of the reports reaching Caiaphas quoted Jesus predicting that not a single stone of the great buildings of the temple would be left on another; that everything would be destroyed. If that wasn't a call for revolution, what was it?

Holy Facts! _____

Tradition puts the location of Caiaphas's luxurious home on the site of the present Church of the Holy Savior (in the Armenian Quarter). In the southeast corner of the church is the small Chapel of the Second Prison of Christ. The first is believed to have been the house of Caiaphas's father, Annas, and where Jesus was taken after his arrest in the Mount of Olives Garden of Gethsemane. Whether either place is genuine is a matter of debate.

Deciding What to Do with Jesus

We know from Scriptures that Jesus was taken before Caiaphas and the Sanhedrin to answer the charge that he had been forgiving people of their sins and claiming to be the Son of God. If Jesus had done so, he committed blasphemy. Under Jewish law he deserved to be put to death. Asked point-blank by Caiaphas about the Son of God claim, Jesus answered, "You have said it." What is more, he said, Caiaphas would one day see the Son of man sitting on the right hand of power and coming in the clouds of heaven.

That was enough for Caiaphas. Ritually ripping open his clothing, he denounced Jesus as a blasphemer. Because only the Romans could carry out a death sentence, Jesus was hauled before Pilate. The timing couldn't have been worse. It was Passover week, and Jerusalem was jammed with Jews from Judea and elsewhere. Because of the recent troubles over the graven images and the slaughter that ended the aqueduct protest, another wrong move could inflame Zealots into a full-scale uprising.

Hesitant about sending to death a man who'd gained a sizeable following, Pilate grabbed what he thought was a way out of the dilemma. Learning that Jesus was from Galilee, he ordered him taken to Herod Antipas for judgment. He surely knew that Antipas had not so long ago executed another troublemaker by the name of John the Baptist, so sending Jesus probably seemed to Pilate to be a great way to get himself off the hook. He may or may not have heard that Jesus had scorned Antipas as "that fox."

Shunting Jesus off to Antipas's palace, Pilate found out just how sly Antipas could be. Instead of sending Jesus to the same fate as John the Baptist, Antipas had a royal robe put on the man who claimed to be "King of the Jews," had a good time mocking him, and sent him straight back to Pilate.

Holy Facts!

As with much of the geography of Jerusalem in the story of Jesus, there's disagreement among scholars about whether Jesus was tried in front of Pilate in the Antonia fortress or in Antipas's palace, where Pilate might well have been staying during his Passover visit to the city.

Reverent Remarks

All the armies that ever marched, all the navies that ever sailed, all the parliaments that ever sat, all the kings that ever reigned, put together, have not affected the life of man on this earth as much as that one solitary life.

—Notable American minister, Dr. James Allan Francis, in a famous 1920s sermon about Jesus

With the problem of Jesus tossed back into his court, Pilate hemmed and hawed for a while, but gave in to the combined demands of the temple establishment. He also had to deal with a mob that was antagonistic to Jesus. He thought a way out would be to take advantage of an old Jewish custom of giving amnesty to one prisoner at Passover. He offered the mob a choice of freedom for Jesus or the murderous Zealot named Barrabas. The crowd picked Barrabas. Pilate made a show of his displeasure by literally washing his hands of "this man" (Jesus). Beaten up by soldiers and forced to wear a crown they'd made out of thorns, Jesus was led from the city to Golgotha (Calvary) and nailed to a cross.

Setting aside the issue of whether Jesus possessed the divinity he'd espoused, no event in the long saga of Jerusalem had a more powerful and lasting significance than the execution of Jesus of Nazareth. Many years later, Josephus noted that to "the present day" the devotion of those who called themselves Christians "has not ceased." As a result, within three centuries Christianity had been decreed the Roman Empire's official religion. After two millennia, the faith would claim more adherents than any other—in a world in which time is divided between the years before the birth of Jesus and those after.

A Religion's Bumpy Road Starts in Jerusalem

Convinced that Jesus had been resurrected, was the Son of God, and that through him all sins had been washed away, his disciples began looking for adherents, not of a new religion, but followers of a Judaism in which the promise of a Messiah had been fulfilled. Based in Jerusalem and evangelizing only among Jews, they had no intention of bringing Gentiles (non-Jews) into the fold. But they soon discovered that their message about Jesus was as unwelcome among ordinary Jews as Jesus' words had been to Caiaphas and the Sanhedrin. Instead of being greeted by receptive audiences, they found themselves in a fight with temple priests.

Jerusalem Gets Its First Christian Martyr

You'll recall that one of the Old City's gates is named for Saint Stephen. (It's the gate that leads to the Via Dolorosa.) Stephen was so significant that four Old City churches bear his name. How he earned sainthood is not a pleasant story.

About three years after Jesus was crucified, Stephen irked members of the Sanhedrin by asserting that God didn't need the temple in Jerusalem, or a building of any kind anywhere, to reveal Himself. Pounced upon, Stephen was dragged outside the city walls and stoned to death. This caused many of Jesus' followers to clear out of town so fast that they didn't stop running until they got to the Greek city of Antioch (in present Turkey). Because they used a Greek word, Christos, (meaning the Messiah), they were soon being called "Christians."

Meanwhile, Back in Jerusalem

Although many fresh converts to Jesus had fled to Antioch, three of Jesus' original disciples— Peter, John, and James—stayed. They were known among Jesus' latter-day followers as "the Pillars" of the fledgling religion. But it's important to note that they felt that they were still Jews.

James was an important figure not only because he was said to be a brother of Jesus, but because he claimed that the risen Jesus had appeared to him. Extremely devout, James would eventually be the leader of the Jerusalem Christians and one of its martyrs. Stoned to death, he's remembered in the Cathedral of Saint James in the Armenian Quarter.

High and Mighty
Identified in the scriptures as Jesus' brother, James was also called "the Righteous Man." His name burst into news headlines in 2003 with the discovery that a first-century ossuary (a box to hold bones) was inscribed in Aramaic (the language spoken by Jesus and his disciples): "James the brother of Jesus." The Israeli Antiquities Authority has determined that the inscription is a forgery.

A Sudden Turnaround on the Road to Damascus

One of the fiercest persecutors of the Jesus people in Jerusalem at this time claimed the rare distinction of being Jewish and a Roman citizen. Little is known about his early years beyond the fact that he'd been born in Tarsus, that he was a tentmaker, had studied Jewish law, and was a Pharisee (a stickler for keeping all the Judaic laws to the letter). Named Saul, he was evidently quite proud of tormenting the Jesus crowd and had taken part in the stoning of Stephen.

Saul was apparently so effective in going after Christians that one day he set on the road to Damascus in order to capture Christians in that city and bring them "bound unto Jerusalem." This plan was interrupted when a bright light appeared in the sky, blinding him and scaring his horse. Thrown to the ground, Saul heard a voice that demanded an explanation as to why he was persecuting—here's the word that riveted Saul's attention—"me." Now Saul asked for an explanation. The voice replied, "I am Jesus."

When Saul reached Damascus, the people who were expecting him to start rounding up Christians were stunned to hear him talking about Jesus as the Christ (Messiah). Barely escaping with his skin intact, he returned to Jerusalem and shocked the Pillars and everyone else by seeking to join their cause. Understandably suspicious, they wanted nothing to do with him, so he left Jerusalem for his hometown and struck out on his own. By converting Gentiles, he put himself at odds with the Jerusalem Christians. They felt that to follow Christ meant being a Jew in all respects, including circumcision. In an historic meeting in Jerusalem between him and what was by now a Christian hierarchy, it was agreed that no one in the Gentile world would have to undergo circumcision.

Free to be the apostle of Christ in the wider world, Saul, now going by the name Paul, preached that belief in Christ alone was all that mattered. Arrested for provoking a riot at the temple in Jerusalem, he was jailed in Caesarea, but invoked his rights as a citizen of Rome to be tried there. Shipwrecked on the way, he survived and was held under house arrest. Caught up in a wave of persecution of Christians in Rome, he was executed (circa 68 A.D.).

Hard Times Hit Jerusalem Again

Approximately two years before Paul's death, with Christianity still in its infancy, Jews began an uprising against Roman rule. Launched in 66 A.D., it was sparked by Roman desecration of the temple. The rebels burned the Antonia, much of the Upper City, and Herod's palace. The Romans counterattacked, led by Emperor Vespasian's son Titus. After a long siege, the city was taken, the temple was destroyed, and a group of Jewish rebels who'd fled to Herod the Great's long-abandoned fortress of Masada chose to commit suicide rather than surrender. Evidence of the sacking of the city by Titus is preserved as the "Burnt House" that you read about in Chapter 2.

No Jews Allowed, and No Christians Either

The residents of Jerusalem who survived Titus's onslaught were exiled or sold into slavery. The ban on Jews from the city, as well as Jews who embraced the still incipient Christianity, held firm until approximately 131 A.D., when a rebel named Bar Koba bristled at news that Emperor Hadrian planned to turn the city into a colony for Romans, many of them ex-soldiers, and name the city Colonia (colony) Aelia Capitolina. Determined to prevent this, Bar Koba and his followers commenced the Second Jewish Revolt. Things went their way at first. They drove out the vaunted Tenth Legion, took the city, and made it a Jewish capital again.

But in the fourth year of this triumph, the full weight of Roman anger descended on Jerusalem in the form of an army led by the emperor himself. The war lasted three years. With all the Jews routed, Jerusalem took on the feel of a Roman city. It had the Cardo that you read about, better walls, triumphal arches, and buildings outside the old boundaries. Emperor Hadrian also imposed a new name on the lands of the Jews. He called it Palestine.

Jerusalem was also emptied of the small number of its Jewish Christians, but this did not mean a total absence of people who had embraced the new faith. Among the colonists imported by Hadrian to populate Aelia Capitolina were Greeks and Syrians who brought their Christianity with them. Because the only approved worship was of Rome's pantheon, the non-Jewish Christians found a house outside the south wall on the hillside the Jews called Mount Zion. The appeal of the house was its "upper room," where the local belief held that Jesus had convened the Last Supper.

If Christians had wanted to see Golgotha (Calvary), they couldn't. It was under the Temple of Aphrodite. Whereas the Place of the Skull had been beyond the city wall when Jesus was led to it, it was now inside the wall that Hadrian had built. Christians could visit the Mount of Olives and Gethsemane if they wished, and nothing prevented a short trip down to Bethlehem to see a cave where the locals said Jesus was born. Jerusalem, however, was a thoroughly Romanized place of gods and goddesses with no patience for either worshiping the God of the Jews or an executed criminal who had claimed to be the Son of God. It would remain out of bounds to Christians for two centuries.

Christianity's Return to Jerusalem Hits a Snag

We now come back to Emperor Constantine, his conversion to the cross of Christ, Christianity's adoption as his empire's official religion, and Constantine's plucky mother, Queen Helena. The year is 326 A.D. and the queen is in Jerusalem to find the places where Jesus was crucified, buried, and put in a tomb that turned out to be only borrowed for three days. You're familiar with the result in the form of the Church of the Holy Sepulchre.

With Constantine's blessing, Christ's followers felt right at home. More churches went up and everything seemed glorious for Christianity in the city they now called Holy.

Flash forward to July 19, 362 A.D. Constantine has departed to claim his reward in heaven. There's a new emperor: Julian. Meeting with a delegation of Jewish elders, Julian gives his permission for them to rebuild the temple. Panic grips Jerusalem's Christians. But on May 27, while Jews are busy clearing the Temple Mount of centuries of rubble, the city is rocked by an earthquake that the Christians interpret as the wrath of God aimed at the Jews. A few weeks later, Julian is killed in battle and a Christian (Jovian) becomes emperor. From him through a series of Byzantine dynasties spanning nearly three centuries, Christianity held sway.

But on April 13, 614 A.D., Persians arrived at the gates with Jews as allies to lay a siege. When the city fell at the end of May, the Persians went on a killing spree, slaughtering more than 66,000 Christians, exiling the rest. They took with them a relic of the true cross, a spear that was believed to have pierced Jesus' side as he hung on the cross, a sponge used to give him vinegar, and an onyx cup—the Holy Grail—believed to have been used at the Last Supper. The victorious Persians put control of the city in the hands of their Jewish allies.

Fifteen years later, the tables turned when Emperor Heraclius took back the city for Christ and ordered that all Jews be baptized. Nine years after that, followers of an even newer religion were at the gates. Claiming Jerusalem in the name of Islam, they would hang onto it for more than four centuries.

Holy Facts! _____

Christian Jerusalem Chronology:

4 B.C.–A.D.30	The lifetime of Jesus.
30–64	Christianity is in its infancy.
	Paul carries Christianity to the Gentiles.
66–73	The First Jewish Revolt results in the destruction of the temple.
132–135	The Second Jewish Revolt is defeated by the Romans.
135	Hadrian names the rebuilt city Aelia Capitolina;
	Christianity's first Jerusalem church is established (the Upper Room).
303	Violent persecution of Christians begins under Emperor Diocletian.
312–313	Emperor Constantine embraces Christianity.
326	Emperor Constantine's mother, Queen Helena, visits Jerusalem and finds Golgotha.
	Christianity flourishes in Jerusalem.
362	Christians rejoice at Jews' failure to rebuild the temple.
380–391	Christianity remains Rome's official religion.
614	Persians take Jerusalem, aided by Jews.
629	Emperor Heraclius recaptures the city and exiles the Jews.

The Least You Need to Know

◆ The Roman Empire named Herod the Great "King of the Jews."

◆ Jesus was crucified.

◆ Christianity struggled to become a religion.

◆ Rome put down a Jewish revolt and destroyed the temple.

◆ Jerusalem became Christianity's holy city.

Chapter 8

City of Allah

In This Chapter

- ◆ Islam wins Jerusalem without a fight
- ◆ A period of religious tolerance and pilgrimages
- ◆ Crusaders sweep in and take over
- ◆ Saladin returns the city to the Muslims
- ◆ Jerusalem becomes part of Ottoman Empire

Beginning with a bloodless takeover of Jerusalem from Byzantine Christians by Muslims in 638 A.D., this chapter covers periods when the city changed hands several times. Spanning more than 12 centuries, it examines the influences of Islam, the Crusaders, and the Ottoman Empire. The saga concludes with the British taking control over Palestine from Jerusalem at the end of World War I.

Sons of Ishmael Go on the March

When the Prophet Mohammad died in June 632 A.D., Arabia had been won for Allah. But with his death a unity that had been welded by the force of his personality fragmented into a traditional tribalism that proved stronger than Mohammed's desire to forge Arabs into the great nation that God had promised to Ishmael. Consequently, Mohammed's successor, Abu Bakr, found himself struggling to hold onto everything Mohammad had achieved. This entailed confronting not only rebellious tribal leaders, but individuals who claimed that they were also prophets of Allah. Although Abu Bakr succeeded in crushing them, he was left with a simmering discontent. Seizing a device that proved a solution for countless rulers who faced internal problems, he turned Arabian energies toward fighting external foes. He found them in the Persians and the Byzantines.

After a year of military campaigns, Abu Bakr died (634) having seen a unified Arab army march into Palestine. He was succeeded by Caliph 'Umar. One of the "Companions of the Prophet," he was a devout Muslim who lived as simply as Mohammad had by wearing an old, threadbare woolen tunic and carrying his own military baggage. Defeating troops of Emperor Heraclius in a battle at Yarmuk on August 20, 636, he and his force had an open road to Jerusalem. When he arrived at the gates of the Christian city, he set up a siege that resulted in Jerusalem's surrender in February 638.

You've read in Chapter 4 that 'Umar declined an invitation to pray in the Christian church on the site of Golgotha because to do so would have converted it into a mosque. Jerusalem historian Karen Armstrong saw 'Umar expressing the "monotheistic ideal of compassion more than any previous conqueror of Jerusalem, with the possible exception of King David." She continued, "Once the Christians had surrendered, there was no killing, no destruction of property, no burning of rival religious symbols, no expulsions or expropriations, and no attempt to force the inhabitants to embrace Islam. If respect for the previous occupants of the city is a sign of the integrity of a monotheistic power, Islam began its long tenure in Jerusalem very well indeed."

> **" " Reverent Remarks**
>
> Glory to God who did take his servant for a journey by night from the sacred mosque to the farthest mosque, whose precincts we did bless in order that we might show him some of our signs. For he is the one who heareth and seeth all things.
>
> —Sura Bani Israel: Verse 1

When 'Umar set out to build what became the Dome of the Rock, he chose the same site as the Jews' second Temple Mount, which had been left a ruin since Titus de-stroyed it in 70 A.D. After the Temple Mount had been cleared of rubble and garbage, 'Umar called in a Jewish convert to Islam, Ka'b ibn Ahbar, to advise on where to place the Islamic holy place.

What's in a Name?

Neither Islamic military control of the city nor construction of an Islamic shrine on the Jews' Temple Mount altered the reality that the religion of the city's majority was

Christianity. Its places of worship dotted the landscape, from the Mount of Olives and the upper room to the imposing Church of the Holy Sepulchre with the majestic dome that would have a rival in grandeur in the Dome of the Rock. But Muslims would do more than alter the city skyline. They eventually gave Jerusalem a name of their own: "al-Quds," meaning "the Holy."

Assassinations and Civil War

In 644, six years after Islam's bloodless conquest of Jerusalem, 'Umar was killed by a Persian prisoner of war. His successor, Uthman bin Affan, also had been one of the Companions of the Prophet. A member an aristocratic clan (Umayyad), he was just as pious as 'Umar, but nowhere as effective as a leader. He died in 646 at the hands of a group of officers. Their choice for the fourth caliph was the Prophet's closest living relative, Ali ibn Ali Talib, who was not a member of the Umayyad clan. The result was civil war. After Ali was stabbed to death by a fanatic in 661, the Umayyad clan returned to power in the person of Mu'awiyah ibn Sufyan, ruler of Syria and Palestine, known to Arabs as al-Sham. Umayyads would rule Islam for almost 100 years.

Upon the death of Mu'awiyah, the caliphate passed to his son, Yazid. But in 680, al-Husayn (the son of Ali ibn Ali Talib and grandson of the Prophet) led an anti-Umayyad rebellion. Greatly outnumbered in a fight at Kerbala in Iraq, he was killed.

Although the Umayyads lost power in another rebellion (683), it was temporary. In firm control of Syria and Palestine, Caliph Abdul Malik ibn Marwan began work on repairing city walls and gates, and then set his mind on the building of the Dome of the Rock that you read about in Chapter 4.

The Umayyads Learn that Nothing Lasts Forever

Everything came tumbling down for the Umayyads in the middle of the eighth century. After Caliph al-Walid was murdered in 744, his son Yazid had to face a rebellion that continued under his successor, Marwan II. Then an earthquake hit (747). It brought down two sides of the Dome of the Rock, wrecked the al-Walid Mosque, flattened the Umayyads' palace, and sent the surviving Muslims into the hills for six weeks. In the aftermath of these problems, the dynasty was challenged by descendants of Mohammad's uncle (Abbas) and other Umayyad opponents.

Defeats on the Za'b River in Iraq and Antipatris in Palestine closed the Umayyad chapter of Jerusalem's history in 749. Authors of the next chapter were the Abbasids (a name derived from that of the Prophet's uncle). Because Jerusalem was so associated with Umayyads, the Abbasids chose Baghdad, rather than Jerusalem, as their capital. From 762 until 775, Jerusalem was treated like a distant cousin. When one caliph was asked to finance badly needed repairs to the al-Walid Mosque, he suggested that the way to pay for the repairs was to strip the gold and silver of the Dome of the Rock, melt it down, and sell it. It wasn't until 775 that Caliph al-Mahdi ordered provincial governors and military commanders to fork over money so that the Haram/Temple Mount could be fixed up, including building the al-Aqsa mosque.

The Caliph of Baghdad and the Christian King

In the year 801, the Abbasid ruler in Baghdad was Caliph al-Harun al-Rashid. Although he was a Muslim, he discovered that he had a friend in the brand new king of the western part of an empire that was now called "Holy Roman." Crowned on Christmas Day 800 by the pope (Leo III), he was given papal approval as the "Emperor of the Romans." He was Charles, King of the Franks, and soon to be hailed by Christians as Charlemagne, and to those who didn't speak French, Charles the Great. Relations grew so friendly between caliph and king that the Muslim invited the Christian to build a hospice in Jerusalem. Charles followed up with an estate for pilgrims in the Kidron Valley. It was, in the words of an Arab warning, "letting a camel stick its nose into a tent."

A Case of Pushing the Envelope

Relations between Muslims and Christians didn't go as swimmingly as Harun had hoped. Followers of Islam were offended by Christian images and "magic rituals." One of these was an Easter ceremony of the "holy fire," in which a white light miraculously appeared in the darkness of the Church of the Holy Sepulchre. Christians swarmed into the streets in ecstasy and shouted "Hasten to the religion of the cross."

Islamic tolerance began to wear thin. In 938 the Christian Palm Sunday processional was attacked, the gate to the church built over Golgotha was set on fire, and the patriarch was dragged to a stake and burned. Evidently as a reminder to the Christians that they'd surrendered Jerusalem to Caliph 'Umar, the first mosque to be built outside the Haram went up provocatively near the Church of the Holy Sepulchre.

Even before Charlemagne, Abbasids had opened Jerusalem's gates to Christian pilgrims, and had profited by such visits. But it was only after the Abbasids lost control to the Fatmid dynasty (750–969) that Muslims began to complain that the city was being overrun by outsiders. In 996, a new Fatmid caliph turned the tide of resentment. A Shii named al-Hakim, he had a Christian mother and an Islamic sensitivity of social justice. He also had mood swings that could be violent. Told in September

1009 that the ritual of the holy fire made "a great impression" on Muslims and introduced "confusion in their hearts," he ordered the church on the site of Golgotha torn down. Attempts were made to coerce Christians and Jews to convert to Islam. Despite this, on balance in the years of Fatmid rule (969–1071) Christians and Jews fared pretty well.

Say Hello and Good-Bye to the Noble Turks

The next takeover of Jerusalem was by Turks who were converts to Islam. Because the leading family of the Turkomans ("Noble Turks") was named Seljuk, this brief period of Jerusalem's saga bears that name. It started in 1071, lasted 27 years, and was notable for its hospitality to scholars. Then Fatmids made a comeback (1098). But as they were settling in, Europe was percolating with reports from the Holy Land of horrendous abuse of Christians at the hands of the Muslims.

The Pope and the Monk's Tale

The story you're about to read may or may not be true. Told by a French monk named Peter the Hermit, it's one that took hold in the mixture of fact and "tradition" that runs through the history of Jerusalem. While on a pilgrimage to the Holy City in 1095, he found that his Christian brethren were suffering at the hands of the Turks. One day while Peter was taking refuge in the Basilica of the Holy Sepulchre, Christ appeared and told him to go back to Europe and proclaim the miseries of Jerusalem's faithful.

During the first millennium of the Christian calendar that split history into time before Jesus' birth (B.C.) and "years of the Lord" (A.D.), successors to the Apostle Peter bore the title "pope." In 1095 the "vicar of Christ" was Urban II. Whether he called upon the Christians of Europe to organize armies to wrest the Holy City from the grip of Islam on the basis of Peter the Hermit's report is another of the many dubious accounts in the city's history.

High and Mighty
Born at Amiens in about 1050, Peter the Hermit was also known as Cucu Peter and Little Peter. A contemporary said he wore "a plain woolen shirt with a hood and over this a cloak without sleeves, both extending to his ankles, and his feet were bare." He lived on wine and fish and hardly ever ate bread. Although he led a "poor people's" march to free Jerusalem, he never reached the city. He died in 1115 at the monastery of Neufmoutier in Liège (Belgium).

The contrary version to Peter the Hermit's claim is that Urban II sprang into action at the request of the Byzantine ruler. Worried about the threat to the eastern lands of the empire by the spread of Islam, and discerning weakness in the Turkoman hold on the Near East, Emperor Alexius Comnenus asked for the pope's help in raising an army.

In a famous speech at the Council of Clermont in the spring of 1096, Urban II declared that Christians in the Holy Land were being oppressed. Attacked! Churches and holy places defiled! Jerusalem groaned under the Saracen (Muslim) yoke. The Church of the Holy Sepulchre had been converted to a mosque. (Not true.) Pilgrims were denied access to the Holy Land. The answer: There must be a march to the defense of the tomb of Christ. Europeans must cease their internal wars and squabble and go against the infidel. Wage a righteous war, and God himself will lead it. The reward for those who took up arms for Christ would be absolution and remission of sins. He concluded his speech by declaring *"Deus vult."* ("God wills it!")

The day after Urban's exhortation, the Council granted privileges and protections that he'd promised. Those who took up arms in the name of Christ to liberate the Holy Land adopted a red cross as their official emblem. The name by which these soldiers of the cross became known is "Crusaders."

Setting out in the spring of 1096, 60,000 soldiers and countless noncombatant peasants and pilgrims, with their wives and children, were followed in the autumn by five more armies. Although later accounts of the Crusades depicted the motivation as greed for the riches of the East, and while some participants acted for that reason, most Crusaders acted for religious reasons and returned home broke.

A Long Bloody Road to Jerusalem

As the first Crusade wound through Europe toward the Holy Land, many of the marchers had more on their minds than liberating it from Muslims. Believing the crucifixion of Jesus by the Romans was the result of trickery and manipulation by the Jews of that time, they attacked "Christ killer" Jews along the way, revealing an anti-Semitism that would mark other Crusades and persist in the history of Europe to this day.

After a year of arduous marching, the Crusaders were at the gates of Jerusalem and occupying the Mount of Olives (June 7, 1099). After laying a siege, they burst into the city on July 15 and went on a rampage. No non-Christian was spared. Ten thousand Muslims who sought safety on the roof of the al-Aqsa Mosque were massacred. Jews were dragged from synagogues and butchered.

Raymond of Agiles described men cutting off the heads of their enemies. Others shot them with arrows. Some tortured Muslims by casting them into the flames. Piles of heads, hands, and feet littered the streets. It was necessary to pick one's way over the bodies of men and horses. At the Temple Mount/Haram al-Sharif where religion had been exalted, Christian warriors rode in blood up to their knees and their horses' bridles. This was, Raymond wrote, "a just and splendid judgment of God that this place should be filled with the blood of unbelievers since it [the Temple Mount/Haram] had suffered so long from their blasphemics."

When the Crusaders stood around the tomb of Christ, the scene to Raymond was one that would be "famous in all future ages, for it turned our labors and sorrows into joy and exultation." It was a day of "justification of all Christianity, the humiliation of paganism, the renewal of faith."

Reverent Remarks

This day, I say, will be famous in all future ages, for it turned our labors and sorrows into joy and exhultation; this day, I say, marks the justification of Christianity, the humiliation of paganism, the renewal of faith.

—Raymond of Aguiles, July 15, 1009

Having won the city, the warriors chose Godfrey of Bouillon to be the ruler. He could have taken the title of king, but he declared that he would not wear a crown of gold in the city where Jesus' crown had been made of thorns. Calling himself "Advocate of the Holy Sepulchre," he showed that the Muslims had been routed by setting up his home and office in the al-Aqsa Mosque and turned the Dome of the Rock into a church called the Temple of the Lord.

When he died a year later of typhoid fever, he was buried in the Church of the Holy Sepulchre. He was succeeded by his brother, Baldwin, who had no qualms about wearing a golden crown or adopting a royal title. Crowned in the Church of the Nativity in Bethlehem, he called himself "King of Jerusalem." To demonstrate that he was nonetheless committed to Christ, he had a cross placed on the top of the Dome of the Rock.

Despite the religious fervor that motivated the Crusaders, the city they'd wrenched from Islam became secular and Westernized. Not since King Herod the Great went on a building spree had the city experienced such a splurge of construction and improvement. Many of the landmarks of the present Old City date to the years of the Crusaders.

More Changes of Hands

As the Crusades were making a new Jerusalem that was entirely Christian, with Jews and Muslims barred, a force was gathering to mount a counterattack. It would be led to victory by a fierce fighter for Islam by the name of Salah al-Din, meaning "the Righteousness of the Faith." He'd be known and feared throughout the Christian world as Saladin.

He and his army crashed into the city of Jerusalem on October 2, 1187. It was the date on which Muslims commemorated the Prophet's night journey. Like Caliph 'Umar five centuries earlier, Saladin chose not to massacre the Christians living in the city. Christians who had money were allowed to ransom themselves. Those who didn't were sold into slavery. Crusader buildings were converted to Muslim uses. Baldwin's cross was removed from the Dome of the Rock.

Upon the death of Saladin of typhoid fever in 1193, his empire was divided by the Ayyub family. Although fresh Crusaders tried to retake the city, it was not until 1229 that a peace treaty between the Sultan al-Kamil of Egypt and Fredrick II, the Holy Roman Emperor of Europe, brought a return of Christians. Muslims were allowed to keep their shrines. Christians got back control of Jerusalem, Bethlehem, and Nazareth. This arrangement outraged both the Muslim and Christian worlds, but the truce held for 10 years.

A last attempt by Crusaders to gain Jerusalem, led by King Louis IX of France in 1248, proved to be a dismal failure. The whole army was captured by the Ayyubs and imprisoned in Egypt (1250). Then the Ayyubs found the tables turned on them by a regiment of European Muslims. Mamlukes who had been conscripted into the army decided to rise up and start their own kingdom (Mamalite). They would reign from 1260 to 1517. It was in this period that Rabbi Moshe ben Nachman started the Ramban Synagogue that you've read about in Chapter 2. It's also when Jews fled the Inquisition in Spain and Portugal and settled in Jerusalem while Christopher Columbus stumbled onto the islands of the Western Hemisphere and mistook them for Asia.

> **Holy Facts!** _____
>
> Reminders of the Mamlukes are found mostly around the Temple Mount/Haram. They constructed beautiful homes, mosques, schools, hospices, markets, and fountains.

> **Holy Facts!** _____
>
> There were seven major Crusades:
>
> - I. 1096–1099
> - II. 1147–1149
> - III. 1188–1192
> - IV. 1202–1204
> - V. 1217–1221
> - VI. 1228–1229
> - VII. 1248–1250

Visitors to Jerusalem today look at buildings and sites remaining from the Crusader period and think of them as interesting relics of the age of knights in shining armor. (One of them, England's King Richard the Lionheart, is perhaps best known from stories about Richard's most devoted and dashing subject, Robin Hood.) But to millions of today's Muslims, the era of the Crusaders is as fresh in the mind as yesterday. The dark memory of the Crusaders allowed Osama bin Laden, Saddam Hussein, and other extremists to inflame the Arabs by demonizing Americans as new "Crusaders."

Bye-Bye Byzantium, Hello Ottomans

In the wider world beyond the boundaries of Jerusalem during the thirteenth century, momentous changes were afoot that were to have a significant impact on the Holy City. A new Islamic power, the Ottoman Empire, had been forged in Turkey by Osman I out of formerly disorganized nomadic tribes. Led by Osman's successors, the Ottomans grew powerful enough to challenge the supremacy of the European powers. By 1453 they had smashed the Byzantine Empire, taken control of Constantinople, and changed its name to Istanbul. They seemed to be an unstoppable Islamic wave rolling westward. The legacy of this Ottoman sweep is found in Muslim populations in the Balkan countries of today.

Even as the Ottomans moved into Europe, their armies were going south into Arabia and Palestine. After defeating the Mamlukes at Cairo, Egypt, in 1516, they were able to take Jerusalem without a fight. The predominant personality of the beginning of the Ottoman period in Jerusalem was Sultan Suleiman al-Azeem.

The Second Solomon

Born in 1494, Suleiman was respected by Europeans as the most significant ruling personality of the late sixteenth century. To Muslims he was the perfect Islamic ruler and "the Magnificent." Because of his wisdom and adherence to the laws of Allah, he was also called the second Solomon. (He was named after King Solomon.) Ottomans called him *Kanuni* (meaning "Law Giver").

Suleiman was not what you'd call a "shrinking violet." He had no qualms about calling himself "master of the lands of Caesar and Alexander the Great." He said he was "powerful with the

> **Holy Facts!**
>
> The kanun were legal issues not covered in the main body of Islamic laws found in the Qur'an, known as the Shari'ah. You could say that a kanun decision is similar to a ruling by a U.S. federal judge as to whether a statute is in keeping with the Constitution. Under the Otto-mans, the kanun was formalized into a code of laws that was independent of the Shari-ah. They are known as "kanun-i Osmani," or the "Ottoman laws."

power of God," "deputy of God on earth," "shadow of God over all nations," and "Sultan of Sultans." In another burst of self-definition, he declared, "I am Suleiman and my name is read in all the prayers in all the cities of Islam. I am the Shah of Baghdad and Iraq, Caesar of all the lands of Rome, and the Sultan of Egypt."

A master politician, he took advantage of European rivalries by waging a campaign of destabilization. He played off Protestants against Catholics and exploited a schism between the Roman Catholic Church and the Holy Roman Empire. To further discord in Europe, he assisted Muslim countries in resisting European expansion.

Suleiman the Builder

Like his Jewish namesake, Suleiman launched a building spree. He set out to make his capital city, Istanbul, not only the center of Islamic civilization, but an architectural showplace with a series of building projects, including mosques, bridges, and palaces. In Jerusalem, he left his mark by restoring the Old City walls and gates, building drinking fountains that are visible in many parts of the Old City today, and expanding souks. He also encouraged settlement that tripled the population.

Suleiman's most significant act affecting Jews was in granting them permission to pray at the Western Wall. Three hundred years after he opened the city's gates to them, the Jews would be the majority of the population.

The Least You Need to Know

♦ Muslims took the surrender of Jerusalem in 638 A.D.

♦ The Islamic name for Jerusalem is "al-Quds," meaning "the Holy."

♦ Pope Urban II called on Christians to retake the city.

♦ Europeans undertook seven Crusades between 1096 and 1250.

♦ The Ottoman Empire took Jerusalem in 1516.

Chapter 9

A European City

In This Chapter

- ◆ The Ottomans give Christians free passage to Jerusalem
- ◆ Jews gain access to the Western Wall
- ◆ Jerusalem expands beyond the Old City
- ◆ Modernity envelops all aspects of Jerusalem life
- ◆ The British army of occupation arrives on the scene

This chapter takes a giant leap in time. From Suleiman's taking of Jerusalem as part of his inroads into Europe, it jumps out of the sixteenth century to the nineteenth, during which the Islamic Ottomans had created an empire as vast and powerful as those of Alexander the Great and the Romans. The difference was that Alexander and company conquered land for their enrichment. Suleiman believed that his empire was God's gift. Whether his successors could hold on to it is a subject that we'll explore.

The Big Picture as Suleiman Saw It

If Suleiman had been cut from the same cloth as Alexander and the Caesars and had marched his men across the map just to see how much land they could grab, his place as a conqueror might not rank as high as it does. The consensus of historians is that Suleiman's motivation was not empire building in Europe, but a reaction to European threats to Islam. He saw Portugal invading Muslim cities in eastern Africa and envisioned a fresh wave of Crusaders coming from Europe into the Muslim world. Rather than taking a defensive stance, he went on the offensive. By taking Corfu, Rhodes, large chunks of Greece, and a major part of the Austrian Empire that put him on the doorstep of Vienna, he rocked the capitals of the continent. As one historian wryly recorded, no ruler in the sixteenth century "was more adept at diminishing the egos" of other rulers. As self-designated protector of Islam, he felt he was entitled to declare himself "Supreme Caliph." Few Arabs were ready to argue the point.

By absorbing Arabia and Palestine, the Supreme Caliph also got Jerusalem. Finding the city a politically unworthy place from which to run an empire, Suleiman settled into Constantinople, now called Istanbul, and controlled the Holy City from there through a governor (pasha). But Suleiman wasn't completely hands-off. One of his first decrees was that the city's dilapidated, and in some parts nonexistent, walls be rebuilt. Those you see today are the ones that went up under Suleiman. When the work was finished in 1541, the walls stretched 2 miles and had 34 towers. The gates were open to anyone with peaceful intentions.

Holy Facts!

In 1553, the estimated population of Jerusalem was about 13,000. Jews and Christians numbered around 1,600. Most Muslims were local Arabs. Others were from North Africa, Egypt, Persia, Iraq, and Bosnia.

In studying Arab provinces of the Ottoman empire, historian Dr. Hala Fattah found that Jerusalem was a city of tolerance for all religions. Although Christians were not considered equal to the Muslims in many instances, the government gave Christians right of free passage into the city and did not interfere with their religious practices. This was not easy. When Franciscan monks moved onto Mount Zion in 1551 and Muslims seized the Monastery of the Cross, the monks were compensated with a grant of other land to build a new monastery. Christians were allowed to construct, renovate, and maintain monasteries and churches in Jerusalem and beyond the walls.

A Wall Becomes a Conduit to God

An order from Suleiman to the government in Jerusalem was called a "firman." While work was proceeding on restoring city walls, one of these edicts concerned a wall that was a great deal older than the others. A buttress that had been built by Herod the Great to support an expanded Temple Mount, it was an exposed stretch of foundation stones. On the west side of the Haram, it was overshadowed by al-Aqsa Mosque and the Dome of the Rock. Because the Western Wall was significant to Jews, Suleiman's firman let them gather there for prayers. Because the area was only 9 feet wide, Jews had to squeeze into it.

With so many faithful eager to stand at the wall and pray, the pressure to move out and make room for others was intense. At some point, someone who obviously believed that God was still present on the site of the first and second temples decided to write his supplication on a scrap of paper and leave it in a crevice between two stones. Jews have been doing so ever since. By the end of the sixteenth century, Jerusalem had gained a distinct Jewish section close to the wall.

Keeping in Touch with One's Roots

This liberal policy toward religions that Islam deemed "infidels" didn't mean that Jerusalem was no longer an important Muslim city, or that Suleiman was too busy confronting Europe to care about al-Quds. Finding the Haram and the Dome of the Rock in a state of neglect, he ordered restoration of both. Mosaic wall tiles were repaired. The lower part of the drum (exterior wall) was sheathed in marble. Surrounding structures were spruced up. All of this enhanced the beauty of the Haram, but it also provided jobs to residents of the city.

A Thriving Little City

As a result of religious tolerance, the city's population in 1553 was a little over 13,000 including approximately 1,600 Christians and Jews. They lived in a city with thriving markets. Workers formed guilds to make such goods as soap, leather, and metalwork products, which were exported in return for textiles, rugs, rice, coffee, and other products. All in all, the life of Jerusalem under Suleiman was certainly better than life had been under the Mamlukes.

Not Even God's Deputy Lives Forever

When Suleiman the Magnificent died in 1566, he left Jerusalem a better place than the city he'd conquered. But the world he had amazed and frightened with his audacity was not only different, it was larger. While God's Deputy ruled his eastern domain, the countries of western Europe sent explorers venturing farther to the west to open a "new world." Suddenly, the gold, silver, and other riches of the Americas were flowing into the treasuries of Europe. Even more disconcerting, Islam's previously unbeatable Islamic navy lost a major battle at Lepanto (1571). As economic and military tides shifted, Suleiman's decades-long policy of delegating governmental administration to pashas was falling apart. Largely on their own, the pashas proved to be less accommodating to the Jews and Christians, resulting in a flight from the city.

Law and order broke down in the countryside. Because of a threat from the Bedouins, the city gates that Suleiman had kept open were shut at night. Emboldened European nations started making demands concerning Jerusalem's Christian holy sites. Franciscan monks began organizing processions of pilgrims to the Church of the Holy Sepulchre along a street that they called the Via Dolorosa, with stops at stations of the cross along the route.

A French visitor in 1784 found Jerusalem "a striking example of the vicissitudes of human affairs." Shocked by the leveled walls and buildings "embarrassed with ruins," he wrote that he could scarcely believe that a "celebrated metropolis, which, formerly, withstood the efforts of the most powerful empires" was in such a mess that "we with difficulty recognize Jerusalem." This was not exactly true. The walls were still up, but the city was not in very good shape.

Napoleon Comes and Goes

If you know the history of the eighteenth century, you should not be surprised that Napoleon would put in an appearance at this point in the saga of Jerusalem. His main objective was not to pray at the tomb of Christ. The aim of his expedition into the Near East was to put his army in the way of British domination of the region. Their big battle would be in Egypt, but he also sent troops into Palestine to take on the Ottomans. Counting on the residents to revolt against the Turks, he was disappointed by the Turks' lack of enthusiasm for overthrowing the Ottomans so that they could submit to him. Before Napoleon could reach Jerusalem, his army was stricken by plague, then beaten by a combination of the British fleet and a Muslim army.

With the Napoleon scare behind them, the people of Jerusalem were still under the Ottomans, but the empire built by Suleiman was on shaky legs. "By the eighteenth century," Karen Armstrong wrote in *Jerusalem: One City, Three Faiths*, "the Ottoman empire seemed to have broken down irretrievably."

A Loosening of the Hands

When the Armenian Catholic community in Jerusalem chose to build a church on property close to a Muslim mystic fellowship, they were allowed to do so, even though the Armenians totaled 22 men and women in 4 houses. Ironically and tragically, as these Jerusalem Armenians were being decently treated, Ottomans in Anatolia (Turkey) were carrying out a genocide of Armenians.

When people of Greek Orthodox faith asked to renovate their church in 1881, permission was granted on condition that Jerusalem's governor determine that the property on which the churches would be built belonged to the community in question, that it did not infringe on Muslim property, and that no force would be used to obtain contributions from Greeks to build the churches.

The Principle of Never Passing Up an Opportunity

During the nineteenth century, European-based religious activity increased through-out the Holy Land because Ottoman land reforms of 1839 and 1856 had allowed non-Ottoman citizens to own land. Europeans grabbed onto this concession to foster religious and cultural penetration. This had the effect of making Jerusalem and the Holy Land, as one historian noted, "an arena of European rivalries."

Remember Edward Robinson and the arches? Charles Warren's shaft? Chinese Gordon and the Garden Tomb? They carried out all their exploring during the time we're now talking about (1800s). None of it would have happened without the approval and encouragement of the Ottomans. It's also the period when Zionism was born and took root in Jewish communities in eastern Europe and Russia.

The Return of the Jews

During the nineteenth century, Jews who had fled oppression in eastern Europe and Russia added significantly to their number in Palestine and Jerusalem. Encouraged by the Zionist movement, Jews established the Jewish National Fund (1901) and began buying up land, including part of the Palestinian city of Jaffa. It became the city of Tel Aviv. In 1910, the Jews outnumbered Muslims in Jerusalem more than 3:1: with a population of 45,000 to 12,000. The Jewish name for this migration was "aliyah," meaning "the return to the land of Israel."

"From being a deserted, desperate city (under Mamlukes)," Karen Armstrong wrote of this period, "Jerusalem was being transformed by modernity into a thriving metropolis, and for the first time since the destruction of the temple, Jews were once again in the ascendancy."

Among Jews of Poland who felt a burning desire for creating a Zionist state in Palestine was David Green. When he finally got there, he kept his first name, but changed Green to Ben Gurion. If you've never heard of him, you'll find out a great deal about him very soon.

The Jerusalem that migrating Jews found in the early years of the twentieth century was not confined to the Old City. Thanks to the likes of Moses Montefiore and Muslims who'd looked for places to build beyond the walls, the city had spread out. Historian Martin Gilbert notes in *Jerusalem in the Twentieth Century* (John Wiley & Sons, 1996) that by 1910 nearly twice as many people lived outside the city walls as inside. Outside the Old City, he wrote, along the Jaffa Road and the Street of the

Consuls, as well as in expanding Jewish suburbs, could be found hotels, shops, and amenities expected of a modern, secular, European city.

Catching Up with the Nineteenth Century

This activity turned Jerusalem into a much different city at the end of the Ottoman reign than it had been a century earlier. In 1892, a railroad connecting Jerusalem to the nearest port city of Jaffa began operating. Reliable roads linked Jerusalem not just to Jaffa, but Ramallah, Nablus, Hebron, and Jericho. By the turn of the century, streets of the new city had been paved. Telegraph lines connected Jerusalem to Egypt and Europe. There was even an infant telephone system, with plans to expand it beyond the first installation in the American Colony to all official points and then businesses and residences.

Late in the nineteenth century a municipal council was created. Its initial activities included installing a sewage system in the 1870s. In the 1890s, regular garbage collection began, kerosene lamps were installed to light streets, and a city park was opened on Jaffa Street in front of the Russian Compound where a military band entertained on Fridays and Sundays. In 1914, a concession was granted by the Jerusalem municipality to provide electricity to the city. Other changes included formation of a city police force (1886), fire department (mid-1890s), and municipal hospital (1891). Between 1876 and 1916, Arabic newspapers and periodicals appeared, including an official government publication, *al-Quds al-Sharif.* The century also brought an expansion in educational opportunities for the city's elite, including girls.

In the midst of this conversion from medieval backwardness to the wonders of the nineteenth century, European powers vied to get an upper hand. They supported missionary activities, archaeology, and scholarship. To keep an eye on political, cultural, and social developments, Britain, France, Russia, Austria, and the United States opened consulates.

Reverent Remarks

Thus the new Jerusalem grows by accessions from every part of the globe. On the streets all sorts and conditions of Jews and Gentiles meet and pass one another; they may be strangers to each other and ignorant of the part they are playing, but I cannot resist the belief that each is doing his part in God's plan for the rebuilding of the city and its enlargement far beyond the borders it has occupied in the past.

—Edwin Sherman Wallace, United States consul in Jerusalem, 1898

Twists and Turns of the Winds of War

In 1914, events unfolding far from Jerusalem would open a new chapter in the city's history. On June 28, in Sarajevo, capital of Serbia in the Balkans, a Serbian nationalist assassinated the heir to the throne of Austria-Hungary, Archduke Franz Ferdinand. A month later, Austria-Hungary declared war on Serbia. Because Serbia had an ally in Russia's Czar Nicholas II, Russia joined the fray. In a matter of weeks the European powers took sides, with Germany aligning with Austria-Hungary against England, the French, and the Russians. By choosing to line up with Germany and Austria-Hungary, the Ottoman Turks handed the British Empire an opportunity to realize an old dream of moving into the Middle East in a big way.

Promises, Promises

Seven months into "the Great War" that was supposed to end all wars and make the world "safe for democracy," politicians in Great Britain and France were already pondering what to do with postwar Palestine. Paying no mind that in March 1915 victory was by no means a sure thing, a Jewish member of Britain's Labor government, Herbert Samuel, proposed the establishment of a British "protectorate" in Palestine. Although not a Zionist, he was keenly aware that most of the people of the United Kingdom were more concerned about the fate of the holy places of Christianity than those of Jews. He also knew that if he were to win support for a protectorate, he would need the help of a colleague in the government, Lloyd George. Samuel knew that his prospective ally, in the words of another member of the government, "does not care a damn for the Jews," but that he looked with horror on Jerusalem, Mount of Olives, Bethlehem, and other Christian shrines "under the protectorate of Agnostic Atheistic France." To win Lloyd George's backing, he pledged that the holy places would not go to the French. They could have their way in Baghdad, he said, but never in Jerusalem.

To encourage the Arabs to rebel against the Turks, the British high commissioner in Egypt promised an "independent sovereign Muslim state." Although Palestine was not mentioned, and no treaty was signed, the Arabs launched a revolt. You can get a good picture of all this in the movie *Lawrence of Arabia*. One of the film's major characters, portrayed by Jack Hawkins, is the commander of the British army, General Edmund Allenby. Keep him in mind; he'll be back in this story in a very big way.

What the Arabs didn't know as Britain talked about an Arab state in Palestine was that the Brits had also made a commitment to Jews to "facilitate" the creation of a

Jewish homeland. The pledge was made in a letter from Foreign Secretary Arthur Balfour to Lord Rothschild on November 2, 1917. It's known as the Balfour Declaration. But in a memorandum two months earlier, Balfour had written that although Britain and France had given their word to set up national governments in the former Ottoman Empire, "we do not propose even to go through the form of consulting the wishes of the present inhabitants of the country."

As to a preference between Arabs and Jews, Balfour stated that Great Britain was committed to Zionism because of "traditions" and "present needs and future hopes of far profounder import than the desires and prejudices" of 700,000 Arabs.

Sweet Music to the Ears of Zionists

When the Balfour Declaration was made public on November 9, 1917, grateful Jews held a "thanksgiving meeting" in the Royal Opera House in Covent Garden. Herbert Samuel spoke. After pledging a "reverent respect for Christian and Mohammedan holy places," he pulled out all the emotional stops. He said:

> I see in my mind's eye those millions [of Jews] in eastern Europe, all through the centuries, crowded, cramped, proscribed, bent with oppression, suffering all the miseries of active minds, denied scope, of talent not allowed to speak, of genius that cannot act. I see them enduring, suffering everything, sacrificing everything in order to keep alight the flame of which they knew themselves to be the lamp, to keep alive the idea of which they knew themselves to be the body; their eyes always set upon one distant point, always believing that somehow, some day, the ancient greatness would be restored; always saying when they met their families on Passover night, "Next year in Jerusalem."

On the March to Jerusalem with General Allenby

On the day that Samuel spoke, advanced units of the Australian and New Zealand Mounted Division were within 20 miles of the town of Latrun, with Jerusalem just beyond the hills. Keep the name of this town in the back of your mind; it will again be a key position as Israelis fight to Jerusalem in 1948 (Chapter 13).

Part of Britain's Egyptian Expeditionary Force, the Australians and New Zealanders, along with Indian troops, were commanded by General Sir Edmund Allenby. In addition to the campaign to take Palestine, he'd had to contend with an enigmatic English officer named Lawrence (whose name would forever be followed by the words "of

Arabia") and the death of a son, Michael, who'd been killed in action on the western front in France.

In advance of a land attack, Jerusalem was subjected to an air raid. The Royal Air Force planes targeted German military headquarters at the Augusta Victoria Hospice. A member of the American Colony noted with relief and satisfaction that the only church hit in the attack was a German one containing portraits of the kaiser and his wife.

On October 31, 1917, Allenby's force of 40,000 caught the Turks in southern Palestine by surprise. Expecting an attack through Gaza, where two previous British assaults had failed, the German commander of the Turkish force, General Kress von Kressenstein, was surprised that Allenby chose to strike against the biblical town of Beersheba. This bold move was planned on the basis of a new tool in warfare. Reconnaissance by airplanes had revealed inadequate defensive measures in the form of barbed wire and anticavalry ditches. Unimpeded by such barriers, Allenby's horsemen quickly took the town. With Beersheba fallen, a third attack on Gaza did the trick. As Turkish troops retreated north toward Jaffa, Allenby seemed to be about to achieve his goal to take Jerusalem.

> **High and Mighty**
>
> Born in England in 1861, Edmund Allenby trained at Sandhurst (Britain's equivalent of the U.S. Military Academy at West Point). Before leading the British forces in Palestine, he commanded the First Cavalry Division and the Third Army in France (1915–1917). After securing Jerusalem, he sent his cavalry to rout Egyptians at Meggido. Appointed high commissioner in Egypt in 1919, he held the post until 1925. He died in 1936.

Jerusalem's Pasha Looks for Scapegoats

The day after Gaza's fall, Palestine's governor, Djemal Pasha, ordered that the Jewish leaders of the Holy City and Jaffa be rounded up. When they were brought to him, he declared them and all the Jews guilty of espionage. Two Jews who had actually been caught spying were ordered executed. Some leaders were imprisoned. While others were let go because of lack of evidence, Djemal Pasha vowed that no Jews would be left in Jerusalem to welcome the British. With Allenby's forces getting closer to the city, he followed through on the threat. Forty Jewish leaders with American nationality and a number of Ottoman citizens who were

> **Reverent Remarks**
>
> Without Jerusalem, the land of Israel is as a body without a soul.
>
> —Elhanan Leib Lewinsky, Zionist leader (1857–1910)

known Zionists were forced to march to Jericho and into Jordan, in the words of a member of the German consulate, "like criminals." Plans were made for the deportation of hundreds more, to begin on December 9.

Allenby Learns that the Road to Jerusalem Runs Uphill

The plan laid out by General Allenby for Jerusalem's capture was a classic pincer movement. One part of his force would advance on the city from the west. A second portion headed to Hebron (King David's capital before he took Jerusalem from the Jebusites). The Hebron flank would press on to Bethlehem from the south and also cut the Jerusalem-Jericho road to the east. But this portion of the attack was delayed for three days because heavy rain turned the ground into a quagmire. Troops advancing north and west of Jerusalem were slowed by heavy Turkish artillery fire. Despite these impediments, on Friday, December 7, 1917, Jerusalem was effectively surrounded. Once again, the shifting tides of history had set the stage for a battle over the city that the world's three great religions called holy.

A Christmas Present for the People of England

On Sunday morning, December 9, two British soldiers foraging for eggs in a valley just three miles north of the city were shocked to see a group of Turkish soldiers carrying a white flag. With them were the mayor of Jerusalem and a multifaith contingent of priests, rabbis, and imams. Carrying keys to the city, they were looking for a general to accept the city's surrender.

According to the official British history, based on reports of the city's citizens, a "sudden panic" gripped the Turks. "After four centuries of conquest," the account noted, "the Turk was ridding the land of his presence in the bitterness of defeat, and a great enthusiasm arose among the Jews." At midnight, the city's governor, Izzet Bey, had gone to the telegraph office to send its employees home, then smashed all the equipment with a hammer. Two hours later, the Turkish force in the city began an evacuation that lasted five hours. As they left, an officer told a puzzled onlooker, "Gitmaya mejburuz." It meant, "We've got to go."

That Jerusalem could be taken without a fight had been the hope of the British government. Now that the moment had come, it would be recorded in history books not as a swaggering entrance into the Holy City, but an arrival marked with appropriate deference to its sanctity. Indeed, orders had gone out well in advance of the surrender that there must be no triumphal parade of men on horseback through the Jaffa Gate. General Allenby would dismount outside the wall, disarm, and enter on foot. He did so on the eleventh of December to the tolling of every bell in the city.

Christians were elated. An exultant British government official hailed the event as a Christmas gift for the people of England. They greeted the news with tolling bells, as did Rome and other cities in Europe.

Arab scholars recalled words of a prophet: "When the waters of the Nile flow into Palestine, then shall the prophet from the west drive the Turks from Palestine." The Arab word for prophet was al-Nabi, and very close to the name Allenby.

Noting that the day of the surrender of Jerusalem coincided with a Jewish holiday, the British official chronicler wrote:

> On this same day 2,082 years before, another race of conquerors, equally de-tested [as the Turks], were looking their last on the city which they could not hold, and inasmuch as the liberation of Jerusalem in 1917 will probably amelio-rate the lot of the Jews more than any other community in Palestine, it was fit-ting that the flight of the Turks should have coincided with the national festival of Hanukah, which commemorates recapture of the temple from the heathen Seleucids by Judas Maccabaeus in 165 B.C.

By substituting 2003 for 1917 Jerusalem in one passage in the official account of the Turks' abandonment of the city, you can understand the feelings of the people of Baghdad after Saddam Hussein's regime was deposed by an American-led coalition. The historian wrote that as Turks fled "townsfolk roused themselves from the leth-argy into which hunger and the Turkish police had plunged them and fell upon a variety of buildings, official or requisitioned for official purposes, and looted them, even stripping roofs, doors, and floors from the Ottoman barracks. It must be admit-ted that, as the government had furnished and maintained itself almost entirely by uncompensated requisitions, the crowd was only trying to identify itself."

As in Baghdad in 2003, Jerusalem in 1917 began a period in which no one could say how long it would remain an occupied city. That stretch of time is covered in the first three chapters of the next part of this book.

Holy Facts!

Ottoman period time line:

1517	Palestine and Jerusalem are taken by the Ottoman Empire.
1538–66	Suleiman the Magnificent rules, restores the city walls, and begins an era of religious tolerance.
1566	The Ottoman Empire begins to decline.
1798	Napoleon fails to conquer Palestine.
1882	The British occupy Egypt.
1880s	Expanded Jerusalem becomes a modern city.
	First large-scale Jewish immigration (aliyah) commences.
1904–14	Second aliyah, mostly from eastern Europe and Russia occurs.
1914	Ottomans ally with Germany as World War I begins.
1917	General Edmund Allenby accepts city's surrender, which begins the start of the British occupation.

The Least You Need to Know

◆ Jerusalem was absorbed by the Ottoman Empire.

◆ Suleiman the Magnificent gave Jews access to the Western Wall.

◆ Jews immigrated in large numbers in late nineteenth century.

◆ The Balfour Declaration pledged a future Jewish state.

◆ The British drove out the Turks and took control of the city.

Part  3

Next Year in Jerusalem

Covering six decades of Jerusalem's history (1917–1979), this part explores why and how Great Britain was granted authority to govern Palestine after World War I, the role of Zionism in laying the foundation of a Jewish state, and what happened when Britain withdrew from the region. It then examines three wars (1948, 1967, and 1973) between Arabs and Jews and their significance.

Chapter 10

Mandate

In This Chapter

+ Britain grants authority to a Zionist organization
+ A planning body sets rules for Jerusalem's development
+ When Muslims riot, Jews organize for self-defense
+ Winston Churchill sides with the Jews
+ The League of Nations "mandates" British control

With the rule of the Ottoman Empire over Palestine ended by Britain's defeat of Turkey's army, the new League of Nations gave Britain a "mandate" to set up a military regime that would smooth the way toward creation of a Jewish state. When Muslims rioted in protest, Jews responded by forming a self-defense force called Hagannah. In a city bubbling with religious tension, the British imposed rules for development of Jerusalem that gave the "new city" a unique architectural character and the Old City's picturesque street names.

Gentlemen, There'll Be No Flag Waving

You no doubt remember TV pictures of the patriotic U.S. Marine covering the face of a statue of Saddam Hussein with an American flag as the towering figure of the dictator was being readied to topple in Baghdad in April 2003. Moments later, the Stars and Stripes were replaced by the Iraqi flag because GIs were under orders not to display Old Glory so that the United States wouldn't be viewed throughout the Arab world as "an occupying power." Well, 86 years earlier, the British government in London had sent essentially the same order to General Sir Edmund Allenby. There would be no unfurling of the Union Jack, or the flag of any other Allied nation. Guards at the holy places of each of the city's three religions were to be adherents of the religion whose shrines they protected.

One of Allenby's aides, Major H. O. Lock, noted for posterity, "Never before had Jerusalem fallen into the hands of conquerors so zealous for the safety of its populace or so concerned for the preservation of the city and all that it contained." This was not exactly in line with the facts. You'll recall that when 'Umar took over Jerusalem in 638, he'd respected Christian sites, and that Suleiman the Magnificent emulated him nine centuries later. Major Lock's lapse of historical knowledge aside, there is no questioning the sincerity of Britain's policy of not offending sensitivities of residents of a city and territory that victory had thrust into British hands. However, this respect for Muslim, Christian, and Jewish feelings didn't mean that Britain intended to go back on the Balfour Declaration's pledge to Zionists that Jews would get a homeland in Palestine.

> **Reverent Remarks**
>
> In the din and tumult of the age, the still small voice of Jerusalem remains our only music.
> —Israel Zangwill, Jewish writer, 1921

Who Speaks for the Jews?

Before publication of the declaration bearing his name, Arthur Balfour had given the pledge of King George V's government that Jews would have a state in Palestine. He made it in a letter to Britain's most influential Jew, Baron Edmond de Rothschild. In mid-December of 1917, the baron's son, James, a British army officer, met with Jerusalem's leading rabbis to solicit their blessing for recruitment of Jews in the continuing war with retreating Turks in central Palestine and Galilee. Rothschild's argument was that raising a Jewish battalion would bolster Jewish belief in the promise of the Balfour Declaration.

Attending the meeting were Orthodox rabbis. Representing four fifths of the city's Jewish population, they believed that a Jewish state would be realized not by any British declaration or group of European Zionists, or even by Jewish warriors, but by the coming of the Messiah. Consequently, Rothschild's meeting failed to win the rabbis' endorsement for the raising of a Jewish fighting force. Undaunted, the British went ahead with their recruiting and put together the 40th Battalion, Royal Fusiliers, with volunteers mainly from Jerusalem. They joined the 38th Battalion—made up of Jews from America—and the 39th, consisting of Jews from Britain—formed by two ardent Zionists, Joseph Trumpeidor and Vladimir Jabotinsky. The latter will turn up later in this chapter in a dramatic way.

Rothschild's frustrating meeting with the Orthodox rabbis would not be the last time that the Brits would throw up their hands and ask in dismay, "Who speaks for the Jews?" When one of the Zionist leaders in Europe, Chaim Weizmann, learned of what he considered Orthodox obstinacy, he fumed, "As long as this *kloitzel* exists, there is no hope for our own [Zionist] institutions to achieve control over the country." Despite this gloomy outlook, Weizmann would become a powerful force in ensuring that the Jewish state would be built in Palestine on a Zionist timetable.

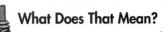

What Does That Mean?

Kloitzel is a derisive term for a small and disorganized synagogue.

A New Voice Speaks for the British

To run Palestine and its chief city, the Roman Empire appointed a military boss called a procurator. The Ottoman's version was a caliph. King George VI's government chose to call him the military governor. Because General Allenby still had a war to fight, he was replaced in mid-December 1917 by a member of the War Cabinet Secretariat. With a laudable 10-year record as an administrator in Egypt, 36-year-old Colonel Ronald Storrs arrived in Jerusalem 5 days before Christmas.

The Colonel Makes a Courtesy Call

Two days after settling into Jerusalem, Storrs got a taste of what a Christian Englishman faced when dealing with Muslims. He went to the Haram to introduce himself to Kamel al-Husseini, the *Mufti* of Jerusalem. After this chat, the Mufti directed a cousin to give Storrs a tour of Islam's third-holiest site. But as they were approaching the Dome of the Rock, Muslim guards made it clear that the shrine was off-limits to non-Muslims.

What Does That Mean?

The **Mufti** was a Muslim city's spiritual leader. He interpreted religious law. The Arabic definition is "one who gives a decisive response." The English word "mufti" refers to clothes worn by an off-duty soldier. It came into popular use in the nineteenth century in British colonies in Islamic regions when officers relaxed in long robes like those worn by Muslims.

That night in his quarters in the Grand New Hotel just inside the Jaffa Gate, Storrs became downright poetic about Jerusalem in his diary. He wrote, "The city is indeed quick with every time and kind of tragic memory and has perhaps passed the age of its productivity, though surely not of its interest and attraction. Not the hopeless beauty of Venice, the embattled majesty of Thebes, the abandon of Ferrara, or the melancholy of Ravenna; but something past yet unalloyed and throbbing, and seems to confound ancient and modern, and to undate recorded history."

A Scene that Rembrandt Could Have Painted

The day after meeting with the Mufti, Colonel Storrs conferred with 20 Ashkenazi rabbis. Ritually Orthodox, they were the descendants of Jews who'd emigrated from eastern Europe during the previous two centuries. Storrs recorded in his diary that he was received with "much ceremony in the council chamber, a long commonplace room on the first floor (approached by an outside staircase) and quite unworthy of the Rembrandtesque fur-gowned, fur-hatted, ringleted Rabbis sitting on either side of me down a long deal table."

What Does That Mean?

Yiddish From the Hebrew word "yehudi," meaning "Judean." The Jewish Almanac defines it as a "Germanic language invented and spoken by Jews in eastern Europe with a vocabulary derived from Hebrew, Slavic, Latin, Italian, French, Russian, Aramaic, and German, and written in slightly modified Hebrew characters."

Most of the Jews spoke only *Yiddish*. A few knew Arabic and French. One was capable of "very tolerable English." Storrs broke the ice by referring to the happy coincidence of Allenby taking the surrender of Jerusalem on Hanukkah. But what concerned the Ashkenazi was a report that out of 15 members of a newly organized city council, only 5 were Orthodox. The rest were Zionists (five), Sephardic (three) with Zionist ideas, and two were "unaffiliated." The Ashkenazi would respond to this Zionist maneuver by forming their own "community council."

On Christmas the new military governor of Jerusalem left the problems of the Jews and the Muslims to another day to observe the first return of Christian authority in Jerusalem since the Crusades.

Three days after Colonel Storrs celebrated Christmas, he formally assumed his duties. On December 31, he received New Year's greetings from the people he would be dealing with. Muslims and Christians came separately, as did the Zionist-dominated city council and the rival Orthodox Ashkenazi community council. Providing a touch of humor in all this seriousness of purpose was a written appeal for a favor from an Arab Christian. He wrote, "I do beseech Your Excellency to grant my request, for the sake of J. Christ, Esq.; a gentleman whom Your Honor closely resembles."

Not Since the Days of the Romans

As the United States learned in Europe after two world wars and in Afghanistan and Iraq in the first wars of the twenty-first century, the first duty of an occupier of a conquered city, even one that was taken without a battle, is to provide inhabitants with good water. Finding Jerusalem's ancient sources not only inadequate but unhealthy, Storrs was faced with building a new water system, and doing it quickly. After surveying the problem, army engineers found the answer in the city's past. In the time of Herod the Great the Romans had solved the water problem with an aqueduct system that brought water from distant springs to a reservoir holding 4 million gallons. The official historian of Britain's Egyptian Expeditionary Force noted that engineers cleared the old channels of "the dust of ages, including the remains of several individuals who may have belonged to almost any period."

The old reservoir was repaired and equipped with pumping machinery Romans could never have imagined. Nine weeks after work began, clean water was flowing at the rate of more than a quarter-million gallons a day. Never at a loss for superlatives, the historian wrote, "Not since the days of the Romans has running water been so plentiful in the Holy City."

If You Seek His Monument, Look Around

Upon the death of London's greatest architect, Christopher Wren, his son provided a Latin inscription for Wren's tomb in the crypt of Wren's greatest achievement, St. Paul's Cathedral. It reads, *Si monumentum requiris circumspice.* ("If you would see the man's monument, look around.") Looking around modern Jerusalem, you'll see Storrs's greatest contribution to the city in its facades. Wielding dictatorial powers with all the vigor of procurators and pashas who'd preceded him, he issued a proclamation on April 8, 1918 in the four languages of the city (English, Arabic, Hebrew, and French) that said, "No person shall demolish, erect, alter, or repair the structure of any building in the City of Jerusalem or its environs within a radius of 2,500 metres from the Damascus Gate (Bab al-Amud) until he had obtained a written permit from the Military Governor."

Banning building fronts made of stucco, corrugated metal, concrete, and wood, he decreed that they be made only of Jerusalem stone. This restored to Jerusalem the unique look that Josephus had described as "a snowy mountain glittering in the sun." The edict is still law.

A New Face in Town and the Thin End of the Wedge

Earlier in this chapter, you read a quote that was anything but flattering to Jerusalem's Orthodox leaders. Three months after the Zionist leader Chaim Weizmann branded them a kloitzel, he arrived in Jerusalem as head of a commission empowered by the British to serve as a liaison group between all of Palestine's Jews and the military government. Storrs promptly arranged a meeting between Weizmann and the Mufti. According to Storrs, Weizmann spoke of "progress together until they [Jews and Muslims] are ready for joint autonomy." The Mufti quoted Islamic tradition: "Our rights are your rights, and your duties are our duties."

It wasn't long before reality overtook this amity. As the Zionist commission flexed its muscles, the city's Arabs felt, as Storrs put it, that it was "the thin end of the wedge, the beginning of a Zionist "government within a government." With these "anxieties and suspicions," Storrs wrote, "the pitch of good relationship was being irreparably" questioned.

Nothing soured Jewish-Muslim relations more than a rejection by the Mufti of Weizmann's offer of 75,000 pounds to pay for demolishing buildings that blocked easy access by Jews to the Western Wall.

Storrs recognized that even if the Mufti were willing to accept the offer, he "would have had to reckon" with "sensitiveness of his own public (quite apart from their growing fear of Zionism) over the slightest rumor of interference even with the ground adjoining the outside wall of the Haram al-Sharif." Storrs later said with regret that acceptance of Weizmann's offer "would have obviated years of wretched humiliations" of Jews and their Wall.

Five decades would have to go by and two wars fought before Jews would clear away obstacles to worship at the Western Wall.

Run These Ideas Up the Flagpole

To say that Arab nerves were on edge during the first year of the British occupation is a mild understatement. They were offended by Zionists adding a subsidy to wages of Jews employed as city clerks, policemen, railway workers, and telephone operators. Arabs registered a protest when the Zionists got the British to change the date for a parade to mark King George V's birthday to a day that didn't take place on the Jewish

Sabbath. When Zionists produced thousands of small white flags with a blue Star of David at the center, the commotion on the part of Arabs was so great that Storrs had to prohibit their display. The first act of a new Congress of Muslim-Christian Association was a memorandum that rejected Zionism. A statement by Palestinian-Arab nationalists called on Britain to "defend Palestine from Zionist immigration."

Storrs noted ruefully, "Jerusalem was growing more difficult and less agreeable. Arab resentment against the Balfour Declaration was now louder as well as deeper."

The Symbolism of a Row of Building Blocks

On July 24, 1918, Jews gathered on Mount Scopus, north of the Old City, for a ceremony laying 12 symbolic stones—one for each of the 12 tribes of ancient Israel. They were the beginning of the Hebrew University. Moved by thoughts of all that had happened to Jews in the thousands of years since Solomon built the temple, and of a beginning of a return of Jews to Jerusalem made possible by the Allied victory in Palestine, Chaim Weizmann said, "Here, out of the misery and desolation of war is being created the first germ of a new life. In this University we have gone beyond restoration. We are creating, even during the war [WWI would not end for another four months], something which is to serve as a symbol of a better future. In the University, the wandering soul of Israel will reach its haven."

City Planning, Parks, Gardens, and Open Spaces

The next idea to spring from Storrs's mind was the Pro-Jerusalem Society. Its purpose was "the protection of and the addition to the amenities of Jerusalem, the provision and maintenance of parks, gardens, and open spaces," protection and preservation "of the antiquities," and "encouragement of arts, handicrafts, and industries." With funding provided by city banks, businesses, and contributions from the United States and Europe, Storrs put the undertaking in the hands of official city planner William MacLean and civic advisor C. R. Ashbee.

The Pro-Jerusalem Society didn't wish to improve the character of the Old City's jumble of streets and alleyways. The scene particularly impressed city official Edward Keith-Roach. "The steps were hemmed in on either side by vegetable shops aglow with colour," he wrote after a tour. "Butchers' shops alongside, selling goats' meat and mutton with very naked fat tails, were festooned with intestines and tripe. Flies were rampant. Laden camels passing up and down caused as much disturbance as a motor lorry passing along an English lane." Of the people: "Most of Jerusalem—Arab, Jew, and European—appeared to be in the overcrowded thoroughfare. Gesticulating, haranguing, expostulating, they went from shop to shop, accompanied by little Arab boys with baskets strapped across their shoulders, turning over, choosing or rejecting the produce. There were no carts within the city walls, nor were the streets wide enough to take them."

While this panorama was fascinating and certainly exciting, below its surface flowed a tide of Arab resentment of the pro-Zionist Balfour Declaration. "In politics," Storrs wrote, "Jerusalem was growing more difficult and less agreeable."

An Agony of Fear and Hatred

On February 27, 1920, Major-General Louis Bobs, who held the title of Officer Administering the Government of Palestine, issued a proclamation shattering Arab hopes that Britain might find a way to wiggle out of the Balfour Declaration's pledge to grant the Jews a state in Palestine. Informed that the British government intended to carry out the promise, 1,500 Jerusalem Arabs poured into the streets in a peaceful protest. Ten days later, Arab mobs attacked Jews on streets and in their shops while shouting "Palestine is our land and the Jews are our dogs." General Bobs reacted with a ban on demonstrations that seemed to put a lid on things. But on Easter Sunday, April 4, 1920, as Storrs was returning home after services at St. George's Cathedral, he was met by his orderly. He blurted in Arabic, "There has been an outbreak at the Jaffa Gate and a man has been wounded to death." Storrs later said that he felt as if the aide had "thrust a sword into my heart."

As other Arab attacks followed, Vladimir Jabotinsky, a Russian who'd fought in the British army, decided to organize a Jewish defense force, called a Hagannah. Its members marched to the Jaffa Gate but were repulsed by British troops. Two days of fighting resulted in the deaths of 5 Jews and 4 Arabs, and more than 200 Jews injured. Rounded up, Jabotinsky and 19 members of Hagannah were sentenced to prison. All but Jabotinsky got three years. He received 15; in response to the public outcry that followed, however, he was released after only a few months. Storrs lamented that "carefully built relations of mutual understanding between British, Arabs, and Jews seemed to flare away in an agony of fear and hatred."

A Visit by the Secretary of State for Colonial Affairs

In the early spring of 1921, a newly appointed Secretary of State for Colonial Affairs, Winston Churchill, traveled to the Holy City from Cairo, Egypt, where he'd presided over a conference to settle boundaries in the former Ottoman Empire. His first stop in Jerusalem was the British military cemetery on Mount Scopus.

The next day (March 28), he got an earful from Arabs on what they thought of Zionists, the Balfour Declaration's "gross injustice," and Jews who had "no separate political or linguistic existence." Along with this came a warning. "The Arab is noble and large-hearted," said members of the Executive Committee of the Haifa Congress of Palestinian Arabs. "[But] he is also vengeful, and never forgets an ill-deed. If England does not take up the cause of the Arabs, other powers will." (Britain and the United States would experience the brunt of Arab resentment of being ignored when Arab nations allied themselves with the Soviet Union during the Cold War, followed by a campaign of terrorism with the issue of Palestine at its core.)

> **Reverent Remarks**
>
> These veteran soldiers lie where rests the dust of the Khalifs and Crusaders and the Maccabees. Peace to their ashes, honour to their memory and may we not fail to complete the work which they have begun.
>
> —Winston Churchill, British Military Cemetery, Mount Scopus, Jerusalem, March 27, 1921

Churchill replied that …

> it is manifestly right that the Jews who are scattered all over the world, should have a national center and a National Home where some of them may be reunited. And where else could that be but in this land of Palestine, with which for more than 3,000 years they have been intimately and profoundly associated? We think it will be good for the Jews and good for the British Empire. But we also think it will be good for the Arabs who dwell in Palestine, and we intend that it shall be good for them, and that they shall not be sufferers or supplanted in the country in which they dwell or denied their share in all that makes for its progress and prosperity.

He then pointed out that because it was the British armies who had driven out the Turks, Britain had earned "the right" to do as it desired.

To members of an also newly formed body, the Jewish National Council, who followed the Arabs in meeting with Churchill, the message of the secretary of state for colonial affairs was music to the ears. "I am myself perfectly convinced," Churchill told them, "that the cause of Zionism is one which carries with it much that is good for the whole world, and not only for the Jewish people, but that it will also bring with it prosperity and contentment and advancement of the Arab population of this country."

High Hopes Clash with Hard Reality

On the fourth anniversary of formal publication of the Balfour Declaration, Arabs surged from mosques with denunciations of the declaration by mullahs ringing in their ears. They went on a rampage, sweeping through the Jewish Quarter of the Old City. They were met by the Hagannah. When the clash was over, four Jews had been killed.

A Fateful Decision

Meanwhile, in April 1922, in San Remo, Italy, far removed from troubled Jerusalem, the newly formed League of Nations met to further seal the Zionist fate of Palestine. Noting that the "Principal Allied Powers" that had won World War I had agreed to give ("mandate") administration of "the territory of Palestine" to one of the powers, the responsibility was accepted by the government of "His Britannic Majesty" in the expectation that Britain place the country "under such political, administrative, and economic conditions" as to secure the establishment of a "Jewish national home," while at the same time safeguarding "civil and religious rights of all the inhabitants of Palestine, irrespective of race and religion."

For "the purpose of advising and cooperating" with the British, the League of Nations required recognition of an "appropriate Jewish agency." It designated the Zionist Organization.

> **Reverent Remarks**
>
> The Mandatory shall see that complete freedom of conscience and the free exercise of all forms of worship, subject only to the maintenance of public order and morals, are ensured to all. No discrimination of any kind shall be made between the inhabitants of Palestine on the ground of race, religion or language. No person shall be excluded from Palestine on the sole ground of his religious belief.
>
> —Article 15, The British Mandate for Palestine, League of Nations, April 24, 1922

A Mosaic of the New and the Old

As the League of Nations was mapping the politics of Palestine, the part of its most venerated city was experiencing a building boom. Following sale of a tract of land in the "new city" outside walled Old City by the Greek patriarchate, shops, cafés, and hotels blossomed on a new street named in honor of a man who had worked to revive the Hebrew language, Eliezer Ben Yehuda. At the same time, thousands of trees were planted and a municipal center constructed, with a Government House fashioned out of what had been the Augusta Victoria Hospice. Eventually a new avenue, named for King George V, was built to link Jaffa Road with the railroad station. Zionist leader Dr. Arthur Ruppin hailed it as "wide and long enough to invite one to walk here."

New structures were a symbol of modernity, but the abiding appeal of Jerusalem was the Old City as described in Cook's guidebook for 1924: "Among these streets, and the hundred and one narrow lanes and byways that are tributary to them there is endless passage of camels, donkeys, sheep, goats and the picturesque natives of the city." This "enthnographical museum" was a bazaar of antiquities and curiosities. Yet beneath the surfaces of Old City and new ran turbulent currents that would vex Jerusalem's British rulers for decades to come.

The Least You Need to Know

- The British military governor was Ronald Storrs.
- Britain's government favored Zionist leaders.
- Orthodox Jews said that only their Messiah could create a Jewish state.
- Arabs rioted against the Balfour Declaration.
- The League of Nations gave Britain a "mandate" in Palestine.

Chapter 11

An Unruly Place

In This Chapter

- ◆ Muslims attack Jews at the Western Wall
- ◆ The Jewish population increases by a third
- ◆ A decade of attacks and retaliations
- ◆ Britain cracks down on Jewish immigration
- ◆ The Irgun declares all-out war on Arabs and Brits

With Jerusalem the capital of the Israel for the first time in more than seven centuries, the city grew rapidly. Leading Zionist organizations, which were based in Tel Aviv, moved their offices to Jerusalem. And as noted in the previous chapter, the Hebrew University of Jerusalem was established on Mount Scopus.

On the west side of the city, developers were busy putting up luxury hotels, reflecting a resurgence in commercial life. The King David Hotel, to be opened in 1931, would bring a new level of accommodation to the city's tourist trade. Across the street, the "handsomest YMCA in the entire world" designed by Q. L. Harmon, an architect who would also build New York's Empire State Building, was going up. The "Y" gave Jerusalem its first heated swimming pool and first indoor basketball court.

Not to be outdone, Arabs opened the nearby Palace Hotel. North of the Old City wall rose the new Rockefeller Museum of Archaeology. These and other projects in the decade following the entry of the British Egypt Expeditionary Force in 1917 had wrought changes outside the Old City walls that justified the area being called the "New Jerusalem."

No doubt impressed and pleased by the advances which had been inspired and achieved under the leadership of Ronald Storrs, the man who had preceded him into Jerusalem, Edmund Allenby, was back in the city on May 7, 1927. He came for the unveiling of a new name for the British Military Cemetery on Mount Scopus, called thereafter the Jerusalem War Memorial Cemetery. Allenby also had a new title: Field Marshal Viscount Allenby. He would lay the foundation stone of the Hospice and Church of St. Andrew's, the patron saint of Scotland, and pay tribute to Scot soldiers who had been among the city's liberators in 1917.

Jerusalem Old and New Gets a Shaking from Mother Nature

Nine weeks after Allenby's return to the city he'd entered on foot out of respect for its holiness, the ground beneath Old and New Jerusalem shifted. Although only one man and one woman died in the earthquake of July 12, 1927, several buildings suffered severe damage, including the Government House in the former Augusta Victoria Hospice, the new Hebrew University on Mount Scopus, the Church of the Holy Sepulchre, and the Abyssinian Palace. At the al-Aqsa Mosque, the quake weakened the central ceiling, floor, eastern transept, and ancient columns. (When a 1938 earthquake inflicted even more damage, the columns would be replaced with pillars of Carrara marble paid for by Italian dictator Benito Mussolini.)

Holy Facts!

In 1925, the Supreme Moslem Council offered a visitors' guide to al-Haram al-Sharif. The 16-page brochure included text and photographs of the "Noble Sanctuary" with its imposing Dome of the Rock, the al-Aqsa Mosque, and other architectural features.

The guide noted that upon entering the Dome of the Rock through the west gate the interior "is almost too dark to see, but as the eye gets used to the subdued light, the beauty of the structure and the splendor of the ornamentation reveal themselves. In the center, vertically below the dome, is the sacred rock, an irregular mass of yellowish stone."

Because of "considerable repairs" to part of the al-Aqsa Mosque supporting its dome, visitors in 1925 were admitted only to the nave and aisles. The guide advised that pillars with Byzantine capitals "of wicker-work design are worth noticing."

Although the natural disaster left large scars on the city, acts of men had a far greater impact on Jerusalem during the 1920s.

Muslims React Angrily to Jews Changing the "Status Quo"

Although Miriam the Prophetess, sister of Moses and Aaron, led the children of Israel in dancing in praise of the Lord after the safe crossing of the Red Sea; Deborah was esteemed as the "mother of Israel"; and Ruth of the Bible was an ancestor of King David, a feature of synagogues was the segregation of men and women during the services. Consequently, though inexplicably belatedly, men who gathered at the Western Wall on September 23, 1928, on the eve of Yom Kippur, put up a screen to separate the women who'd also come to pray. Because this had not happened before, Muslims saw it as a change in the British-imposed "status quo." Asserting that the screen was a deliberate provocation, they claimed that the screen blocked passage, despite the fact that the "right of way" was a dead end.

Because it was a holiday and no Jewish police were available to handle the crisis, British constables arrived. Inspector D. V. Duff asked that the screen be removed. The Jews not only balked, they complained to Duff that he'd interfered with their prayers. Duff's polite request became an order. Ignored, the inspector directed his men to take down the screen. Shoving ensued. Fists flew. The police used night sticks. Several Jews, men and women, were hurt. The screen was hauled away.

When the dust-up had settled, the Mufti spoke for the Muslim Supreme Council. "The Jews' aim," he warned the British authorities, "is to take possession of the Mosque of al-Aqsa gradually." Within hours, Muslims took to an overlooking rooftop to conduct their own prayers at the top of their voices.

Jews Show that Arabs Aren't the Only Ones Who Don't Forget

On August 15, 1929, young Jews who were apparently fed up with the Muslim prayers from the rooftop, and evidently miffed that the British had done nothing about it, poured onto the Haram waving Star of David flags and singing Zionist songs. Muslims retaliated the next day by flocking to the Western Wall to chase away a handful of Jews, beat up the Jew in charge, and tear up and burn Hebrew prayer books. A day later, a Jewish boy who'd gone after a football that he'd unintentionally kicked into an Arab garden was stabbed. He died in a hospital three days later. Following his funeral on the morning of August 23, a throng of irate Jews set out to invade the Muslim Quarter but were stopped by the police at the Jaffa Gate.

When Muslims departed the Noble Sanctuary after prayers the next Friday, thousands headed for the Jewish Quarter. Working in an office outside Damascus Gate, a British official heard "faint distant shouting, like the ominous buzz of bees." Looking out a window, he watched Muslims attack every Jew caught in sight. Worse was happening in Jewish homes beyond the Old City. A mob of Muslims broke into the houses on a murderous rampage. By that afternoon, Arabs had attacked Jewish settlements in more distant suburbs.

The riot went on for three nights with a Muslim mob destroying a synagogue and Jews vandalizing a mosque. By the time British troops flown in from Egypt quashed the rioting, nearly 4,000 Jews had been forced to abandon their homes and seek the protection of the British in Jerusalem.

Mufti Haj Amin al-Husseini put the blame on Jewish provocation in the form of a "Zionist demonstration" on August 15 when they had walked "unauthorized" on Muslim streets to the Western Wall and "illegally hoisted" the Zionist flag. Arab leaders sent a letter to the British High Commissioner demanding disarmament of Jews, establishment of a Palestinian parliament, and repudiation of the Balfour Declaration.

> **Reverent Remarks**
>
> Jerusalem has now been a city of death for eight days during which work has ceased and people are starving. Hundreds are receiving bread rations. Everywhere it is deadly quiet, and everyone is nervous.
>
> —Reuters news report, August 30, 1929

Arab Students Call for a Boycott of Jewish Businesses

On September 11, 1929, Arab students called for economic warfare by means of a boycott. They issued a proclamation that said in part:

> O Arab! Remember that the Jew is your strongest enemy and the enemy of your ancestors since olden times. Do not be misled by his tricks for it is he who tortured Christ, peace be upon him, and poisoned Mohammed, peace and worship be with him. It is he who now endeavors to slaughter you as he did yesterday. Be aware that the best way to save yourself and your Fatherland from the grasp of the foreign intruder and greedy Jew is to boycott him. Therefore boycott him and support the industry of your Fatherland and God.

The Palestine Zionist Executive declared, "We are convinced that were it not for the fact that through circulation of deliberately false reports calculated to stir up their feelings, such as the allegations the Mosque of Omar had been bombed, looted or burnt, the Arabs of Palestine would have continued to live in peaceful relations with their Jewish neighbors, as it is still the wish of the overwhelming majority of the Arab population."

Arabs Look Around and See More and More Jews

The accompanying chart shows that five years into British rule, Jerusalem had about 20,000 more Jews than Muslims. Although the Muslim population had increased by 1931, the Jewish majority had also widened. The number of Christians had more than quadrupled.

Jerusalem's Post WWI Population Growth

Year	Jews	Muslims	Christians	Total
1922	33,971	13,411	4,699	52,081
1931	51,222	19,894	19,335	90,451

Alarmed by the rise in the Jewish population, the Mufti, Haj Amin al-Husseini, called for a World Islamic Conference. It convened in Jerusalem on December 6, 1931, and concluded 11 days later with a decision to establish a permanent Islamic Congress. Based on a belief that Jews intended to drive Muslims from the Haram and take it over, the conference voted to deny Jews access to it.

Denouncing the wave of Jewish immigration, the Mufti blamed it on what he saw as Britain's pro-Zionist policies.

Although the Mufti was complaining that the British government was all too eager to give Zionists everything they requested, the British denied a plan proposed by the head of the Political Department of the Jewish Agency, Chaim Arlosoro, that Jerusalem be divided into Jewish West (New City) and Muslim East (Old City), with religious sites protected. The formal British government response viewed "with disfavor any proposal for the partition of Jerusalem." Britain's High Commissioner, Sir Edwin Samuel (son of the Herbert you read about earlier), feared "immediate proximity to each other would be almost to invite friction."

While the British government struggled to make up its mind about what to do with Jerusalem and Palestine, there would be friction aplenty, as the following sampling of nasty incidents between Arabs and Jews in 1936 shows:

 ◆ **April 22.** Arab youths threaten Jewish and Arab merchants for not joining a general strike.

◆ **May 14.** Two Jews are shot point-blank in the Jewish Quarter. The Mufti justified these deaths by declaring, "The Jews are trying to expel us from the country. They are murdering our sons and burning our houses."

◆ **May 16.** Three Jews die when an Arab gunman opens fire in the new Edison Film Theater.

What had begun as a general strike by Arabs quickly turned into a full-scale campaign of violence against Jews. A *Palestine Post* headline asked, "War of Extermination?" Citing Jewish "restraint" and Jewish "moral repugnance for murder," the article wondered "who can now guarantee that Jews, outraged to their depths, will not undergo a change of outlook on the sacredness of human life?"

Britain's response was a royal commission to review the mandate and the causes of the violence. Arabs boycotted the commission at first, but in the end the Mufti appeared before the panel. Defiant and demanding independence for Palestine, he was asked if Palestine could assimilate its Jewish population. He replied, "No." The commission found the Mufti and the Arab Higher Committee responsible for "protracting the strike" and for not condemning "the acts of sabotage and terrorism which became more frequent as the strike continued."

Holy Facts! ─────────

In the rioting between 1936 and 1939, the death toll in Palestine was 500 Jews, 160 British, and more than 3,000 Arabs (about one third of the Arab deaths were caused by other Arabs).

The panel's formula to resolve the issue of Palestine was two states: Jewish along the coast and in Galilee, Arab on the West Bank of the Jordan River, the Gaza Strip, and the Negev Desert. A corridor between the sea and Jerusalem would be neutral. The proposal's likelihood of taking off was the same as that of a lead balloon because the Arabs immediately rejected it.

The Mufti Cozy Up to the Nazis

While Jews and Arabs were at each other's throat and the British were trying to keep the peace in Palestine throughout the 1930s, King George VI's ministers in London were watching events across the English Channel. Since 1933, the German government had been in the hands of Adolf Hitler and his Nazi party. Hitler's policy on what to do with Jews in Germany was the same as that of the Mufti of Jerusalem, Haj Amin al-Husseini. The Mufti wanted them gone from Palestine. Hitler wanted them expunged from Germany.

On July 16, 1937, British tolerance of the man they identified as the main trouble-maker in Jerusalem ran out. When they learned that the Mufti had met with the German consul and known Nazi in Jerusalem, the Brits issued an order for the Mufti's arrest. Tipped off, he rushed to the Haram and claimed sanctuary. Three months later, he slipped out of the city, reportedly dressed as a woman, and made it to Beirut, Lebanon. But the escape didn't spell the end of his agitation against Jews. In 1943, he was heard on the radio broadcasting from Rome on the birthday of the Prophet (March 19). He spoke of the "dangerous aim" of Jews and their "wish to occupy the holy Islamic institutions." He also read a statement by German Foreign Minister Joachim von Ribbentrop that the "basic tenet of German policy" was "obliteration of what is called the Jewish national home."

Jews Read a British "White Paper" and See Red

As the Nazis pursued a policy of repression of German Jews, the result was an exodus of Jews who could pay for transportation to the land Arabs called Palestine and Jews called Israel. Alarmed Arabs demanded that Britain stop the flow of these refugees. Worried about the fate of the Middle East in case of another war with Germany, and fearing that Arab nations (Egypt, Syria, Saudi Arabia, Yemen, and Iraq) might side with the Germans, the British published a "White Paper" on May 18, 1939, that restricted Jewish immigration to Palestine to 75,000 for a period of 5 years. After that, the territory's "majority" (the Arabs) would have the right to veto further arrivals.

When several hundred Jews in Jerusalem rioted in response to the policy, the commander of the British troops in Palestine summoned Jewish leaders. One of them called on was David Ben-Gurion, to whom you were introduced in Chapter 10 as David Green. You'll be reading a lot more about him in the next chapter. The British general said there must be no more riots. "If blood is to be shed," he warned, "that blood will be on the head of the Jews." Unfortunately, the British officer was talking to the wrong group of Jews.

Eye for Eye, Tooth for Tooth, Hand for Hand, Foot for Foot

The preceding "eye-for-eye" guideline for a just response to a wrong is found in the Old Testament (Exodus 21:24). As Arabs continued to attack Jews, a Jewish group calling itself *Irgun Zvai Leumi* (IZL) took the biblical formula for revenge to heart.

What Does That Mean?

Irgun Zvai Leumi means "National Military Organization." Its initials—IZL—were spoken as a word: *Etzel.*

Holy Facts!

The 1960 movie *Exodus,* based on the novel of that title by Leon Uris, provides a dramatic portrayal of the dispute over strategy that led to militants splitting from the Hagannah to form the Irgun.

Militant members had split from Hagannah out of frustration over the Jewish armed force's preference for negotiations with the British. Irgun took its inspiration from Vladimir Jabotinsky (whom you also met in Chapter 10). An explanation of this split was provided by a man whose name would loom large in the annals of the Irgun in the years immediately after World War II and even more importantly as Israel's prime minister in 1979. In a personal history of Irgun (*The Revolt; Steimatzky's Agency Ltd.,* 1952), Menachem Begin wrote, "The official Zionist leaders, especially those of the Left [Hagannah] were fanatically opposed to its developing a military nature." When Jabotinsky called for a Jewish army, Begin continued, "he was denounced by the Left as a 'militarist' and a 'Fascist' for daring to utter such a thought."

When the British House of Commons voted to approve of the White Paper on May 23, 1939, Irgun leaders viewed it as a sham and an exercise in cynical betrayal. Begin would write that the White Paper "liquidated" the Jewish claim to Palestine.

The Irgun immediately called for Jews to take Palestine by force and establish a state with boundaries of the Israel of the Bible. Six days after the Commons vote, Irgun bombs exploded in a movie theater, injuring 10 Arabs and 5 constables (2 British and 3 Arab). On the same day, Arab buses were fired on in the Romema neighborhood, close to gates of the city.

The British responded by arresting Irgun suspects and instituting a citywide curfew. On May 26, Arabs killed a German Jew who'd come to Jerusalem following his release from the Dachau concentration camp. On June 2, an Irgun bomb in a melon market killed nine Arabs, including a policeman. Hours later, Irgun bombs exploded in manholes and cut off phones in half of the city. While John F. Kennedy, a son of Joseph P. Kennedy (U.S. Ambassador to the United Kingdom) was visiting Catholic holy sites early in June, the city was plunged into darkness by 14 Irgun bombs that shut off the city's electrical system.

Although Hagannah leaders deplored the violence, the British were not satisfied. "Lip service to nonviolence is useless," said the Military Commander of Jerusalem, Major General Richard O'Connor, "if the Jewish community does nothing to check its criminal members or to assist the authorities in their efforts to maintain public security."

Reverent Remarks

Of my own free will and consent, and without any coercion, I swear to be a loyal soldier in the Irgun Zvai Leumi in the Land of Israel who will defend the national property, life, and honor, and will help to bring about the full restoration of our people in the land of their forefathers. I accept obedience without any reservations, and promise to keep total secrecy in regard to all I know about the Irgun. I will obey my commanders and carry out all their orders at any time. So help me the Guardian of Israel.

—The Irgun Oath

A Harvest of Inevitable Tragedy

With the assistance of the Irgun and the Hagannah, Jews fleeing the Nazi campaign to round them up and send them to concentration camps attempted to reach Palestine on ships. Britain's policy was to block their departures from eastern European seaports, and if that failed, intercept them at sea and turn them around.

They justified such treatment in part by saying that German spies disguised as refugees might penetrate the Middle East and endanger British interests. When one of these ships, the *Struma*, arrived off the coast from Romania with more than 700 Jews, it was ordered back. Halfway back to Romania, it sank, taking everyone with it. Reacting to what Menachem Begin called "a harvest of inevitable tragedy," Britain announced that such ships would thereafter be diverted to Mauritius. "Illegal immigration" to Palestine, declared Britain, would not be allowed.

The British began to put refugees in camps on the island of Cyprus. At the high point of these detentions approximately 50,000 Jews were imprisoned.

Holy Facts!

On June 6, 1946, President Truman urged the British government to relieve the suffering of the Jews confined to displaced persons camps in Europe by accepting 100,000 Jewish immigrants. Britain's Foreign Minister, Ernest Bevin, replied that the United States wanted displaced Jews to immigrate to Palestine "because they did not want too many of them in New York."

The Story of the Refugee Ship *Exodus*

As the detention camps were filling up, an American journalist in Jerusalem, Ruth Gruber, learned that a former American pleasure boat, renamed the *Exodus 1947*, had been attacked by five British destroyers and a cruiser as the ship attempted to deliver

4,500 Jewish refugees, including 600 children, to Haifa. Arriving at the seaport, she saw the *Exodus* entering the harbor "like a matchbox splintered by a nutcracker." To block the ship's progress, the British rammed it and opened fire with guns and tear gas. The *Exodus* crew of mostly Jews from America and Palestine retaliated with potatoes, sticks, and cans of kosher meat. During the battle, the second officer was clubbed to death while trying to keep a British soldier from the wheelhouse. Learning that the prisoners from the *Exodus* were being transferred to Cyprus, Gruber flew there and waited for their arrival. After photographing prisoners living in tents behind barbed wire with little water or sanitary facilities, she cabled the New York Herald, "You had to smell Cyprus to believe it."

Discovering that the British had changed plans and would send the *Exodus* prisoners to where they had originated (Port de Bouc in southern France), Gruber rushed to that location and arrived as the prisoners were refusing to leave the ship. After 18 days of stand-off, the British decided to ship them to Germany. By now the world's press had picked up the story, but only Gruber was allowed by the British to accompany the refugees. Aboard the prison ship *Runnymeade Park*, she photographed refugees defiantly raising a British flag on which they'd painted a swastika. The photo became *Life Magazine's* "Picture of the Week."

Reverent Remarks

Dark night, the darkest of all nights, descended on the Jewish people in Europe. All appeals to what Jews hoped was a sensitive British conscience was fruitless.

—Menachem Begin

Gruber published a book about what she'd observed, and much of what she reported provided inspiration for Leon Uris's best-selling novel and movie, *Exodus*. In the fictionalized account, one of the characters, Dov Landau (played by Sal Mineo), explained that on his arrival in Israel he would join the Irgun to kill British soldiers because "they know how to do it."

It was against this background that Jews would vent their ire against the British. Leading the fight would be a new terrorist organization, proudly calling itself a "gang," that you'll meet in the next chapter.

The Least You Need to Know

♦ Muslims feared that Jews planned to take over the Haram al-Sharif.

♦ Jerusalem was racked by religious riots.

♦ British policy restricted Jewish immigration.

♦ The Irgun resistance group urged Jews to conquer Palestine.

♦ Jews fleeing Nazi oppression in Europe were turned back.

Chapter 12

Exodus

In This Chapter

- ◆ Jerusalem during World War II
- ◆ The British try to keep out Jewish refugees
- ◆ A campaign of terrorism by the Stern Gang
- ◆ The Irgun blows up the King David Hotel
- ◆ The British decide to throw in the towel

It's fair to say at this point in the story of Jerusalem (1939) that a lot of people in England were wishing that when the League of Nations "mandated" Palestine to Great Britain back in 1922, George V's government would have declined to accept it. As you've read, the Brits got nothing but two decades of headaches. Believing the issue of what to do with Palestine could be solved politically by "partition," they ran into a religious division as old as the Bible.

It's also fair to say the Brits thought all they had to do was get Jews and Muslims to resolve everything by sitting down and talking to one another. But Jews were Old Testament "eye for an eye," and Arabs, in words of one of their leaders, were a people who could never forget a wrong.

Consequently, when Britain issued its White Paper, Jews interpreted it as a betrayal of the Balfour Declaration's promise of a Jewish state in Palestine. Arabs viewed it as opening a door to a gradual takeover through Jewish immigration.

A Divided City Finds Itself Between a Rock and a Hard Place

What might have happened in Palestine if there hadn't been a war in Europe in 1939 can never be known. Maybe the partition would have worked. But war there was, Britain found its own existence hanging by a thread, and the Palestine issue was put on a back burner. Arabs adopted a policy of wait and see. Jews took a look at the Nazis and chose the time-tested and proven view that "the enemy of my enemy is my friend." This policy was enunciated by Zionist leader David Ben-Gurion.

A Man Who Put First Things First

A visionary with a unique combination of personality, vigor, and determination, Ben-Gurion both symbolized and embodied the dream of a Jewish state in the Holy Land as a sanctuary for Jews after centuries of Diaspora and persecutions. The Zionist movement for Eretz (new) Israel had begun long before he was born in Poland. He learned of its existence and its goals in his father's Hebrew school. Liking the Zionist idea, he dedicated himself to working to achieve it. He joined the Socialist-Zionist group Poalai Zion at age 18 and at 20 emigrated to Palestine. Working on a kibbutz (farm), he immersed himself in Zionist politics, but with a new name. David Green became David Ben-Gurion.

One of the founders of a Jewish self-defense group, known as Hashomer, he studied law in Istanbul until he was ordered out of the country at the outbreak of the First World War by the Turkish government. Settling in the United States, he married Brooklyn, New York, nurse and fellow Zionist Paula Monbesz, with whom he had three children. With the defeat of the Ottoman Empire and the creation of a British mandate in Palestine, he returned to the Holy Land and served as a soldier in the Jewish Legion of the British army. Elected secretary-general of the General Federation of Labor (Histadrut), he held the post until 1935. Under his leadership, Histadrut became not only a trade union, but the most important political, social, and economic force in Zionism.

At the time of the White Paper, he was the acknowledged leader in the Zionist movement in Eretz Israel and chairman of the Jewish Executive Agency. "What matters," he declared, "is not what the Gentiles [British] say, but what the Jews do." His policy was to help the British destroy the Nazi menace, then deal with them over the unacceptable conditions of the White Paper.

The Difference Between a Statesman and a Politician

A word portrait of David Ben-Gurion was drawn by another Jewish leader you'll be reading a great deal about from now on. Her name was Golda Meir. She eventually became prime minister of Israel. In her 1975 autobiography she wrote of Ben-Gurion as "one man, above all others, on whose remarkable qualities of leadership and stunning political intuition we all relied and were to continue to rely in the years that lay ahead." This woman, who at the time she published her life story was one of the most famous people in the world, wrote that Ben-Gurion would be "known to Jews and non-Jews alike even in a hundred years." She also wrote that he was "not a man one could be close to," that he was "certainly not a man with whom anyone disagreed lightly," and "even in theory when he was quite wrong, he would usually be proved right in practice, and that, after all, is the difference between a statesman and a politician."

High and Mighty

Golda Meir was born Golda Mabovitz in Kiev, Russia, in 1898. She knew the terrors of pogroms against Jews and what it meant to be poor. "There was never enough of anything," she wrote in her 1975 autobiography. "I was always a little too cold outside and a little too empty inside." When the family emigrated to the United States in 1906 and settled in Milwaukee, Wisconsin, the hunger and fear ended. As a public school teacher, she became active in a Zionist labor organization. Married to Morris Myerson in 1917, she emigrated with him to Palestine in 1921. When she and Morris separated after the birth of a second child, she took the Hebrew name Meir, meaning "to burn brightly."

Jews Take Up Arms Beside the British

In 1940, Jews were allowed to enlist in Jewish companies attached to the British East Kent Regiment. Three battalions were moved to Egypt and Cyrenaica and assigned mostly to guard duty, but were denied permission to participate in fighting and the right to display the Jewish flag. Only after Chaim Weizmann wrote to British Prime Minister Winston Churchill in 1944 was a Jewish fighting force formed. The "Jewish Brigade" consisted of infantry, artillery, and service units. After training in Egypt, approximately 5,000 soldiers took part in the final phase of the war on the Italian front under the command of Canadian-born Jew Brigadier Ernest Benjamin. In May 1945, the brigade moved to northeast Italy and encountered survivors of the Holocaust. In the summer of 1946, the British disbanded the brigade, but, as you will soon read, they would use the fighting skills they'd learned for other purposes.

Say Hello to the Deadly Dreamers

You'll recall that in 1931, a group of Hagannah members broke with the policy of restraint from retaliation favored by the Jewish establishment represented by Hagannah and formed an armed resistance movement called the Irgun. One of the men who took that path was a firebrand named Avraham Stern.

> ### High and Mighty
>
> Born in Poland in 1907, Avraham Stern immigrated to Palestine in 1925 and attended Hebrew University. After winning a scholarship in classical languages and literature offered by the University of Florence, he returned to Jerusalem (1929), joined Hagannah, and devoted himself entirely to liberating Eretz Israel from the British occupation.

A follower of Vladimir Jabotinsky, who'd died in 1940, and also a close friend of the head of the Irgun (David Rahziel), Stern was against the Irgun policy of suspending attacks on the British until the war with Germany was over. The Irgun had adopted the policy because they believed that the Nazis were a more immediate threat to Jewish survival than that posed by the British White Paper. Stern and others, however, blamed the British for the deaths of Jews who were denied entrance to Palestine. In a break with the Irgun, these dissidents organized Lohamei Herut Israel (meaning Fighters for the Freedom of Israel). The group's initials, LEHI, meant "jawbone" and was a reference to Samson's killing of Philistines with the jawbone of an ass.

Before long, the British gave LEHI its own nicknames. The group was mocked as the "Deadly Dreamers" and feared as the "Stern Gang." The Stern Gang caught British attention on January 9, 1942, when they robbed a bank. They killed two Jewish employees and two British officers who'd witnessed the robbery. Infuriated, the Brits launched a massive manhunt and arrested or killed most of the gang. On February 12, 1942, Stern was cornered inside his hideout in Tel Aviv and shot to death. The British explained that the bullet hole in his back occurred when he was "trying to escape." His defenders claimed that before he died he had been tortured. If the British thought it was the last of the Stern Gang, they were wrong.

An Idea Floated in a Hotel in Manhattan

Convinced that Great Britain would never implement the Balfour Declaration, but still believing that the way to deal with the Brits was through negotiations, Zionist leaders met at what they called the "Extraordinary Zionist Conference" in New York City's Biltmore Hotel in May 1942.

A Zionist Vision of a New World Order

One of the most significant declarations in Israel's history, "The Biltmore Program: Towards a Jewish State," adopted at the conference on May 11, 1942, called for "fulfillment of the original purpose of the Balfour Declaration and the [British] Mandate." The conference affirmed "unalterable rejection of the White Paper of May 1939" and denied its "moral or legal validity."

It also noted, "The White Paper seeks to limit, and in fact to nullify Jewish rights to immigration and settlement in Palestine, and, as stated by Mr. Winston Churchill in the House of Commons in May 1939, constitutes 'a breach and repudiation of the Balfour Declaration.'"

Asserting that the policy of the British White Paper was "cruel and indefensible in its denial of sanctuary to Jews fleeing from Nazi persecution" at a time "when Palestine has become a focal point in the war front of the United Nations, and Palestine Jewry must provide all available manpower for farm and factory and camp, it is in direct conflict with the interests of the allied war effort."

The Conference also declared that "the new world order that will follow victory cannot be established on foundations of peace, justice and equality, unless the problem of Jewish homelessness is finally solved."

> **Reverent Remarks** _____
>
> In "The Biltmore Program," Zionists urged that "the gates of Palestine be opened; that the Jewish Agency be vested with control of immigration into Palestine and with the necessary authority for upbuilding the country, including the development of its unoccupied and uncultivated lands; and that Palestine be established as a Jewish Commonwealth integrated in the structure of the new democratic world. Then and only then will the age-old wrong to the Jewish people be righted."

The Zionists proposed that Britain empower the Jewish Agency to create a Jewish state, but not immediately. Instead, the nation of Israel would come into being only when the Jews became the majority in Palestine. This would happen slowly by way of controlled immigration.

The flaw in the daring proposal was that it left Arabs with the unacceptable choice of resigning themselves to a future minority status or packing up and moving into neighboring Arab countries that had no interest in taking them.

Menachem Begin Declares War to the End

Reverent Remarks

The fighting youth will not flinch from tribulation and sacrifice, from blood and suffering. They will not surrender until they have renewed our days of old, until they have ensured for our people a homeland, freedom, honor, bread, and justice.

—Menachem Begin, February 4, 1944

On November 1, 1943, members of the Stern Gang who'd been tossed into prison shocked the British by breaking out and getting back into business with a new leader, Nathan Friedman-Yellin. As if this weren't bad enough, on February 4, 1944, a new head of the Irgun, Menachem Begin, issued a statement declaring, "Our people is at war with this [British] regime—war to the end." It could be avoided only by "immediate transfer of power in Eretz Israel to a provisional Hebrew government." Otherwise, the ultimatum warned, "We shall fight; every Jew in the homeland will fight. The God of Israel, the Lord of Hosts, will aid us. There will be no retreat. Freedom—or death."

Like a Flame Across the Country

Thirty years after the Irgun's declaration of war against the British, the prime minister of Israel, Menachem Begin, recalled in his autobiography, *The Revolt*, that the "chief bearer" of the Irgun message was the Assault Force. "It gave the enemy no respite," he wrote. "It penetrated the heavily defended centers of government. The superior forces of the British army did not help." Buildings and barracks were speedily reduced to rubble.

Attacking in small units before and after midnight, the Jews had not only the element of surprise in their favor, but a high degree of skill in the use of explosives and a continual cover of machine gun fire. The only day the enemy could count on not being attacked was the Sabbath. "The British knew this," Begin wrote, "and consequently looked forward to the Jewish Sabbath more than to Sunday." The Assault Force, he said, "swept like a flame across the country."

Jerusalem Celebrates V-E Day

With the announcement of Germany's surrender on May 8, 1945, the people of Jerusalem celebrated Victory in Europe Day by taking to the streets. The *Palestine Post* reported, "Hundreds of flags and pennants and bunting flying from most of the buildings in the center of the town and decorating the squares sprang into life in the cooling breeze. Cars and buses and trucks, also beflagged, sounded their horns, and suddenly empty streets were jammed with crowds. On the steep slope of Ben Yehuda Street, wine flowed freely. By 6:20, 8,000 glasses had been poured."

The next day, Jews demanded of the British that 100,000 refugees, survivors of Nazi concentration camps being held in British pens on the island of Cyprus, be permitted to board ships for Haifa. One of these aging craft, *Palmyra*, renamed *Exodus*, defied the ban and succeeded in reaching Haifa. This dramatic episode was made into a novel by Leon Uris and subsequently into a movie starring Paul Newman. The book and film provided an insight into the war that broke out between the Irgun and the British army. In one of the ships, a young Polish survivor of the Holocaust, Dov Landau (played by Sal Mineo) vows to kill Englishmen by joining Irgun "because they know how to do it."

Britain offered yet another plan for partition. Bearing the name of the chief justice in the Mandatory administration, Sir William Fitzgerald, it would set up two self-governing boroughs, Jewish and Arab, each with four members on an administrative council. Two more members would be named by the British high commissioner. The council would control the Old City and the holy places. The "Fitzgerald Plan" was deemed dead on arrival by both sides.

A Scene that Would Inspire a Hollywood Screenwriter

When British Labor Party member of Parliament Richard Crossman checked into the King David Hotel on March 6, 1946, the lobby was a scene that would have had a writer of movie thrillers reaching for a pencil and notebook. Crossman had come to Jerusalem with the Anglo-American Committee of Inquiry, an organization set up by the British to review the issue of Jewish immigration to Palestine. He found the King David bristling with "private detectives, Zionist agents, Arab sheikhs, special correspondents, and the rest, all sitting around about discreetly overhearing each other."

Holy Facts! _____

The plush King David Hotel hosted several refugees during the war. In 1936, the emperor of Abyssinia, Haile Selassie, fled an Italian invasion of his country and found a haven in Jerusalem. When the German army grabbed Yugoslavia and Greece, the King David provided respite to King Peter II of the former and King George III of the latter. The first of the exiled monarchs, Spain's Alfonso XIII, had arrived in 1931 soon after the hotel opened. He had been forced to abdicate by Republican rebels. It was also the residence of Britain's high commissioner for Palestine, the headquarters of the high command of the army, and the center of Britain's intelligence service in the Holy Land.

The Brits Raid the Jewish Agency

Three and a half months after the scene in the King David lobby that had fascinated Richard Crossman, a British raiding party barged into the offices of the Jewish Agency. Long known to the Brits as "Jewish headquarters" and the place where the Irgunists plotted their attacks, the offices had been considered safe by Jewish Agency leaders because Jerusalem enjoyed "international status." But on June 29, 1946, the British decided it was fair game.

The Agency was, as suspected, a treasure trove of information on Irgun activities, past and in planning stages. There were many "secret documents," noted Irgun leader Menachem Begin, "which a wisely run organization in such circumstances would never have allowed to be there." The "booty" which the British carried away, Begin recalled, was "considerable." The material "gave the lie" to emphatic denials David Ben-Gurion had recently made to the Anglo-American Committee that the Jewish Agency knew nothing about Irgun actions. Among the documents was an unfinished report of a speech by an Irgun leader to the Zionist Council in which he praised the blowing up of bridges and explained the political significance of such activities. In response to the raid, the Irgun began developing an "eye-for-an-eye" plot in which the target was to be British headquarters in the King David Hotel.

Hatching a Plot Codenamed "Chick"

The first codename for the plan to attack the King David Hotel was the Hebrew word "malonchik," meaning "little hotel." As the planning went on, it was shortened to "Chick." The daring scheme was initially opposed by the top leadership of Hagannah, but on July 1, 1946, they sent a letter indicating a change of heart and calling for Chick to be carried out "as soon as possible." Menachem Begin recalled, "We were well aware that this was the largest of our operations to date and that it might turn out to be unique in the history of partisan wars of liberation."

The Plan

Five hundred pounds of explosives were to be packed into large milk cans. Each contained a synchronized timer and a triggering device that would detonate if a can were opened. To prevent that, a note would be put on each can: "Mines. Do not touch." The cans would be taken to the Regence Café in the basement of the government wing of the hotel (east) by robed men disguised as Arab employees of the hotel. As to the timing of the attack, because the café would be crowded at lunchtime, the planners chose eleven o'clock. Fifteen minutes before, a female Irgun "telephonist" would call the hotel with a notification that bombs had been planted and warn everyone to "evacuate the whole building." Calls would also be placed to the *Palestine Post* and to the adjacent French consulate.

Reverent Remarks

It is no simple matter to penetrate the very heart of the military government, to deliver a blow within the fortified headquarters of a military regime. I doubt if this operation had any precedent in history.

—Menachem Begin, *The Revolt*, 1975

The date was set: July 22.

Minutes before the detonations, some firecrackers would be set off outside to scare off people who might be heading for the hotel. The bombing was to be carried out at the same time as an attack by the reconstituted Stern Gang on another site of British offices, the David Brothers Building. This action was codenamed "Operation Your Slave and Redeemer." But at the last minute, the second operation was called off.

What a Difference an Hour Can Make

According to Menachem Begin's account of the execution of Chick, because of "consultations" about the cancellation of the David Brothers Building action, "the time of the attack was delayed by one hour and began at twelve o'clock instead of eleven." At first, all went as planned. Fifteen overwhelmed Arab employees—cooks and waiters—were locked in a side room. But as the milk-can bombs were being put in place, two British soldiers appeared with guns drawn. Bullets flew. At the same time, Irgunists outside the hotel clashed with military patrols. Plans for surprise went up in gun smoke, the bombs' timing mechanisms were started, "do not touch" signs were posted, and the men in the hotel escaped through the smoke from the diversionary firecrackers.

At 10 minutes past noon, the telephonist placed her calls to the *Post* and the French consulate. When she informed a British officer in the hotel that everyone should evacuate, he retorted, "We are not here to take orders from the Jews. We give them orders."

The bombs exploded at 12:37 P.M. Jerusalem shook from the force of the blast. A mixture of TNT and gelignite going off in the confined basement space brought down six floors of concrete, Jerusalem-stone facing, and steel. A reporter for the British Broadcasting Corporation told shocked listeners in Great Britain and around the world by shortwave radio that the entire wing of the King David Hotel was cut off "as with a knife."

A total of 91 British, Arabs, and Jews were killed. Scores more were injured. The Jewish Agency denounced "the dastardly crime" by a "gang of desperadoes." The Jewish Community Council saw an "abyss opening before our feet by irresponsible men" who committed "a loathsome act." Although the British did not hold an inquiry, the commanding general of Britain's army in the Mandate told the troops, "I am determined that they [Jews] should be punished and made aware of our feelings of contempt and disgust at their behavior." He warned of "hypocritical sympathy expressed by their leaders and representative bodies" and "protestations that they are not responsible and cannot curb the terrorists."

Half a century later, leaders of Israel would use almost the same words concerning Palestinian officials regarding terrorism aimed at Israelis in Jerusalem and elsewhere (see Part 4).

Everyone Was Lashing Out

For months after the King David Hotel bombing, a full-scale war raged between Jews and the British army. When Jewish prisoners were flogged, Irgun retaliated with whippings of 4 captured British soldiers (18 lashes each) on December 29, 1946.

A public notice written by Menachem Begin carried a warning. "If the oppressors dare in the future to abuse the bodies and the human and national honor of Jewish youths, we shall no longer reply with the whip. We shall reply with fire."

In the ensuing months, the Irgun and the Stern Gang unleashed a series of attacks. A British officers' club was bombed, killing 20 and wounding 10. Two oil transport trains were wrecked, and a refinery in Haifa was burned. In April 1947, the Stern group attacked an army transport near Rehovot. In an attack on a Cairo to Haifa train, 8 British were killed and 27 hurt. But the most spectacular action came on May 7 when Jews shot their way in and out of the British prison at Acre, freeing 120 Jews and 131 Arabs. (This daring escape was vividly reenacted at the prison, which in 1962 was used as a mental institution, in the movie *Exodus*. But in blowing up a wall for the reenactment, one of the inmates managed to mingle with the actors and escape.)

Humiliated by the success of the Acre Prison action and fed up with the Jews' unrelenting attacks (the British called it terrorism), the government of Great Britain decided that they'd had enough. They dumped Palestine into the lap of the successor to the League of Nations, telling the brand-new United Nations on April 2, 1947, that the British army intended to leave Palestine in May 1948.

The UN Calls on Jerusalem to Be a *Corpus Separatum*

On August 14, 1947, a special commission on Palestine (UNSCOP) recommended establishment of two states, one Jewish, one Arab, with Jerusalem a separate entity (*corpus separatum*) that would be administered by the UN. After 10 years, Jerusalem residents would vote on which state they wanted to join. The Jewish Agency accepted the proposal. But the Arab Higher Committee rejected it. Meanwhile, the British remained in control.

Holy Facts!

Jerusalem chronology (1939–1947):

1939	Britain issues a White Paper on Palestine.
	The Irgun calls on Jews to take Palestine by force.
	World War II starts.
1940–45	Jerusalem is relatively peaceful.
	The Jewish Brigade is established by the British army.
	Illegal Jewish immigration swells the Jewish population.
	David Ben-Gurion states that the end of the war will signal the start of the Zionist struggle for an independent Jewish state.
1946	March: The Anglo-American Committee arrives in Jerusalem.
	June 29: British raid offices of Hagannah.
	July 22: Irgun blows up a wing of the King David Hotel.
	Irgun/Stern Gang initiate terrorism campaign.
1947	April 2: Britain announces plans to quit Palestine.
	United Nations plan for Palestine calls for Jerusalem to be an international city for 10 years.

The Least You Need to Know

- The Jewish leader in Palestine was David Ben-Gurion.

- Britain allowed formation of a Jewish Brigade of its army.

- After WWII, the Irgun and the Stern Gang launched attacks.

- Irgun bombs destroyed a wing of the King David Hotel.

- The British decided to let the UN worry about Palestine.

13

Israel

In This Chapter

♦ The United Nations okays partitioning Palestine

♦ The Irgun and Stern Gang are accused of a massacre

♦ When Israel declares independence, Arab nations attack

♦ Battles rage for possession of Jerusalem

♦ The war ends in an armistice

Meeting at Lake Success, New York, on November 29, 1947, the General Assembly of the United Nations voted 33 to 13 to let Jews and Arabs form states in Palestine. Ten Arab and Muslim nations disapproved. Ten countries abstained, including Great Britain, and one—Thailand—chose not to vote. Assenting nations included the United States and the Soviet Union.

The UN Makes a Decision that Satisfies No One

General Assembly Resolution (No. 181) on the Future Government of Palestine, known as the "Partition Resolution," noted that the British Mandate for Palestine "shall terminate as soon as possible but in any case not later than 1 August 1948." The armed forces of the mandatory power "shall be progressively withdrawn from Palestine, the withdrawal to be completed as soon as possible but in any case not later than 1 August 1948."

Great Britain was directed to advise the Commission, "as far in advance as possible, of its intention to terminate the mandate and to evacuate each area," and "use its best endeavours to ensure that an area situated in the territory of the Jewish State, including a seaport and hinterland adequate to provide facilities for a substantial immigration, shall be evacuated at the earliest possible date and in any event not later than 1 February 1948." Independent Arab and Jewish states and a "Special International Regime for the City of Jerusalem" were to come into existence in Palestine two months after the evacuation of the British armed forces had been completed, but in any case not later than October 1, 1948.

The partition plan of UN General Assembly Resolution 181.

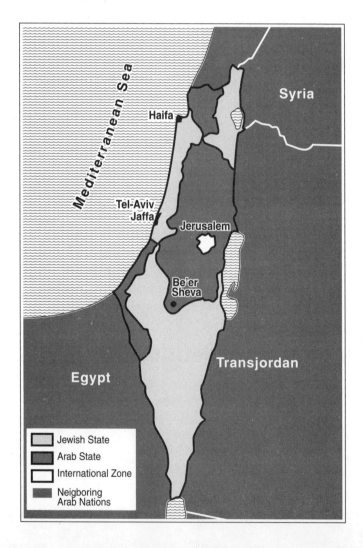

During a "transitional period," a United Nations commission would be established consisting of one representative of each of five UN member states elected by the General Assembly "on as broad a basis, geographically and otherwise, as possible." Administration of Palestine would be gradually turned over to the commission and would "act in conformity" with General Assembly recommendations, under the guidance of the Security Council. On its arrival in Palestine, the commission would "proceed to carry out measures for the establishment of the frontiers of the Arab and Jewish states and the city of Jerusalem in accordance with the general lines of the recommendations of the General Assembly on the partition."

After consultation with "democratic parties and other public organizations of the Arab and Jewish States," each state would "as rapidly as possible" form a provisional government council. Their activities were to be carried out under the general direction of the commission. During the transitional period, the councils would have "full authority in the areas under their control," which included matters of "immigration and land regulation." The provisional council of government of each state was to recruit an armed militia from the residents of that state, sufficient in number to maintain internal order and prevent frontier clashes. Each armed militia would be under the command of Jewish or Arab officers, but general political and military control, including the choice of the militia's high command, would be exercised by the commission.

Finally, the provisional council of each state would, "not later than two months after the withdrawal" of British forces "hold elections to the Constituent Assembly which shall be conducted on democratic lines."

Holy Facts!

According to the UN resolution, qualified voters were to be anyone—male or female—over 18 years of age who were (a) Palestinian citizens residing in that state; and (b) Arabs and Jews residing in the state. People living in Jerusalem had to sign a "notice of intention to become citizens, the Arabs of the Arab State and the Jews of the Jewish State," before they would be entitled to vote in the Arab and Jewish states respectively.

During the transitional period, no Jew would be permitted to establish residence in the area of the proposed Arab state, and no Arab would be allowed to establish residence in the area of the proposed Jewish state, unless permission was granted by the commission. This would lead to difficulties in the future, when Israel built settlements in Palestinian areas.

The constituent assembly of each state would draft a democratic constitution and choose a provisional government to succeed the provisional council. Each legislative body would be elected by universal suffrage and by secret ballot, based on proportional representation. An executive body responsible to the legislature would also be chosen.

All international disputes in which one of the states might be involved was to be settled "by peaceful means in such a manner that international peace and security, and justice, are not endangered." Each state was expected to "refrain in its international relations from the threat or use of force against the territorial integrity or political independence of any State, or in any other manner inconsistent with the purpose of the United Nations." Each would also guarantee "to all persons equal and nondiscriminatory rights in civil, political, economic, and religious matters and the enjoyment of human rights and fundamental freedoms, including freedom of religion, language, speech and publication, education, assembly, and association."

As for the city of Jerusalem itself, "freedom of transit and visit" was to be guaranteed to "all residents and citizens of the other State in Palestine and the City of Jerusalem, subject to considerations of national security."

What Tomorrow Shall Bring

"With the dawn in Jerusalem," noted the *Palestine Post*, "the Zionist flag could be seen draped from buildings, strung to lamp posts, and fluttering from cars and trucks." But not everything in the UN decision was to the Jews' advantage. In the splitting of the map of Jerusalem, one sixth of the Jewish population was in the Arab section, leaving them dependent on Arabs for power, water, and food supplies. The cut-off areas included Mount Scopus and the Hebrew University. By day's end, Arabs had attacked a Jewish ambulance on its way to Hadassah Hospital, machine-gunned buses on the road to Jerusalem, and murdered a Jerusalemite on the boundary between the Arab city of Jaffa and Jewish Tel Aviv. The next day (December 1), the Arab High Committee called a three-day strike and a boycott of Jewish businesses. Less than 24 hours later, the commercial center of the Old City was under attack by Arabs shouting "Death to the Jews."

On the morning of December 5, the Jewish Agency called on all men and women, ages 17 to 25, to take up arms. After 2 weeks of violence in the city and on surrounding roads, the death toll was 74 Jews, 71 Arabs, and 9 British. Many Arabs and British had been killed by members of the Irgun and the Stern Gang. Including a bomb attack on the Damascus Gate bus station that killed 5 Arabs, a British tally showed that in a period of 6 weeks following the UN vote to partition, 1,669 Arabs, 769 Jews, and 123 British were killed; an average of 46 per day.

How to Make a 100 Percent Jewish City

Finding themselves under constant attack, Arabs living in the New City began leaving in droves. The result pleased Ben-Gurion. He told a meeting of Jewish leaders in Tel Aviv on February 5, 1948, "Since Jerusalem's destruction in the days of the Romans, it has not been so Jewish as it is now. In many Arab districts in the west one sees not one Arab. I do not assume this will change."

But Ben-Gurion's joy over the evacuation of West Jerusalem by its Arab population was dampened by the inability of Jews to travel to the Jewish Quarter of the Old City without being shot at by Arab snipers. In an effort to deal with this threat, Jewish civil guards in blue uniforms were posted on all roads. To move food and other supplies from West Jerusalem to the isolated Jewish Quarter of the Old City, armed guards accompanied convoys by way of the Zion Gate.

> **Reverent Remarks**
>
> No city in the world, not even Athens or Rome, ever played as great a role in the life of a nation for so long a time, as Jerusalem had done in the life of the Jewish people.
>
> —David Ben-Gurion, 1947

Despite Ben-Gurion's assertion that Jerusalem was the capital of Israel, fighting and bombings made it a very dangerous place to conduct the business of government. Consequently, more and more officials abandoned the city and returned to Tel Aviv. Along with them went large numbers of ordinary citizens. One estimate put the number of Jews who chose to leave at 30 percent of the prepartition Jewish population of 100,000. Although Jerusalem was the avowed "heart of the nation" and Israel's "eternal capital," one official noted, "Tel Aviv is the capital in practice."

The Arab Higher Committee Pulls Up Stakes

Ordinary Jerusalem Arabs weren't alone in getting out of town. The Arab Higher Committee decided that a better place to take care of its business was Damascus. It also decreed that when the time was ripe, a provisional Arab government would be set up in Jerusalem under the presidency of Haj Amin al-Husseini, the Mufti who'd spent his time during World War II on the side of the Nazis and making broadcasts from Rome. However, said the Arab Higher Committee, if making Jerusalem the Arab capital should prove not to be a good idea, the city of Nablus would do just as well. This was not what you would call a strong endorsement of Jerusalem as an Arab capital city.

A Bloody Stain on the Jewish Cause

As noted, Arab forces had engaged in sporadic and unorganized ambushes since December 1947 in an attempt to cut off the highway between Tel Aviv and Jerusalem. One of the strategic points on this route was the Arab town of Deir Yassin, population about 750. On a half-mile-high hill less than a mile from Jerusalem suburbs, it provided a commanding view of the road. To take it out, the Irgun and the Stern Gang devised a plan named Operation Nachshon. When Hagannah commander David Shaltiel heard about it, he told the planners, "I have no objection to your carrying out the operation provided you are able to hold the village. If you are unable to do so I warn you against blowing up the village which will result in its inhabitants abandoning it and its ruins and deserted houses being occupied by foreign [Arab] forces."

The Irgun force attacked on April 9. According to Menachem Begin, the assault was carried out by 100 men. Other sources say there were as many as 132 men from both groups. Begin claimed that a truck with a loudspeaker had parked at the entrance of the village and broadcast a warning to evacuate the area. In other accounts, no warning was issued because the truck had rolled into a ditch.

The battle lasted several hours. The Irgun counted 41 casualties, including 4 dead. The *New York Times* reported more than 200 Arabs killed, 40 captured, and 70 women and children released. The Arabs claimed the Jews had committed a massacre and many women had been raped.

The Jewish Agency immediately expressed "horror and disgust" and sent a letter expressing shock and disapproval to Transjordan's King Abdullah. The Arab Higher Committee hoped that exaggerated reports about a "massacre" at Deir Yassin would shock the Arab countries into bringing pressure on their governments to jump into Palestine. The immediate result was a Palestinian exodus and retaliation. Four days after the reports from Deir Yassin, Arabs ambushed a Jewish convoy on the way to Hadassah Hospital, killing 77 Jews, including doctors, nurses, patients, and the director of the hospital.

Holy Facts!

The Deir Yassin "massacre" and the Hadassah Hospital ambush attracted little attention from the world. But Deir Yassin has remained controversial ever since, with both sides maintaining contradictory Internet websites.

Caught in the Middle, the British Hand Off to the UN

Denouncing "such deeds as Deir Yassin" and "the butchery" on the road to the Hadassah Hospital," a *Palestine Post* editorial put part of the blame upon the "constituted Authority in this land, which, in the purpose of the Government of the United Kingdom, stands by helpless and humiliated." But as these attacks took place, the 20-year-old British Mandate had just 2 weeks to go before responsibility for Palestine transferred to a United Nations Truce Commission. The Commission consisted of the consuls of the United States, Belgium, and France, with headquarters in the French consulate near the frequently embattled Jaffa Gate. What was left of the British Chief Secretariate and army headquarters was ensconced in the King David Hotel.

At 7:30 A.M., on Friday, May 14, 1948, as many officials departed in a motorcade, an honor guard and High Commissioner General Sir Alan Cunningham saluted the lowering of the Union Jack. Within 10 minutes of the finale to British rule in Jerusalem, Hagannah soldiers were occupying vacated British army posts on the Jaffa Road, the General Post Office, telephone exchange, the Russian Compound, and the imposing Barclay's Bank Building, providing a panoramic view of the Old City from the northwest corner to the Jaffa Gate.

A Country of Their Own, If the Jews Could Keep It

For the first time in 13 centuries, the land that the Jews called Israel was not under the heels of foreigners. The United Nations had given Jews a homeland and had decreed international status for Jerusalem, with guarantees of access to Judaism's most holy place, the Western Wall. To claim that legal right, the Jews had been fighting Arabs almost constantly since the UN voted on partition. And now the time had come for the realization of the Zionist dream. It happened not in Jerusalem, but in Tel Aviv.

At 4:40 in the afternoon of May 14 at the Tel Aviv Museum on Rothschild Boulevard, with a large portrait of Theodore Herzl placed on a wall behind a conference table, David Ben-Gurion cleared his throat and said to 13 members of a provisional government, "I shall now read the Scroll of Independence." Reading it would take him a quarter of an hour. When he came to paragraph 11, Golda Meir recalled, his tone changed and his voice rose as he read:

> Accordingly, we, the members of the National Council, representing the Jewish people in the Land of Israel and the Zionist movement, have assembled on the day of the termination of the British mandate for Palestine, and by virtue of our

natural and historic right and of the resolution of the General Assembly of the United Nations, do hereby proclaim the establishment of a Jewish state in the Land of Israel—the State of Israel.

It would be, said Ben-Gurion, "open to Jewish immigration and the gathering of exiles." He added, "Even amidst the violent attacks launched against us for months past, we call upon the sons of the Arab people dwelling in Israel to keep the peace and to play their part in building the state on the basis of full and equal citizenship and due representation in all its institutions, provisional and permanent." To surrounding Arab nations went out "the hand of peace."

The Palestine Philharmonic Orchestra played the nation's anthem, "Hatikvah." With a final rap of his gavel, Ben-Gurion said, "The State of Israel is established. The meeting is ended." The state of Israel would become a reality at the stroke of midnight.

Holy Facts!

One of Israel's earliest cultural icons was a symphony orchestra founded long before the creation of the state of Israel by Bronislaw Huberman. A Zionist who had foreseen the Holocaust, he started it in Palestine in order to provide employment for Jewish musicians who'd fled Europe. Called the Palestine Orchestra, it gave its first concert on December 16, 1936, under the baton of the world-famous conductor Arturo Toscanini. Because so many members were renowned musicians, it was called "an orchestra of soloists."

Renamed the Israel Philharmonic Orchestra, it played on Israel's Independence Day in 1948, on Mount Scopus after the city had been reunified, at army outposts and hospitals after the Six-Day War, at Christmas in Bethlehem's Nativity Square (1968), on the Lebanese border (1977), and at Massada (1988). Famed as Israel's musical ambassador to the world, it's rated among the world's 10 best symphony orchestras.

A President and a King Give Fateful Orders

At 12:25 A.M., May 15, 1948, in the White House President Harry S. Truman's press secretary, Charles Ross, handed out a statement announcing that the United States recognized "de facto" (the fact) Israel's declaration that it was now a state. The formal, legal recognition (*de jure*) would come on January 31, 1949. Truman noted in his presidential memoirs that the decision had been made long before. He wrote that while disappointed that the UN plan for partition "was not taking place in exactly the peaceful" way he'd hoped, "the fact was that [Jews] were controlling that area in which their people lived" and "were ready to administer and defend it." Thus, the United States became the first nation to accept the existence of the Jewish state. It's a choice that has determined the course of American policy in the Middle East into the twenty-first century and made the United States a target of Arab suspicion, animosity, and terrorism.

In the very moment that Jews hailed the birth of Israel and its existence received recognition by the United States, troops of the Arab Legion, led by a former British officer, Major-General John Bagor Glubb, awaited an order from Abdullah, King of Transjordan. Standing on a bridge named for General Allenby that spanned the Jordan River, he fired a revolver and commanded "Forward!"

The goal set by Abdullah was to quickly take not only the Old City, but all of Jerusalem, and then sweep westward to drive the Jews to the coast and into the sea. But General Glubb knew "the extent of Jewish preparations" and that "the Arabs had no plan and that there was no cooperation between them." Although Glubb hoped that the United Nations would intervene to impose a cease-fire and spare Jerusalem from a full-sale Arab Legion attack, the king insisted that Glubb move against the city "in force."

Destruction, Death, Pain, and Shattered Nerves

The problem confronting Jewish commanders was how to bolster the defenders of the Jewish Quarter to keep it from falling into Arab hands. One plan called for an assault by the commando arm of the Hagannah, known as the Palmach. But the commander of its Harel Brigade—and future Israeli prime minister, Yitzhak Rabin—thought that dynamiting through the Zion and Jaffa gates would be doomed to failure. Rather than "charging head first right into a wall," he proposed encircling the Old City and isolating it from Arab forces before trying to break through. Unable to do either, the Jews' only recourse was to hold on to the Jewish Quarter and hope for improved conditions. One resident wrote of explosions of Arab artillery "leaving behind a trail of destruction, death, pain, and shattered nerves."

Cut off from the world except for a radio, and nearly out of ammunition and grenades, the Jewish Quarter defenders held for nine days. On May 27, an Arab flag was hoisted to the roof of Hurva Synagogue, signaling Arab control of one third of the Jewish Quarter. The next day, the defenders radioed Hagannah headquarters, "There is no possibility from a military point of holding out here." At 9:15 that morning, rabbis carrying a white sheet tied between poles went to an Arab post at the Zion Gate to ask for a cease-fire. Observing this from a position on Mount Zion, Yitzhak Rabin was "horrified."

Holy Facts! _____

In the last week of fighting to save the Jewish Quarter, the Jews lost 62 men, with 200 wounded. At the time of the surrender, only 35 Jewish defenders were found unhurt. In all, 340 Jewish soldiers were sent to a prisoner-of-war camp in Amman, Jordan. Thirteen-hundred old men, women, and children were allowed to go to West Jerusalem.

Conditions of the surrender were that the Arab Legion would take over the Jewish Quarter, and that all Jewish fighters be taken to Amman, Jordan, as prisoners of war. When the Arabs' commander, Major Abdullah al-Tel, saw how few weapons the Jews had, he said, "If I'd known this was your situation, I swear I would have conquered you with sticks."

The Arab capture of the Jewish Quarter meant that no Jews would be living there for the first time in the Old City's history, and that Jews could have no access to the Western Wall. Almost 30 years later (1976), a pamphlet published by the United Mizrahi Bank Ltd. for a United Jewish Appeal National Conference (called "This Year in Jerusalem") bitterly recalled the 1948 surrender and what took place after it. Author N. Bar Glora wrote of the Arabs' "systematic design to obliterate every vestige of Jewish presence." The passage continued, "In berserk wantonness, an Arab mob burst in, wrecking everything in sight, demolishing and plundering synagogues without pity or restraint."

Among the "ravaged" synagogues were the Tiferet Israel, the Yochanan Ben Zakkai, Istambul, Emtzai, and the Hurva. You'll recall from Chapter 2 that the Hurva is the synagogue that Israel didn't rebuild but instead commemorated with an arch. In addition to destroying buildings, Arabs "shamefully defiled" scrolls of the law. Ritual "appurtenances" and prayer books were "pillaged or ripped to pieces, or consumed in the flames of Arab bonfires." Major al-Tel admitted in memoirs published in Cairo in 1959 that "operations of calculated destruction" had been "set in motion" because the Jewish Quarter "had no strategic value. Its buildings and shrines were not destroyed in battle. All this took place after military activities had come to a standstill."

Jews Build a "Burma Road" to Get Supplies to Jerusalem

In Chapter 2, you read that along the road to Jerusalem from Tel Aviv are relics of the fight that took place for control of the road in 1948. Hulks of wrecked armored vehicles stand as monuments to the convoys that, in the words of markers, "forced their way through to Jerusalem." According to the Bible, it was also here where Joshua took on the Amorites and the sun and moon stood still while he finished them off. Nearby, the Macabees defeated the Seleucids. Richard the Lionhearted came this way, too. So crucial to control of the route in 1948 was the hilltop Arab town of Latrun that David Ben-Gurion demanded that it be taken. Among the troops assigned to take the town were refugees of the Holocaust. Many were so new to Israel that their names weren't yet registered. Thrown into the fight with barely a week of training, with no common language, and outdated weapons, they wore bright shirts and sandals.

What was intended to be a surprise predawn attack got started late and quickly fell apart in the face of withering heat and Arab sharpshooters. The Israeli losses included many of the men who'd survived the death camps. A second attack, commanded by former American colonel Mickey Marcus, also failed. Hopes for taking the town were abandoned. Instead, a new road was ordered built well out of Arab artillery range. Laboriously cut through steep and rocky hills, it got the name "Burma Road," after a road that had been carved into mountains in that country during World War II to open a supply line from India to China.

> **High and Mighty**
>
> The Israelis achieved the amazing feat of building the "Burma Road" in eight weeks. Fifteen miles long, it is officially named Valour Road and has been memorialized in the town of Latrun.

The UN Calls Time-Out and Appoints a Referee

With the Arab onslaught against Jewish territory blunted, the warring sides accepted a United Nations call for a cease-fire on June 11. The stalemate left Arabs in control of the Old City and areas to the east, north, and southwest. Jews held the New City and territory to the west. Between them was "no man's land." The Tel Aviv-Jerusalem road was again open. The truce gave the UN until July 7 to find a permanent resolution of the crisis. This unenviable task was assigned to Swedish diplomat Count Folke Bernadotte.

Bernadotte arrived in Jerusalem on June 12. Sixteen days later, he came up with a plan that would make Jerusalem part of Transjordan, but give Jews "municipal autonomy." Holy places would be protected by "special arrangements." Israel's provisional government rejected the proposal. When the UN asked for extension of the truce for 10 days, the Arabs refused.

The Jews Reshuffle Their Defense Forces

Serving in the double-role of Israel's prime minister and the minister of defense, David Ben-Gurion worried that defenders of the new state weren't a unified whole and were often completely unaware of the other's whereabouts and activities. They were split into three parts: the official Hagannah army known as the Palmach, the Irgun, and the Stern Gang. The problem was so acute that on June 21, the Palmach sank an Irgun supply ship with 900 men onboard and a load of arms and ammunition. With great reluctance, the Irgun agreed to meld into a consolidated defense called Zvah Hagannah Le Yisrael, (Israeli Defense Force, or IDF). By July 1948, it had a small navy, a tank battalion, and a tiny air force. It included three American B-17 "Flying Fortress" heavy bombers that had raided Germany by the thousands during World War II. Israel bought the bombers through an arms black market based in Czechoslovakia.

Whereas the Irgun merged with the IDF, the Stern Gang refused to do so. Their refusal provoked an order from a furious Ben-Gurion for a raid on a Stern Gang training camp (September 7). Stern leaders reacted by denouncing Ben-Gurion for accepting a truce and demanding that Count Bernadotte be banned from the country.

The Stern Gang Pays a High Price for Making a Big Mistake

On September 17, 1948, Bernadotte left Jerusalem for a visit with the Jewish military governor, Bernard Joseph, in Rehavia, a town that Bernadotte had chosen as his winter headquarters. The UN mediator was in high spirits. After months of negotiations with King Abdullah, he'd won the Jordanian monarch's acceptance of a plan in which Arabs and Jews would share Jerusalem, and the city would be internationalized and demilitarized.

But Bernadotte never got a chance to share the news with Joseph. On his way to the meeting, the Stern Gang ambushed his transport and murdered the count. The Stern Gang had gone too far, and Bernard Joseph and Israel's military commander in Jerusalem, Lieutenant Colonel Moshe Dayan, agreed that, in Joseph's words, "the only practicable way of dealing with the situation was by way of a large-scale military operation to round up the whole Stern Gang."

Ben-Gurion agreed. His order began, "One, arrest all Stern Gang members. Two, find and surround all Stern bases and confiscate all arms. Three, kill any who resist." Although 184 Stern Gang members were arrested in Jerusalem, others left town. The Stern Gang was dismantled, but the identity of the person who killed Bernadotte was never learned.

An American career diplomat, Ralph Bunche, took over the job of UN mediator. Recognized for his efforts, he became the first black man to be awarded the Nobel Peace Prize, and the first American to receive that honor since President Woodrow Wilson.

The Deal that Was Supposed to Guarantee Peace

Two months and eleven days after the Bernadotte assassination, Moshe Dayan and Lieutenant-Colonel Abdullah al-Tel agreed on a "complete and sincere cease-fire in the Jerusalem area." Under the terms accepted on November 28, 1948, Jews were allowed access twice a month to resupply a Jewish enclave on Mount Scopus. But Jews would continue to be banned from the Western Wall.

When Chaim Weizmann, who'd been asked to accept the presidency of Israel, learned this, he counseled Israelis who'd turned out to greet his arrival in West Jerusalem, "Do not worry because part of Jerusalem is not now within the State. All will come to pass in peace." On February 2, 1949, the Israeli government announced that West Jerusalem was no longer "occupied territory." Twelve days later, the Knesset convened in the Jewish Agency Building on King George V Avenue and formally elected Weizmann president of Israel. On March 17, King Abdullah imposed Jordanian rule in all areas his army controlled, thereby squashing the aspirations of Palestinian Arabs to see Jerusalem as the capital of their state.

Holy Facts! _____

1948–1949 War Combat Forces and Losses:

Nation	Forces	Losses
Israel	140,000	6,000
Palestine	50,000	2,000
Egypt	300,000	2,000
Jordan	60,000	1,000
Syria	300,000	1,000

Although the formal UN armistice agreement (signed on April 3, 1949) partitioned Jerusalem and guaranteed Jews access to the Western Wall, no Jew would stand in prayer before its ancient stones for the next 19 years. How they got there in 1967 is the subject of the next chapter.

The Least You Need to Know

◆ The UN voted to give Jews and Arabs their own states.

◆ When the Jews declared the state of Israel, Arabs attacked.

◆ The Jewish Quarter and Western Wall were captured by Arabs.

◆ UN mediator Bernadotte was assassinated by the violent Jewish Stern Gang.

◆ An armistice in 1949 left Jerusalem divided.

Capital City

In This Chapter

- ◆ Jerusalem becomes Israel's capital city
- ◆ Arab nations are defeated in the "Six-Day War" of 1967
- ◆ The Jewish Quarter and Western Wall are reclaimed
- ◆ United Nations resolutions condemn Israel
- ◆ A third war ends in an Israeli victory

The UN armistice of 1949 settled boundaries between Arabs and Jews according to the territories held by their forces at the end of the fighting. Israel stretched between Lebanon on the north and Egypt on the south (including the Gaza Strip), Syria to the northeast, and the Kingdom of Jordan on the east side of its namesake river. Jordan controlled an area of old Palestine that was now shown on maps as the "West Bank." At the eastern end of a bulge containing the vital Tel Aviv-Jerusalem road was Jerusalem. A "green line" separated Jordanian-controlled East (Old City) and the Jewish West Jerusalem, with Mount Scopus designated a Jewish enclave in East Jerusalem.

Organic and Inseparable

While the United Nations clung to its pre-1948 war policy of an international, partitioned Jerusalem (*corpus separatum*) with no national identity, David Ben-Gurion left no one in doubt how he felt. "Jewish Jerusalem," he declared in December 1949, "is an organic and inseparable part of the State of Israel, as it is an inseparable part of the history of Israel and the faith of Israel and of the very soul of our people. Jerusalem is the heart of hearts of the State of Israel."

After the United Nations rejected an Israeli compromise in which the Old City would become internationalized under UN control with guarantees that the Western Wall be open again to Jews, the Israeli Cabinet, at Ben-Gurion's insistence, declared that Jerusalem was Israel's capital. Meeting there in January 1949, the Knesset recalled biblical Jewish kingdoms and proclaimed Jerusalem "once again" the Jewish capital.

A Deadly Royal Miscalculation

You might think that at this point the king of Jordan would have countered Israel's move by elevating the status of East Jerusalem by declaring it the capital of an Arab state in Palestine. (Had King Abdullah done so, he might have spared the world a half century of violence between Palestinians and Israelis.) What he did was make East Jerusalem and the West Bank part of his kingdom, with the capital in Amman. The effect was to reduce the third holiest city of Islam to provincial status at a time when the Jews were elevating their Jerusalem. This would be commented on by a future mayor of Israeli Jerusalem, Teddy Kollek. Noting that Arabs had never made a capital in one of their holy cities, he pointed to Saudi Arabia. "They have Mecca, Medina, to build their capital there, [but they took] a village called Riyadh and turned it into a capital. The Jordanians had Jerusalem, but they built a capital in Amman and not Jerusalem."

On July 20, 1951, Jordan's King Abdullah arrived in Jerusalem for prayers at the al-Aqsa Mosque. Surprised at finding himself surrounded by bodyguards, he said to their commander, "Why do you imprison me between close lines of soldiers? Let them fall back. This is God's house. Everyone is safe here."

Moments later, Abdullah, with his grandson (and future King Hussein) at his side, was shot dead by a Palestinian, Mustafa Shukri Ashu. Killed in a burst of gunfire by the very bodyguards whom Abdullah had scorned, he was victim of a conspiracy devised by the former Mufti and arch troublemaker, Haj Amin al-Husseini (if you don't remember him, see Chapter 11). In addition to blaming Abdullah for banning him from returning to Jerusalem, he'd branded Abdullah a traitor for making peace with the "infidel" Israelis.

Life on Opposite Sides of the Green Line

Visitors to Jerusalem in the early 1950s found two very different parts of a city separated by a "green line" that UN diplomats saw as the solution to keeping Jews and Arabs apart and at peace. The UN policy was formally called the Statute of Jerusalem. The Israeli ambassador to the world body, Abba Eban, called it a "completely unrepresentative and unrealistic document." The Palestinians were also displeased. With it adopted, no more resolutions with regard to the city's fate would come before the UN for 16 years.

East Is East and Arab

While the New Jerusalem of the Jews was experiencing a building boom in the 1950s, Arab East Jerusalem languished in Jordanian indifference. Although its status was elevated from baladiya (municipality) to amama (not quite a capital), it suffered from such neglect that its Arab mayor, Ruhi al-Khatib, griped, "See the palaces being built in Amman [that] should have been built here in Jerusalem, but were removed from here, so that Jerusalem would remain not a city, but a kind of village."

The British consul-general was so dismayed that he advised the government of the United Kingdom to make it clear "that we are not prepared to allow [the Jordanian government] to treat the Old City of Jerusalem as though it were a provincial townlet in Jordan, without history or importance." Regardless, Jordan went ahead with its systematic political downgrading.

With a truce in place, many Arabs who'd fled Jerusalem during the war began to return. By June 1953, about 20,000 refugees had been registered. From the end of the 1948–1949 war and the second war in 1967, the population of Jordanian-controlled Jerusalem would almost double, from 42,000 to 70,000. Many of these refugees were housed in adjoining villages in makeshift homes.

West Is West and Jewish

In contrast, West Jerusalem had a new Hadassah Hospital, Hebrew University was getting a new campus, and a Palace of the Nation was built at the city's entrance. Chosen as the site of the first Zionist Congress since the movement's birth (1897), the hall was described as a "workmanlike, even artistic accomplishment."

Holy Facts! —————

Between 1948 and 1967, the population of West Jerusalem went from 100,000 to 195,700.

In 1953, on land adjacent to the Military Cemetery on Mount Herzl, work began on a memorial to the 6 million Jews who'd died in Nazi concentration camps. Named Yad Vashem, meaning "a name and a place," it recalled God's promise to Jews in the Book of Isaiah: "Even unto them will I give in mine house and within my walls a place and a name [that] will give them an everlasting name, that shall not be cut off."

Christians Get Shut Out in the Shuffle

The British consul-general who'd worried about the indifference of the Jordanian government to its part of Jerusalem also noted an "anti-Christian tendency" on the part of Jordan that was often "open warfare" against Christian institutions. This was seen in the shutting out of Christians from jobs they had traditionally held in government agencies, business, and tourism. A result was a dramatic decline in the Christian population of the Old City, from 19 percent (31,400) in 1956 to less than 5 percent (12,900) in 1967. A series of laws banned Christian institutions from buying property. In addition to the economic squeeze, they found that religious holidays that had been recognized prior to 1949 were no longer officially observed.

Historian Bernard Wasserstein notes in *Divided Jerusalem*, "Christian Jerusalem thus shrank not only demographically but also in the political consciousness of the Christian world." But, as you will read in Part 4, Israel would eventually find powerful allies among American Christian fundamentalists in its struggle with Palestinians following Arab-Israeli wars in 1967 and 1973 and later Palestinian "intifada" uprisings.

Setting the Stage for a War with Egypt

Although the so-called Suez War of 1956 had little immediate impact on Jerusalem, you need to know its basics to understand why there was another war in 1967. (For a broader picture of the history of the Arab world beyond the city of Jerusalem, read *The Complete Idiot's Guide to the Middle East Conflict, Second Edition,* by Mitchell G. Bard, Ph.D.) In a nutshell, here's the part of interest to you now: When the 1948 war ended with Israel still in existence, President Gammal Abdul Nasser of Egypt, head of the largest of the Arab nations, declared that Israel was like a Western dagger in the heart of Arabia. In a fit of anger against the United States for refusing to bankroll a dam at Aswan on the Nile River, he not only turned to the communist Soviet Union for help, but announced the nationalization of the Suez Canal, thereby taking it over from Britain. This meant shutting down shipping to Israel.

Understandably irritated at losing the canal they'd built, the Brits decided to take it back, with help from France and Israel. The war began on October 29, 1956, with an attack by Israel. The Israelis quickly gained total control of the Sinai Desert, Gaza, and the coast of the Red Sea, but lost a portion of its border with Syria known as the Golan Heights. Over the objection from some Israelis, including Menachem Begin, Israel appealed for a peace treaty with its Arab neighbors that would return territory it had taken in return for guarantees of Israeli safety.

Israel's peace overtures were rejected. Egypt's Nasser, who was in no mood for negotiating, retorted, "The danger of Israel lies in the very existence of Israel as it is in the present and what she represents." The Arab goal was "full restoration of the rights of the Palestinian people" and "the destruction of the State of Israel."

By 1965, Israel was being raided from Egypt and shelled from the Golan Heights by Syria. On May 22, Egypt ordered a UN "Emergency Force" stationed in the Sinai to leave the area. Two days later, the "Voice of the Arabs" radio announced, "The sole method we shall apply against Israel is total war, which will result in the extermination of Zionist existence." On May 22, Egypt blocked the Straits of Tiran, blockading all supplies and oil to Israel. In the language of international law, the act was a justification for war.

The Six-Day War

It began on June 5 on Israel's terms. Rather than sit and wait for an attack by Egypt, Israel struck first with an air attack that smashed most of Egypt's air force on the ground. An Israeli appeal to King Hussein to keep Jordan out of the war was met with this radio message from Hussein to Jordanian troops: "Israel's end is in your hands. Strike at her everywhere, until victory!"

Mayor Teddy Kollek retorted from West Jerusalem, "We shall not be conquered." At 11:15 A.M., Jordanian artillery opened fire while Hussein's army crossed the green line south of the city. During 10 hours of shelling, 10 Jews were killed in West Jerusalem and 100 were wounded. Foreign and local journalists sought shelter in the Knesset building, along with David Ben-Gurion, Golda Meir, and other government officials. Despite a shell that exploded close to the parliament, shattering windows in a cafeteria, the refugees were reported by the *Jerusalem Post* to be "all in high spirits and good humor."

On the morning of June 6, battles raged at Mount Scopus and other strategic locations. By midday, Israelis held most of the land outside the Old City and stood atop Mount Scopus. Looking over the city below, Israeli Defense Minister Moshe Dayan exclaimed, "What a fantastic view." Moments later, he was handed a message that had been intercepted between Hussein and Nasser. Dayan read, "The situation rapidly worsens. In Jerusalem it is hopeless."

At a press conference on Mount Scopus, Mayor Kollek was asked if he expected to soon be mayor of all of Jerusalem. He answered, "Every Jew has dreamed of this for 2,000 years. But we are aware that it cannot be done in a hurry."

The next day, a *Jerusalem Post* editorial ventured the following:

> In a hard and costly fight, the [Old] City has been surrounded, and it is not expected to resist very long in this condition. The Jews of Israel will once more practice the ancient custom of visiting the Western Wall of the ancient temple of prayer and remembrance. Israel cannot permit itself to be locked out of the Old City again or to rely on the uncertain services of the United Nations for its right of access. The division of the city has been a painful and expensive anomaly for twenty years.

The order of the day to Israeli troops on June 7 was concise: "Today Jerusalem is to be liberated. In the center and in the north, the city of our ancestors is in our hands. Our army is poised. Men of the Regional Command, be resolute. Do not waiver." At 9:45, Colonel Mordechai Gur was in a tank at St. Stephen's Gate (Lion's Gate). He found the portal unguarded. Moments later, he was standing on the Haram. In a jubilant message to his boss, General Uzi Narkiss, he exclaimed, "The Temple Mount is ours. I'm standing near the Mosque of Omar right now. The Wailing Wall is a minute away."

When foreign correspondent Robert Musel reached the Western Wall, he found tough Israeli troops "covered with dust" and weeping "like small children." As General Narkiss arrived, the weeping "became sobs, full-throated, an uncontrolled emotional outburst." The Wall had been reclaimed at the cost of 180 Israeli soldiers and 14 civilians killed. Jordanian losses numbered 350 troops and 249 civilians. Moshe Dayan stood before the Wall and said, "We have united Jerusalem, the divided capital of Israel. We have returned to our holiest of holy places, never to depart from it again. To our Arab neighbors we extend, also at this hour—and with added emphasis at this hour—our hand in peace. And to our Christian and Muslim fellow citizens, we solemnly promise full religious freedom and rights. We did not come to Jerusalem for the sake of other peoples' holy places, and to interfere with the adherents of other faiths, but in order to safeguard its entirety and to live there together with others, in unity."

In two wars and six days of fighting, Israel tripled its size, from 8,000 to 20,000 square miles, including the Sinai Desert, Gaza, the Golan Heights, the West Bank, and all of Jerusalem. Those victories came even though, as the following chart demonstrates, Israel was vastly outnumbered in men and arms.

	Israeli	Arab
1956 War		
Troops	60,000	200,000 (half Egyptian)
Tanks	300	600
Planes	170	650
Warships	15	0
1967 War		
Troops	270,000	500,000
Tanks	800	2,500
Planes	350	800
Warships	20	100
Artillery	250	2,400

Sign and Symbol of a New Era

With the Western Wall secured, structures and a narrow passageway that were for so long an obstacle to access to the holy site were cleared. Also removed were barriers and barbed wire that had cut the Old City in two. "More than anything else," said Golda Meir, "those hideous barricades have signified the abnormality of our life, and when they were bulldozed away and Jerusalem overnight became one city, it as like a sign and symbol of a new era."

Among those celebrating the opening of the Wall area was French philanthropist Baron Edmund de Rothschild, whose grandfather's offer to buy the land in 1887 from the Muslims was refused.

Ten days after the taking of al-Haram al-Sharif, Moshe Dayan ordered the Islamic holy site returned to the control of Muslims and that it be open to all Muslims in Israel and the West Bank. On June 24, 1967, 5,000 faithful flocked to it for prayers.

Two days later, the Israeli government announced that as of the next day, Jerusalem would be declared officially reunited.

The UN Jumps Back In

On November 22, 1967, the United Nations Security Council voted for Resolution 242. It set out a formula for Arab-Israeli peace in which Israel would give up territory taken in the war and the Arabs would abandon violence. Although this UN document would be cited as the basis for a settlement, it remained unrealized through decades of negotiations and mutual violence that are the subject of Part 4.

Six days after Israel celebrated the twentieth anniversary of its declaration of independence, the United Nations Security Council passed another resolution (252). Voted on June 21, 1968, it said that all "measures and actions taken by Israel [since the 1967 war], including expropriation of land and properties thereon, which tend to change the legal status of Jerusalem, are invalid and cannot change that status."

This is what Resolution 252 said:

> Expressing its [the United Nation's] continuing concern with the grave situation in the Middle East,
>
> Emphasizing the inadmissibility of the acquisition of territory by war and the need to work for a just and lasting peace in which every State in the area can live in security,
>
> Emphasizing further that all Member States in their acceptance of the Charter of the United Nations have undertaken a commitment to act in accordance with Article 2 of the Charter,
>
> 1. Affirms that the fulfilment of Charter principles requires the establishment of a just and lasting peace in the Middle East which should include the application of both the following principles:
>
>   (i) Withdrawal of Israel armed forces from territories occupied in the recent conflict;
>
>   (ii) Termination of all claims or states of belligerency and respect for and acknowledgment of the sovereignty, territorial integrity and political independence of every State in the area and their right to live in peace within secure and recognized boundaries free from threats or acts of force;
>
> 2. Affirms further the necessity
>
>   (a) For guaranteeing freedom of navigation through international waterways in the area;
>
>   (b) For achieving a just settlement of the refugee problem;

(c) For guaranteeing the territorial inviolability and political independence of every State in the area, through measures including
the establishment of demilitarized zones;

3. Requests the Secretary-General to designate a Special Representative
to proceed to the Middle East to establish and maintain contacts with
the States concerned in order to promote agreement and assist efforts
to achieve a peaceful and accepted settlement in accordance with the
provisions and principles in this resolution.

While the UN Talks, Israel Acts

Israel's answer to UN objections to what it was doing came on April 1, 1969, with
a vote by the Knesset "to bring the Jewish Quarter to life again and dignify it as a
national, religious, and cultural center, stressing its special characteristics and quality."
The act created "The Company for the Reconstruction and Development of the
Jewish Quarter of Jerusalem." You've read in Chapter 2 about its restoration of synagogues and uncovering of ancient ruins, such as the Burnt House and the Cardo.
High on its agenda was clearing a wide area in front of the Western Wall and creating
a broad plaza to accommodate thousands of worshipers.

The Last Thing Anybody Needed

On a sunny August day in 1969, a deranged visitor who'd traveled all the way from
Australia to Jerusalem made his way to al-Aqsa Mosque and set it on fire. The blaze
began at the twelfth-century cedar pulpit and quickly engulfed the ceiling and dome.
Identified as a deranged fundamentalist Christian, 28-year-old Dennis Michael Rohan
explained that he hoped that by setting fire to one of "Satan's temples," he would be
proclaimed "king of Jerusalem" and that "sweet Jesus" would return and pray in a
rebuilt temple.

When an Arab commission investigated, it placed the blame on the Israelis. Mayor
Kollek replied, "Logically, the Arabs in Jerusalem knew we were in no way responsible. But deep in their hearts they wanted to believe we were. Ultimately they interpreted the al-Aqsa incident as divine punishment because the holy places were under
the control of infidels. The infidels in question happen to be Jews, but it would have
been the same if the British, the UN, or the Pope were ruling Jerusalem." With
Israeli assistance, the mosque was repaired. But suspicions of Israeli intentions weren't
so easily fixed.

The Yom Kippur War

On the Jewish holiday Yom Kippur, October 6, 1973, Egyptian and Syrian military forces struck Israeli positions on the Suez Canal in the south and the Golan Heights in the north. Other Arab states provided troops and financial support. Although the attack had been in the works for months, it was just hours before the invasion that Israeli Prime Minister Golda Meir agreed to a limited mobilization of Israeli defense forces. Meanwhile, hordes of Egyptian infantrymen crossed the Suez Canal and overran Israeli defenses. Israel's reserve troops were thrown back to defensive positions that stopped the advance 6 miles east of the canal.

Faced with the possibility of annihilation from Arab forces in the Yom Kippur War, Prime Minister Meir ordered an urgent phone call to Secretary of State Henry Kissinger. Told that it was the middle of the night in Washington, she retorted, "I don't care what time it is. Call Kissinger now! In the middle of the night! We need the help today because tomorrow it may be too late."

With resupply assured by the United States, the Israelis went on the offensive. In a daring drive led by General Ariel Sharon, the IDF cut through a gap between two Egyptian armies and occupied the main Suez highway. After heavy fighting, Israeli troops crossed to the west bank of the canal, captured oil refineries and offices of the Egyptian government, and surged toward Cairo. In the Golan Heights, Syrian forces threw 1,100 tanks against 157 Israeli tanks and threatened to sweep down to Lake Kinneret. Counterattacking on October 8, the Israelis pushed Syria back to the 1967 cease-fire lines. Five days later, they'd driven the Syrians back and occupied Syrian territory, and Israeli jets were in the skies over Damascus. At this crucial moment, the Nixon administration sent a U.S. airlift of weapons and supplies to aid Israel. Operation Nickel Grass flew resupply missions for a month. It consisted of 815 flights that delivered 56 combat aircraft and 27,900 tons of munitions and supplies.

> **Reverent Remarks**
>
> The U.S. airlift of tanks, ammunition, clothing, medical supplies, and air-to-air rockets turned the tide of battle. Golda Meir said that the operation's huge Galaxie transport planes "looked like some kind of immense prehistoric monsters."

> **Holy Facts!**
>
> The toll in lives in the Yom Kippur War was 2,700 Israelis, 3,500 Syrians, and 15,000 Egyptians.

Following a UN–ordered cease fire, Israel held the entire western side of the Suez Canal, stood within 42 miles of Cairo, and had Syrian forces back to within 40 miles of Damascus at a cost to Syria of all of its tanks. When the fighting ended on October 22, 1973, the Security Council passed Resolution

338. It called on all parties to begin implementation of Security Council Resolution 252 "in all its parts" through negotiations. Israel now held an additional 165 square miles of Syrian territory and was solidly established on the west bank of the Suez Canal.

The Brutal Language of Bombers

While Americans who happened to be in Jerusalem on July 4, 1975, were celebrating their country's birthday, 39-year-old Ahmad Jbarah was placing a discarded refrigerator packed with an explosive outside a shop in Zion Square. When it detonated three quarters of an hour later, the blast killed 14 people and wounded 70. Responsibility for the bombing was claimed by the "Jerusalem Committee" of an Arab organization calling itself the "Palestine Liberation Organization" (PLO).

Formed around the festering issue of Palestinians living in many refugee camps, the PLO was born during the first meeting of the Palestinian Congress in 1964. Its "Palestine National Charter" called for the destruction of Israel. Through the years, the PLO would divide into factions, including the Popular Front for the Liberation of Palestine (PFLP), Popular Democratic Front for the Liberation of Palestine (PDFLP), and the Movement for the Liberation of Palestine, or *FATAH*. In 1969, the PLO chose as its chairman and leader 39-year-old Mohammed Yasser Abdul-Ra'ouf Qudwa al-Husseini, soon to be known to the world as Yasser Arafat.

Remember the name of Ahmad Jbarah, the refrigerator bomber. He reappears in the history of Jerusalem in Chapter 19 as a Palestinian hero freed from an Israeli prison after serving 28 years and given a warm welcome by Yasser Arafat.

What Does That Mean?

FATAH is a reversed acronym of the initials H, T, and F of an Arabic phrase "Harakat al-Tahrir al-Watani al-Filastini." The Arab word fatah means "conquest by means of jihad" (holy war).

High and Mighty

The official PLO biography of Yasser Arafat states that he was born on August 24, 1929, in the Gaza Strip. But Christophe Boltanski and Jihan El-Tahri, claim in a 1997 biography of Arafat that he was born in Cairo, Egypt, attended King Saud University in Egypt, and earned a Bachelor's degree in engineering in 1951.

Looking for a Master Plan for the New Jerusalem

While the United Nations warned Israel about making changes in the Old City, the Israelis went about rapidly remaking the skyline of West Jerusalem. Suddenly, high-rise buildings seemed to be going up everywhere. Most notable was the Plaza Hotel. On the crest of the Mount of Olives, it was a modern edifice that provided a breathtaking vista of the Old City. But in the view of many observers, its modern architecture was both an affront to centuries of small buildings and a sacrilege to the Mount and the Garden of Gethsemane. Just as offensive to traditionalists were the Wolfson Towers that overshadowed the Monastery of the Cross and Sacher Park, a 22-floor addition to the King David Hotel, and a Hyatt Hotel on the slopes of Mount Scopus. Some buildings had also ignored the tradition of facades made of Jerusalem stone.

Attempts at coming up with a master plan to shape the New Jerusalem were met with protests. And following the refrigerator bombing, there was added to the mix of a city on the move a sense of foreboding. American Jewish writer Saul Bellow described Jerusalem as "a modern city with modern utilities," but one in which bombs were "exploding everywhere."

The Least You Need to Know

- When Jordan took over East Jerusalem, it downgraded its political status.
- Israel created a Holocaust memorial called Yad Vashem.
- Wars in 1956, 1967, and 1973 ended in Arab defeats and Israeli takeover of Arab territory.
- Israel ignored UN demands for it to pull out of Arab territory.
- The Palestine Liberation Organization (PLO) was formed in 1964; its charter called for the destruction of Israel.

Part 4

Long and Twisting Road

In this part, you will travel down a long and twisting road as the United States begins a 30-year-long effort to negotiate peace between Arabs and Israelis. The journey begins in the company of Egyptian President Anwar Sadat as he makes an historic trip to Jerusalem. Included in this odyssey of hope and disappointments are three conferences at the presidential retreat, Camp David, and a secretive meeting in Oslo. You will also spend nervous nights in Jerusalem during the first Gulf War with Iraq as Scud missiles are launched against Israel.

The recent past of Jerusalem has been the scene of much violence and fear as a string of suicide bombers have unleashed their fury in Jerusalem to protest Israel's occupation of Arab territory. Amidst all the bloodshed, another glimmer of hope has begun to shine, as President George W. Bush encourages both sides to follow a "roadmap" to peace.

15

What Took You So Long?

In This Chapter

- ◆ Israelis look for someone to blame for the 1973 war
- ◆ Golda Meir resigns as prime minister
- ◆ Egypt's president makes an historic trip to Jerusalem
- ◆ The United States brokers an Egypt-Israeli peace treaty
- ◆ A decade of terrorism

On November 11, 1973, in a tent at Kilometer 101 on the road that stretched between Cairo and the Suez Canal, Israel's General Aharon Yariv and Egypt's General Abdel Gamasy signed a six-point agreement on the "disengagement and separation of forces under the auspices of the United Nations." The war that Israel had come frighteningly close to losing ended in Israeli victory. Israel's prime minister, Golda Meir, wrote of that moment, "For the first time in a quarter of a century there was direct, simple, personal contact between Israelis and Egyptians."

History Is Written at Kilometer 101

Although talk of how to keep the peace pervaded the air at Kilometer 101, a dramatically different atmosphere existed in the streets of West

Jerusalem and inside Israel's parliament. People were obsessed with placing blame for Israel's lack of preparation for the war. Accusing fingers pointed to Prime Minister Meir and Defense Minister Moshe Dayan.

"Much of the outcry was genuine," Meir wrote. "Most of it, in fact, was a natural expression of outrage over the fatal series of mishaps that had taken place. It was not just my resignation or Dayan's that was being called for in that storm of protest; it was a call to eliminate from the scene everyone who could possibly be held responsible for what had happened and to start all over again with new people, younger people, people who were not tainted by the charge of having led the nation astray." The ultimate result of the finger-pointing was tumult in the Israeli government and Meir's resignation.

> **Reverent Remarks**
>
> There is a limit to what I can take, and I have now reached that limit.
>
> —Golda Meir, announcing her resignation in 1978

High and Mighty

Prime Minister Golda Meir had been secretly fighting cancer for years. When she died on December 8, 1978, in Jerusalem, obituary writers heaped praise on this extraordinary woman. She was called the "mother of Israel" and a "lioness of Israel."

Meir's life had begun in Russia and matured in the United States. She had labored for the founding of the Jewish state, had become its first minister to the Soviet Union, and served six years as Israel's only woman prime minister. Although her middle-of-the-night appeal to Secretary of State Henry Kissinger for American help in the Yom Kippur War turned the tide of battle, she died blaming herself for unpreparedness that cost 2,500 Israeli soldiers and civilians their lives.

A Hawk Turns into a Dove

The logical successor to Meir was Dayan, but Israel's most famous warrior—at least since David picked up a slingshot to slay Goliath—was also on the receiving end of blame for Israel's brush with defeat in the Yom Kippur War. The job of prime minister went to Minister of Information Shimon Peres.

A Side Note on Moshe Dayan

Moshe Dayan had devoted his life to working for the creation of a Jewish state and defending its right to exist on battlefields. Born on May 20, 1915, on a pioneer collective farm (kibbutz), Deganya Alef, near the Sea of Galillee, he was raised at another kibbutz, Nahalal. As a member of the Hagannah, he'd learned guerilla warfare tactics on night patrols from British Captain Charles Orde Wingate. When the British outlawed the Hagannah in 1938, he was arrested and jailed for two years.

Released in 1941, he found a greater cause than battling the British. While fighting with the British army in the liberation of Syria and Lebanon from the control of Nazi collaborators in the French government at Vichy, he lost his left eye and began wearing a black eye-patch. At the end WWII, he returned to the Hagannah with the goal of persuading Britain to come through with the promise of the Balfour Declaration. When the British proved reluctant to grant Israel independence, and banned the immigration of survivors of Nazi death camps in Europe, he was in command of the defenses of Jewish settlements along the Jordan River, then against Egyptian forces on the southern front, and the commander of Israeli forces in a fight for Jerusalem. Named chief of operations in 1952 and chief of staff in 1953, he was a central figure in the 1956 war with Egypt, Syria, and Jordan. Leaving the military in 1958, he entered politics. Elected to the Knesset in 1959, he served as minister of agriculture (1959–1964), and was minister of defense in the 1967 war. At 10:15 A.M., June 7, he'd raised the Israeli flag over Jerusalem and prayed at the Western Wall for the first time.

High and Mighty

In 1977, Moshe Dayan would be rescued from likely political oblivion by a new prime minister. Menachem Begin named him minister of foreign affairs. Dayan accepted the post because he believed that he could "significantly influence Israel's moves toward achieving a peace arrangement with our neighboring Arab States and with the Palestinian inhabitants of Judea, the West Bank, and the Gaza Strip." As the lead negotiator in peace talks, he was described as acting "alternately with dash and deliberation" and "advancing and stalling," while "vacillating between surprising compromises and inexplicable intransigence." A romantic-looking figure with the band of his black eye-patch stretched at a jaunty angle over a bald head, he first met with Egyptians at Geneva, Switzerland.

An Egyptian with a Sacred Mission to Knock Down Walls

Three years after the 1973 war, a student of modern Arab history wrote that the president of Egypt who had launched the war, Anwar Sadat, was a great actor—one who loved an audience. As a young man he'd briefly tried his hand at acting. But in the aftermath of Egypt's defeat, he stepped into the spotlight of a world stage for what he called "a sacred mission."

Aboard an Egyptian airliner in 1977, he was heading to a place where no Arab leader had set foot since 1948. On the way to the Holy City, he explained to *Time* magazine's Cairo bureau chief, Wilton Wynn, "What I want from this visit is that the wall created between us and Israel, the psychological wall, to be knocked down."

How to Get from the Nile River Delta to Jerusalem

The life journey of Anwar Sadat began on December 25, 1918, in the village of Mit Abul Kim in the Nile River Delta. Graduating from the Egyptian Military Academy, he met another young officer, Gamal Abdel Nasser, and joined him in forming a group dedicated to freeing Egypt from British rule. Imprisoned twice during World War II, and after a period as a businessman and a try at acting, he renewed the association with Nasser in a revolutionary group called the Free Officers Organization. When it staged a coup that toppled Egypt's obese and corrupt King Farouk on July 23, 1952, he became Nasser's public relations minister and closest advisor. Nasser declared Egypt a "nonaligned nation" in the Cold War struggle between the West and the Soviet Union. Encouraged by the Soviets, Nasser committed Egypt to three Arab wars against Israel (1948, 1956, 1967) that ended in disastrous losses.

As vice president of Egypt when Nasser died in 1970, Sadat took power of a nation that had suffered the most in the wars, losing five times as many men in the 1967 Six-Day War as allies Syria and Jordan. Determined to tackle Egypt's domestic problems, he appealed to Moscow for assistance. When Moscow failed to provide it, he expelled all Soviet advisors from the country and put out peace feelers to Israel. When Israel ignored Sadat's entreaties for peace, he launched in the Yom Kippur War, an effort to drive Israel out of the Sinai Desert and with the hope that Israel would be forced to make peace at last. As you know, Egypt, along with its ally Syria, once again found itself on the losing end of the war. But the conflict brought about a series of peace negotiations marked by "shuttle diplomacy" conducted by American Secretary of State Henry Kissinger.

Sadat was frustrated by the slow pace of progress of Moshe Dayan and the Geneva peace conference and alarmed by a "poisonous atmosphere" that threatened yet another Arab-Israeli war. With American help, he succeeded in obtaining an "interim agreement" that returned the western part of the Sinai to

> **" " Reverent Remarks**
>
> There is no time to lose. I am ready to go to the ends of the earth if that will save one of my soldiers, one of my officers, from being scratched. I am ready to go to their house, [to] the Knesset, to discuss peace with the Israeli leaders.
>
> —Egyptian President Anwar Sadat, Cairo, 1977

Egypt. Still beset by his domestic troubles, which included several riots, he decided that the time had come for a bold gamble that the Israelis were as weary of incessant warfare as the Egyptians. Eager to provide a "peace dividend" to both countries, he told the Egyptian parliament in 1977 he was willing "to go anywhere" to negotiate peace.

The World Watches an Astonishing Spectacle

To the world's amazement, Israel's Prime Minister Menachem Begin, the ex-guerilla fighter, responded to Egyptian President Sadat's peace entreaty by extending to him a formal invitation to Jerusalem. The flight from Cairo to Tel Aviv's Ben-Gurion Airport took only 28 minutes. Waiting to meet Sadat's plane were Begin, former premier Yitzhak Rabin, Foreign Minister Moshe Dayan, and the soldier known as Israel's "General Patton," Ariel Sharon, whose tanks had pushed all the way to the Suez Canal in 1973 and across it to the suburbs of Cairo.

Three Days in Jerusalem that Shifted the Course of History

Sadat had been in Jerusalem only one other time. In 1955 he'd come in his capacity as secretary-general of the Muslim Congress. He never left the Arab section of the city and had joined in denunciations of Israel. But now, as an honored guest of the Israeli government, he was the one whom Arabs—at least members of the Palestine Liberation Organization—were denouncing.

Addressing the Knesset, Sadat recalled the history of Arab-Israeli relations since the birth of the Jewish state in 1948:

> We used to reject you, true. We refused to meet you anywhere, true. We referred to you as the so-called Israel, true. At international conferences our representatives refused to exchange greetings with you, true. At the 1973 Geneva Peace Conference our delegates did not exchange a single direct word with you, true. Yet today we agree to live with you in permanent peace and justice; Israel has become an accomplished fact recognized by the whole world and the superpowers. We welcome you to live among us in peace and security.

Following his speech, he joined Prime Minister Begin and others at a news conference. When it was former prime minister Golda Meir's turn to speak, she turned to the visitor from Egypt whose forces hers had defeated in 1973 and asked, "What took you so long?"

Reverent Remarks

It will take a monumental mess-up to derail Sadat's initiative. But if it fails, there will be war.

—U.S. Secretary of State Henry Kissinger

Naming Anwar Sadat "Man of the Year," *Time* magazine noted that the "astonishing spectacle was global theater." Within three weeks, Israeli diplomats and journalists were flying into Cairo to be met "with astounding warmth and joy by Egyptians." Critics of the peace policy, Sadat said, were "dwarfs."

Sadat's bold move paved the way for a 1979 peace treaty, which Sadat and Begin hammered out at Camp David under the mediation of U.S. President Jimmy Carter.

Sadat Gets a Prize and Pays the Price for Peace

Sadat and Begin signed the Camp David Accords on the lawn of the White House. Although the agreement did not mention Jerusalem, Sadat and Begin provided side letters stating their views on the fate of the city. Sadat's letter to President Carter stated that Arab Jerusalem was an "integral part of the West Bank" and that legal and historical Arab rights in the city "must be respected and restored." Begin wrote that the policy of Israel as stated by the Knesset was that "Jerusalem is one city, indivisible, the capital of Israel." So although there was peace between the two countries, they clearly disagreed on the fate of the "Holy City."

Holy Facts!

Since 1979, there has been a peace treaty between Egypt and Israel.

For his daring stroke, Sadat, along with Menachem Begin, was awarded the Nobel Peace Prize. But the era of domestic harmony and economic progress that Sadat had hoped to realize for Egypt did not come about. Despite desperate gambles to deal with Egypt's internal problems, he came under increasing criticism by fundamentalist Muslim groups. The criticism turned violent on October 6, 1981. On that day, as he was reviewing Egyptian troops, several armed men jumped from passing trucks, opened fire into the grandstand, and assassinated him.

High and Mighty

Moshe Dayan died 10 days after Anwar Sadat was assassinated. In the months after Sadat's historic journey for peace, Dayan, like Sadat, had spoken in opposition to Prime Minister Begin's policy of Israeli confiscation of undeveloped Arab land in the West Bank close to Jerusalem. Dayan had quit his post as foreign minister in 1979, bitter that he hadn't been named to lead talks with Palestinians on creating a Palestinian state. (Those talks had been prompted by Sadat's visit.) In 1981 he formed the Telem party, to push for unilateral Israeli disengagement, but he died of colon cancer soon thereafter. He was buried at Nahalal, the kibbutz of his youth.

Jerusalem, Complete and Undivided

By a vote of 99 to 51 on July 22, 1980, the Knesset passed a bill to annex East Jerusalem. The measure began with the declaration that "Jerusalem, complete and undivided is the capital of Israel." It also authorized granting to Israeli institutions "special economic, financial, and other priorities to the development of Jerusalem."

> **Reverent Remarks**
>
> No historic imagination should be affronted by the idea that the responsibility [for Jerusalem] has come to repose upon the people that gave [it] its original fame and its universal resonance.
>
> —Abba Eban, Israeli diplomat and historian, July 1980

Israel and the World Learn a New Arab Word: *Jihad*

Despite protests in the United Nations and world capitals against "prolonged occupation of Arab territories, including Jerusalem," Begin announced that he was moving the prime minister's office to East Jerusalem. When British Foreign Secretary Lord Carrington decried the move, Begin informed Carrington in a public statement that it was "not his business to advise the prime minister of Israel where to site his office." Begin added, "Jerusalem was a capital, a Jewish capital, long before London became the capital of the United Kingdom. When King David moved the capital of his kingdom from Hebron, where he reigned for 7 years, to Jerusalem, where he reigned for 33 years (1 Kings, 2:11), the civilized world had not yet heard of the city of London."

Although Begin eventually gave in to pressure and changed his mind about his office location, annexation of East Jerusalem remained the goal of his government. Infuriated by this policy, Prince Fahd of Saudi Arabia declared that if Israel didn't change its policy of annexation, the Arab world would retaliate with a *jihad*, meaning "holy war."

As if tensions in Jerusalem weren't bad enough in April 1982, an American named Alan Harry Goodman went to the Haram carrying an automatic rifle and opened fire, killing an unarmed Muslim guard. In a statement disturbingly reminiscent of Australian arsonist Denis Rohan (see Chapter 14), Goodman said that his purpose was to liberate the Temple Mount and that he wanted to be crowned the "king of Jerusalem."

> **Reverent Remarks**
>
> We pursue our goals [in Arab East Jerusalem] expecting neither sympathy nor gratitude from a population [Arabs] which cannot alienate itself from its national emotions.
>
> —Mayor Teddy Kollek, March 1985, on plans for the "physical revitalization" of the Muslim Quarter of the Old City

Outraged Muslims reacted by launching a raid on the Mount of Olives and smashing Jewish tombstones.

A Blast from the PLO

The dissatisfied voice of the PLO was heard in December 1983, when 5 Israelis were killed and 43 injured in a bus explosion in West Jerusalem. The Palestine Liberation Organization claimed responsibility for the attack and said that the targets had been 40 Israeli soldiers. Two months later, a grenade tossed into a Jaffa Road clothing store injured 21 Israelis, the Arab owner of the shop, and his son.

Violence at the Dung and Damascus Gates

At an October 1986 military graduation ceremony at the Western Wall, radicals hurled three grenades at the celebrants as they left the Old City through the Dung Gate. One Israeli was killed and 70 were wounded. When the attackers were arrested, they said they belonged to the "Islamic Jihad," based in Gaza and the West Bank. A month later, a young religious Jew, Eliahu Amedi, was stabbed to death in the Old City by three Arabs who said that they'd picked him at random and because he'd been alone. While his body was being carried for burial on the Mount of Olives, his mourners went on a rampage against the Arab shops at the Damascus Gate.

Bewildered and worried by escalating violence from both sides, Mayor Teddy Kollek pleaded, "We have to find a compromise in the city, to live together in tolerance, understanding, and mutual respect."

The Start of a Whole Lot of Shaking

Remember this Arab word: *intifada*. It means "a shaking off" and "uprising." It burst into the news on December 9, 1987, and again (as you will soon read) in 2002. The first method of the "shaking off" was a tactic that Muslims had used previously as a means of protest: economic boycott. But this time, rather than shunning Jewish merchants, the Arabs closed their shops, and then defied the orders of the Israeli army to open them. The shutdown spread to Arab-owned bus lines, attacks of Jewish vehicles, and assaults on anyone who looked Jewish. When police and army units moved in to quell the unrest, they were greeted with cascades of rocks and stones. Police spokesman Rah Levy warned, "Those who take part in disturbances have to take into account the fact that the police will respond."

Six days after the intifada began, Israel's minister of industry and trade, Ariel Sharon, took over and moved into an apartment in the Muslim Quarter. It was an act, said one irate Arab, "like a finger poked in your eye." The next two years brought a series of provocations and clashes:

An Intifada Chronology

Jan. 15, 1988	Israeli police fire tear gas into Palestinian protestors at the Dome of the Rock and the al-Aqsa Mosque.
May 12, 1988	Israeli troops attack Palestinian demonstrators after Friday prayers.
July 2, 1988	Israel's Ministry of Religious Affairs begins digging a tunnel near the Haram.
Nov. 14, 1988	The Palestine National Congress declares a Palestinian independent state with East Jerusalem as its capital.
Jan. 12, 1989	Israel imposes a curfew in East Jerusalem.
Feb. 15, 1989	Ariel Sharon calls for arrest of PLO's "political arm."
Feb. 27, 1989	The "Unified Leadership of the Uprising" calls for "the masses of our people in Jerusalem" to boycott elections and a strike to "paralyze" public transportation.
July 6, 1989	Prime Minister Yitzhak Shamir vows, "There will be no negotiations as long as [Arab] violence continues."
Dec. 23, 1989	South African Archbishop Desmond Tutu visits the Old City and announces support for a Palestinian state and Israel's "independence and territorial integrity."
Dec. 30, 1989	A 2½-mile "human chain for peace" around the Old City, formed by 15,000 Arabs and sympathetic Jews, is fired on by Israeli forces with water cannons, tear gas, and rubber bullets.
Jan. 1, 1990	The Israeli Defense Force demolishes an unfinished Arab house on grounds that builders threw stones at them.
March 27, 1990	The Knesset declares that Jerusalem is under Israeli "sovereignty" and there will be no negotiations about its status.
April 27, 1990	The Church of the Holy Sepulchre is closed for the first time in 800 years to protest Israeli settlers on St. John's Hospice grounds.

May 17, 1990	A new Israeli police unit (Gid'onim) is formed to deal with security problems and to "engage in intelligence missions" in Jerusalem.
Oct. 7, 1990	Ariel Sharon announces a plan to increase the pace of Israeli construction in East Jerusalem and more than double the number of units built each year.
Oct. 22, 1990	Israeli police surround Jerusalem with roadblocks to keep out Palestinians from the West Bank.
Nov. 19, 1990	Sharon says a special effort is being made to build Jewish housing in East Jerusalem.
Jan. 17, 1991	Israel imposes a curfew on East Jerusalem, West Bank, and Gaza.
Jan. 18, 1991	Israel is attacked with Scud missiles from Iraq in the opening days of the Gulf War (see the next chapter).
March 15, 1991	Israel's Religious Affairs Ministry announces plan to build a Jewish cemetery in the West Bank in violation of international rules on use of occupied territory.
July 21, 1991	U.S. and British governments reaffirm Palestinians' right to choose their own representatives.
Aug. 8, 1991	Egyptian President Hosni Mubarak asserts that the PLO must be involved in peace talks.
Oct. 9, 1991	Hundreds of Jews occupy eight Palestinian homes in Silwan, outside the Old City walls; when an Israeli court rules against them, they are evicted (December 13).
Nov. 18, 1991	Israeli forces raid Islamic court offices and seize documents pertaining to Palestinian property rights.

Holy Facts!

Between 1987 and 1992, 695 Arabs were killed by the Israeli army, including 78 children under age 14; and 528 Arabs died at the hands of other Arabs for "collaborating" with Israel or for violations of Islamic law. Thirteen Israeli soldiers and twelve civilians were killed in knife attacks.

America Decides the Road to Holy Land Peace Begins in Spain

During the intifada, changes in the governments of Israel and the United States opened the door to peace negotiations, if only by a crack. In Jerusalem, right-wing Likud party leader Yitzhak Shamir put together a coalition with himself as prime minister. In the United States, George H. W. Bush succeeded Ronald Reagan as president. With the problem of the Middle East high on the agenda following a quick defeat of Iraq in the 1991 Gulf War, the new administration's secretary of state, James Baker, traveled to Jerusalem and held the first meeting of a top American official with Palestinian leaders. The result was an agreement by the Palestinians that if they were included in a peace conference, they would not press for immediate discussion of the status of Jerusalem.

The talks convened in October 1991 in Madrid, Spain. The fate of Jerusalem was not on the agenda. Although they failed to resolve the so-called Palestinian issue, the conference did end with a "framework" for future talks. The leader of the Israeli delegation would be a new prime minister, Yitzhak Rabin, along with a new foreign minister, Shimon Peres.

These political changes set the stage for working out an agreement in the capital of Norway that would be formally titled Declaration of Principles. Popularly known as the Oslo Agreement, it's discussed next.

The Least You Need to Know

- Israelis blamed Prime Minister Golda Meir for the Israeli army's unpreparedness in the 1973 war; she ended up resigning from her post.

- Egyptian President Anwar Sadat, in a bold move, entered into a peace agreement with the Israelis. He was assassinated in 1981, after having received the Nobel Peace Prize.

- In defiance of UN resolutions, Israel moved to take over Arab-occupied East Jerusalem.

- Palestinians launched an uprising called the intifada, which started a multiyear cycle of clashes between Palestinians and Israelis.

Chapter 16

Caught in the Middle

In This Chapter

- ◆ Jerusalem fears Iraqi missiles during 1991 Gulf War
- ◆ Prime Minister Rabin talks about making peace
- ◆ Israelis and Palestinians strike a deal at Oslo
- ◆ A White House ceremony and three Nobel Prizes
- ◆ An assassin shakes up the peace process

In January 1991 the people of Jerusalem learned that they could not shut out events taking place in the rest of the Middle East. This fact was driven home when a coalition of nations led by the United States responded to Iraq's invasion of the small Persian Gulf Kingdom of Kuwait. As the forces of Operation Desert Storm gathered to repel the takeover, Iraq's dictator, Saddam Hussein, warned that any attack on Iraq would result in the burning of "half of Israel" by Russian-built Scud missiles carrying chemical warheads.

Jerusalem Under Attack

With the liberation of Kuwait underway, Saddam followed through on his threat by launching 39 Scuds at Israel. Although most of them would fall harmlessly and contain conventional warheads, Israelis prepared for the worst by seal-ing off rooms and carrying gas masks.

> **Holy Facts!**
>
> During one of the Iraqi Scud attacks, American violinist Isaac Stern was taking part in a concert in Jerusalem given by the Israel Philharmonic Orchestra. While members of the audience put on their masks, Stern stood at center stage without one, tucked his violin under his chin, and played a Mozart solo until the all-clear sounded.
>
> That the violin virtuoso did so came as no surprise to Israelis. Isaac Stern had been performing in Israel since the day it became a state. During the Six-Day War in 1967 and in the Yom Kippur War in 1973 he canceled all commitments so that he could play for troops and in hospitals. When the United Nations Educational, Scientific, and Social Organization suspended its music programs in Israel in 1974, he organized a boycott by musicians of UNESCO events.

Writing about the feeling of terror that had gripped Jerusalem during the Gulf War, historian Martin Gilbert noted that while each incident was "unnerving," Jerusalem was still the "cultural and spiritual magnet" that its Jewish settlers had envisioned at the heart of a nation called Israel.

A Hawk Turns into a Dove

In the year after the Gulf War (July 1992), Yitzhak Rabin became Israel's eleventh prime minister in 34 years. He was assuming the post for the second time, as he had also served as prime minister in the 1970s. This time, in addition to taking on the role of prime minister, Rabin also assumed the cabinet positions of minister of de-fense, and acting minister of religious affairs and labor and social affairs.

> **Reverent Remarks**
>
> The history of the Arab lead-ers in the search for peace is that they have never missed an opportunity to pass up an oppor-tunity.
>
> —Abba Eban, Israeli diplomat and historian

Enough of Tears and Blood

With the exception of the late distinguished leader, diplomat, and historian Abba Eban, there's been lit-tle in the way of notable and quotable speeches by Israeli political leaders that compares favorably with addresses by President Franklin D. Roosevelt in the Great Depression and World War II and those throughout most of the twentieth century by Win-ston Churchill. But you can add to that short list the inaugural address that Rabin gave in Jerusalem on July 13, 1992. Declaring that he wanted to send a message to the Palestinians, he said:

> We have been destined to live together on the same piece of land in the same country. Our life proceeds alongside yours, with you, and against you. You have failed in your wars against us. A hundred years of bloody terror on your part only inflicted suffering, pain, and bereavement upon you. You have lost thousands of your sons and daughters, and you have constantly lost ground. For over 44 years you have been deluding yourselves, your leaders have been leading you by the nose with falsehoods and lies. They missed all the opportunities, they rejected all our proposed solutions, and they have led you from one disaster to another. You, the Palestinians in the territories, living in miserable exile in Gaza and Khan Yanus and in the refugee camps in Nablus and Hebron, you who have never in your lives known even one day of freedom and happiness: You had better listen to us, if only this time. We are offering you the most fair and realistic offer we can put forth today: autonomy, self-rule, with its advantages and limitations. You will not get all that you want. We, too, may not get everything we want. Once and for all, take your fate into your own hands. Do not once again miss the opportunity which may never recur. Take our proposal seriously. Give it the seriousness it deserves to spare yourself yet more suffering and bereavement. Enough of tears and blood!

High and Mighty

A Jerusalem native, born in 1922, Yitzhak Rabin joined the Palmach in 1940 and in the 1948 war commanded the Harel Brigade on the Jerusalem front. In the 1956 war he was in charge of northern command operations. In the years 1959 to 1964, he was chief of operations and deputy chief of staff. After commanding the Israeli Defense Force (IDF) in the Six-Day War and a year in "retirement," he returned to government as ambassador to the United States until the spring of 1973. As a Labour party member of the Knesset, he was Golda Meir's minister of labor. Chosen to serve as prime minister on June 2, 1974, he emphasized strengthening the economy, dealing with social problems, and strengthening the IDF. At the urging of the United States, he had signed disengagement agreements with Egypt and Syria (1974) and a Memorandum of Understanding between Israel and the United States, assuring Israel of U.S. support. Following the formation of a national unity government in September 1984, he served in the Knesset as a member of the Labour party in opposition and as a member of the Foreign Affairs and Defense Committee. Between 1984 and 1990 as minister of defense he handled the withdrawal of IDF forces from Lebanon and the establishment of a security zone along Israel's northern border. Elected chairman of the Israel Labour party in its first nationwide primaries (February 1992), he led the party to a victory in the 1992 Knesset elections that made him prime minister for a second time.

Getting Around Problems by Way of a Back Channel

Peace negotiations had practically come to a standstill, and both sides were getting frustrated. To speed up the process the Israelis, Palestinians, and the United States opened a "back channel" using Norwegian mediators. The result of negotiations between Israel and PLO officials was the "Oslo Agreement." The accords served as a "Middle East peace process" that recognized the right of each side to exist within borders of Palestine/Israel and called for an improvement of relations between their peoples. This "framework for a solution" provided that Israeli forces would withdraw from unspecified areas in the Gaza Strip and an area around Jericho, followed by election of a Palestinian government. Meanwhile, Palestinian affairs would be handled by a "Palestinian National Authority," headed by Yasser Arafat.

What to Do About Jerusalem?

The thorny issue of what to do about Jerusalem was taken up by Israeli Deputy Foreign Minister Yossi Beilin and a close advisor to Arafat named Mahmoud Abbas, also known in the PLO leadership as Abu Mazen. (Remember Mazen's name—he will figure prominently in Chapter 19.) Between the autumn of 1993 and the spring of 1995, these men met about 20 times to try to determine the fate of the 3,000-year-old city.

Agreeing that it should be "an open and undivided city with free and unimpeded access for people of all faiths and nationalities," they came up with a proposal to divide it into Jewish and Arab boroughs based on their populations, with each represented on a "Joint Higher Municipal Council." On all questions affecting the Palestinian boroughs, the council would be required to have the "consent" of the government of Palestine, and Jewish borough issues would need Israeli government approval.

A Capital City with Two Names

Beilin and Abu Mazen agreed that the Jerusalem of the Israelis be called Yerushalayim and Jerusalem of the Arabs be known as al-Quds. The sovereignty of areas outside either Yerushalayim and al-Quds, but within "the present boundaries of Jerusalem," would be determined "as soon as possible." Freedom of worship and access to all the holy sites for all religions would be guaranteed, and the Old City would be granted a "special status" that was not defined. The "state of Palestine" was to be granted "extraterritorial sovereignty" over the Haram and "the present status quo regarding right of access and prayer for all" was to be "secured." The Church of the Holy

Sepulchre would be within a Palestinian borough, but the Joint Parity Committee would look into granting Christianity's holiest site an extraterritorial status. No mention was made of the Western Wall.

Historian Bernard Wasserstein wrote in *Divided Jerusalem* that in spite of the questions that the Beilin–Abu Mazen agreement left unresolved, the deal "represented a surprising achievement" that could be formalized in a treaty and signed by Rabin and Arafat.

On September 13, 1993, the whole world looked on in amazement via television as Israel's ex-warrior and the head of the world's most notorious terrorist organization (PLO) shook hands on the lawn of the White House while President Bill Clinton beamed as if he had just become a new father. So pleased and excited by this agreement were the committee members that handed out the Nobel Peace Prize that they voted to award it jointly to Yitzhak Rabin, Yasser Arafat, and Shimon Peres.

The Law of "You Can Never Satisfy Everybody"

Rabin and Arafat had barely returned home when critics on both sides claimed that too much had been given away.

The Palestinians predicted the Oslo accords would lead to establishment of "bantustans" in Palestine—a comparison to the supposedly autonomous regions created for blacks by the apartheid government in South Africa. The critics noted that "Oslo" and later agreements did not specially mention the creation of a Palestinian state. They would soon note that since the signing of the accords, Israel had settled about 30,000 people in the West Bank, in violation of the treaty.

Israeli critics of the accords claimed that the Palestinians had nothing to give to guarantee Israel's security beyond their word and that the Palestinians were acting in bad faith.

Acting on God's Orders with No Regrets

Among a crowd of 100,000 Israelis who'd gathered to hear Yitzhak Rabin address a peace rally held in King's Square in Tel Aviv on Saturday evening, November 4, 1995, was 25-year-old Bar Ilan University law student Yigal Amir. As the 73-year-old prime minister and war hero walked to his car, Amir drew a pistol and fired twice. One bullet hit Rabin in the arm; the other was a fatal shot to his back.

Captured immediately and soon identified as having been involved in right-wing causes, Amir said, "I acted alone on God's orders and I have no regrets." Two days later at his arraignment he said that he killed Rabin because Rabin wanted to "to give our country to the Arabs." Despite the claim that he'd acted alone, a court found that he'd conspired with a brother, Hagai, and a friend, Dror Adani, and that they'd also intended to kill Palestinians. Judge Amnon Starshov called the three young men "sons of evil."

As Rabin's body lay in state at the Knesset on November 5, 1995, an estimated 1 million people, in a nation of 5 million, filed past the bier.

Reverent Remarks

At a memorial ceremony, Jordan's King Hussein said that Rabin had "lived as a soldier" and "died as a soldier for peace." To President Hosni Mubarak of Egypt, Rabin was a "fallen hero for peace." President Clinton called him a "martyr for peace" and "a man completely without pretense." PLO leader Yasser Arafat, who'd been advised not to attend the funeral for security reasons, said in a formal statement that he was "very sad and very shocked for this awful and terrible crime." The statement continued, "He is one of the brave leaders of Israel and the peacemakers. I hope that we will have the ability, Israelis and Palestinians, to overcome this tragedy."

Rabin's body was carried from the Knesset to Mount Herzl Cemetery in a slow 2-mile procession through downtown Jerusalem streets. "Among the Israelis who mobbed the route to say farewell," noted one news organization, "were hospital patients who ran toward the street in their robes." As the coffin arrived at the cemetery, sirens sounded across Israel to signal two minutes of silence in his honor. At the Tel Aviv square where he'd been shot, thousands mourned by lighting candles and observing a silent vigil. Others gathered outside the apartment building where he'd lived in the northern Tel Aviv suburb of Ramat Aviv. His widow, Leah, told the crowd that "two bullets killed this great, wonderful man."

Putting Together Two Governments

Eleven days after Rabin's assassination, Israeli President Ezer Weizman asked acting–prime minister, Shimon Peres, to form a new government. Its foreign minister would be Ehud Barak, a figure who will play a significant role in the peace process in the next chapter. The day after Peres was designated to form a new Israeli government, PLO Chairman Yasser Arafat convened a meeting of the PLO Executive Committee on the future of the peace process. Fourteen members of the committee attended, making it the highest turnout since the PLO's Declaration of Principles in

1993. At the same time, Palestinians started registering for the balloting to elect a provisional government, as called for in the Oslo accords.

High and Mighty
Born Shimon Perski in Poland in 1923, Shimon Peres moved with his family to Palestine in 1934. His first political job was carrying messages for David Ben-Gurion. In the 1948 war, he was responsible for arms purchases and recruitment, and in 1956 planned Israel's brilliant military campaign in the Sinai Desert. A founder of the Labour party, he headed various ministries and served as prime minister and vice-premier in a unity government until 1990, and then as foreign minister until Rabin's assassination made him prime minister.

In keeping with the Oslo Agreement, the Israeli army completed a withdrawal from the West Bank town of Jenin on November 13, 1995. The Israeli forces were replaced by 1,000 Palestinian police. Six days later, Arafat visited the town and told thousands of Palestinians, "In the name of God, in the name of the Palestinian people, I declare Jenin liberated, liberated, liberated." At the same time, a group known as Hamas (Islamic Resistance Movement) announced the formation of a political wing to partic- ipate in the election. It also said that it would suspend its attacks against Israel.

Seventy percent of Palestinians went to the polls to choose a president on January 20, 1996. It is widely acknowledged that the Palestinian vote was rigged to guarantee that Arafat would be chosen president of the Palestinian National Authority. As expected, Arafat won in a landslide, garnering 83 percent of the vote.

Israelis Also Get a Chance to Cast Ballots

Although Israel's new prime minister, Shimon Peres, nurtured no illusions that he could garner the kind of majority that Arafat enjoyed, he was confident enough in his party's prospects that he moved up the date of a legally required parliamentary election. The key issue in the election would be the terms of the Oslo Agreement— especially those concerning the status of Jerusalem. Leading the opposition right- wing Likud party was 45-year-old Benjamin Netanyahu.

Unlike Rabin and Peres, who supported the return of some land to the Arabs as a means of winning security, Netanyahu believed that security should come first, and that the return of land should take place slowly and only accompanied by Palestinian moves to reduce militant violence.

High and Mighty

Born in Tel Aviv in 1949, Benjamin Netanyahu attended high school in the United States, where his father was a history teacher. In 1967, he served in the Six-Day War in an elite IDF commando unit and was wounded in a rescue of hostages at Ben-Gurion Airport. A brother, Jonathan, would become a posthumous hero when he was killed leading a dramatic rescue raid against a hijacked airliner in Entebbe, Uganda, in 1976. As Israel's deputy chief of mission in Washington for two years, Netanyahu was Israel's best-known spokesman in the United States. Elected to the Knesset in 1988, he was appointed deputy foreign minister. A profile of him by the British Broadcasting Corporation noted, "To his supporters, he came across as young, handsome, energetic, articulate in English, and a master of how to handle the Western media. In short, a man of the age." Known as Bibi to his friends and enemies alike, he was the first Israeli prime minister to be born after the creation of the Jewish state.

The Most Dangerous Bus Route in the World

Thirty-six days after the Palestinian election, progress toward peace ran into a major roadblock. On February 25, 1996, a member of Hamas, with explosives hidden in his clothing, boarded Jerusalem's number 18 bus. In the first such "suicide bombing," 25 people perished and 50 were wounded. Within days there was a second suicide bombing. On March 3 another Hamas member boarded a bus on the same route and set off a bomb that killed 18 riders.

A Dramatic Change of Faces and Direction

Shaken by the bus bombings and Rabin's assassination, Israelis voted in favor of security over peace. Elected prime minister by the narrowest of margins, Netanyahu represented a turning point in the politics of Israel and the peace process. Although he'd vowed he would never compromise on the issue of land for peace, he did so under American pressure, and alienated his supporters on the right. Others saw the doom of the Oslo accords with Netanyahu in power.

As the violence continued, a *Palestine Post* editorial on May 2, 1997, was not ready to give up. "Rumors of the death of the peace process," it declared, "are premature." It went on to say that "[t]he Oslo process was never meant to be an end in itself, but a trial run leading to a stable, final agreement. Oslo was supposed to build each side's confidence in the other's ability to make tough choices and to abide by its commitments …. No one ever said Oslo was perfect or sacred, but it is an agreement. The only way to adjust it in midstream, without undermining the prospects for future agreements, is to balance the changes in favor of both sides."

Bill Clinton Puts On the Pressure

Undaunted by the failure of his White House predecessors (Carter, Reagan, and George H. W. Bush) to get Israelis and Arabs to stop fighting and live side by side peacefully, President Bill Clinton brought Netanyahu and Arafat face-to-face on a historic plantation named Wye in Maryland in September 1998.

With a little arm-twisting by Clinton, Netanyahu agreed to an Israeli giveback of 13 percent of the West Bank over a period of 3 months, and Arafat agreed to arrest Palestinian terrorists and suppress anti-Israeli propaganda. Although Netanyahu carried out the first phase of land givebacks (about 9 percent) and freed some Palestinian terrorists, Arafat reneged on his part of the deal. Terrorists who were to have been quashed by Arafat remained unrestrained and continued their deadly attacks.

Blaming Netanyahu for offering concessions to the Palestinians without getting anything substantial in return, the Knesset called for a new election to be held in mid-May. Netanyahu's principal opponent would be a relative newcomer to Israeli politics, but a man well-known and admired as an IDF general: Ehud Barak.

A Candidate Whose Name Meant Lightning

Born Ehud Brog on a kibbutz in 1942, he adopted the Hebrew name Barak, meaning "lightning." The son of eastern European immigrants to Palestine, Barak didn't look like a boy who would become the most decorated military officer in Israeli history. Joining the IDF in 1959, he served 35 years and rose to the rank of lieutenant general—the highest rank in the IDF—and chief of staff. Barak was awarded the Distinguished Service Medal and four other citations for courage and military excellence. He earned degrees from Hebrew University in Jerusalem and Stanford University. In politics, he'd served as minister of the interior (1995) and minister of foreign affairs (1995–1996). Elected to the Knesset in 1996, he was a member of the Foreign Affairs and Defense committees. Leader of the Labor party, he was seen as the rightful inheritor of Rabin's policy of making peace with the Arabs through mutual concessions.

The defining issues in the election were how to proceed with the peace process requirement that Israel give up territory taken in 1967 and whether there would be a Palestinian state. Netanyahu was for going slowly on land givebacks and was solidly against the creation of a Palestinian state. Barak was open to compromise that could lead to Palestinian sovereignty.

The People Want to See Change

Visiting a polling place in Jerusalem on election day, Monday, May 17, 1999, Ehud Barak told reporters, "The people want to see a change, unity and hope, and we are determined to bring it." His campaign was given a boost the previous weekend when three minor party candidates withdrew from the contest—they would have drained votes from Barak had they stayed in the race. Also bolstering him was support from young and more secular-minded voters, immigrants from the Soviet Union, and many Arabs holding Israeli citizenship. Netanyahu's base of support came from working-class immigrants from the Middle East and North Africa and strictly ortho-dox Jews.

As 4.29 million eligible voters cast blue paper ballots, no one but the most devoted party loyalist was prepared to predict the outcome. Finally, with 93.6 percent of the votes counted late Monday night, Barak led Netanyahu by 56 to 43.9 percent. But parties aligned with Barak claimed only 51 of the 120 seats in the Knesset, with 53 in Netanyahu's column. This meant that Barak had to form a coalition government. With exit polls projecting a Barak sweep, Netanyahu conceded the election and said that he would give up leadership of the Likud party. As his supporters chanted "Bibi, Bibi,"—his nickname—he said, "I want to congratulate Ehud Barak on his victory in the elections. This is how it has to be in a democracy."

President Clinton Sees a Prime Minister to Do Business With

Analyzing Barak as prime minister, Jerusalem historian Bernard Wasserstein found that Barak had to contend with "a rambunctious coalition that stretched from the leftist Meretz party to the National Religious party," as well as a diminished Labour party. But Barak called upon the same qualities that had made his military career so successful: "boldness, ability to see through to the heart of a problem, and readiness to take calculated risks."

From the vantage point of Bill Clinton's oval office in the White House, these were qualities with considerable appeal. Facing the end of his second term as president, Clinton looked ahead to what the historians and journalists called his "legacy" and decided that he wanted to be remembered as the president who at last brought peace between the Jews and Arabs. And what better place bring about that peace than the rustic presidential retreat, Camp David, where Jimmy Carter had secured his legacy as a peacemaker by bringing together Anwar Sadat and Menachem Begin? What happened at Clinton's summit with Ehud Barak and Yasser Arafat, and the consequence of the meeting, is the subject of the next chapter.

The Least You Need to Know

- ◆ The Oslo Accords laid out a plan for a divided Jerusalem.

- ◆ An Israeli radical assassinated Prime Minister Yitzhak Rabin not long after he had signed a historic framework for peace between the Israelis and Palestinians.

- ◆ In the spring of 1996, Hamas suicide bombers blew up two buses in Jerusalem.

- ◆ Rabin's successor, Shimon Peres, lost an election to Benjamin Netanyahu.

- ◆ Ehud Barak was elected prime minister on a peace platform.

Chapter 17

Glimmers of Hope

In This Chapter

- ◆ Israel's "Basic Guidelines" for peace
- ◆ A Camp David summit collapses in failure
- ◆ How Yasser Arafat rose to the top and stayed there
- ◆ Ariel Sharon makes a provocative visit to the Haram
- ◆ Palestinians launch another intifada

You've read that Israelis and Palestinians in meetings in Oslo, Norway, drafted what was to be a blueprint for peace. Among the many agreements were that Israel would begin withdrawing from Jericho and Gaza and that Palestinians would hold elections to set up a provisional government known as the Palestinian Authority (PA). Yasser Arafat won the presidential election in a landslide.

Another result of the Oslo agreement was the signing of a peace treaty between Israel and Jordan (October 26, 1994). This was followed in October 1998 by a conference at the Wye River Plantation in which Israel and the Palestinian Authority pledged to continue what had begun in Oslo.

Traveling the Road that Started in Oslo

Pleased and confident with the two nations' progress toward peace, President Clinton said, "No doubt, as peace gains momentum, forces of hate, no matter how isolated and desperate, will once again lash out. They know this, the leaders, and they are prepared to face it. Staying on the path of peace under these circumstances will demand even greater leadership and courage. The work at Wye River shows what can happen when the will for peace is strong."

Prime Minister Netanyahu declared ...

> Today's a day when Israel and our entire region are more secure. Now this has required sacrifice from both sides and reaching into what Lincoln called the better nature of mankind. This is an important moment to give a secure and peaceful future for our children and the children of our neighbors, the Palestinians. We have seized this moment. I'm asking all people of goodwill, of honesty and candor, I'm asking all of them to join us in support for this important step for a secure future, a future of peace. We are more secure today because, for the first time since the signing of the Oslo accords, we will see concrete and verifiable commitments carried out ... This means that our world today will be safer for our children and for our neighbors' children. But it has been said here, and it's true, that we are just at the beginning or maybe in the middle of the road to a permanent peace.

Said Yasser Arafat ...

> This is an important and a happy day, a day of achievement that we will always remember with optimism and hope. It is true that whatever we achieved is only temporary, that has been late. But our agreement in the Wye River underscores that the peace process is going ahead and that whatever we agreed upon in Madrid, Oslo, and in Washington and Cairo is being implemented on the same basis that have been agreed to and that we will never go back. We will never leave the peace process, and we will never go back to violence and confrontation— no return to confrontation and violence ... This reconciliation between the two peoples, the Palestinian and the Israeli people, will not divert its path, and will go through negotiations on the table and not through tanks, grenades, and barbed wires. We have achieved today a large step, but it is important, my co-partner, Mr. Netanyahu, it is important in establishing the peace process because this is the peace of courageous people.

No one was happier about all this than President Bill Clinton. He saw himself achieving a peace between Jews and Arabs that had eluded American presidents for 50 years. It's no wonder, then, that he welcomed an opportunity to do a little self-congratulation.

Bill Clinton Cuts a Ribbon at a New International Airport

The occasion was the formal opening of an international airport at Gaza City on December 14, 1998. After cutting a red ribbon, Clinton told the crowd that he was there to "celebrate a place that will become a magnet for planes throughout the Middle East and beyond, bringing you a future in which Palestinians [can be] connected to the world."

Noting that he was "the first American president to address the Palestinian people in a city governed by Palestinians," he said, "I was sitting here thinking that this moment would have been inconceivable a decade ago, no Palestinian Authority, no elections in Gaza and the West Bank, no relations between the United States and Palestinians, no Israeli troop redeployments from the West Bank and Gaza, no Palestinians in charge in [the cities of] Gaza, Ramallah, Bethlehem, Hebron, Tulkarem, Jenin, Jericho, and so many other places."

Turning to Yasser Arafat, Clinton said the following words:

> I thank you, Mr. Chairman, for your leadership for peace and your perseverance, for enduring all the criticism from all sides, for being willing to change course and for being strong enough to stay with what is right. You have done a remarkable thing for your people. America is determined to do what we can to bring tangible benefits of peace. I am proud that the roads we have traveled on to get here were paved in peace ... But make no mistake about it, all this was made possible because of what you did because five years ago you made a choice for peace, and because through all the tough times since, when in your own mind you had a hundred good reasons to walk away, you didn't.

A Window of Opportunity to Gain a "Peace of the Brave"

When Prime Minister Ehud Barak rose to address the Knesset on July 6, 1999, to talk about a "window of opportunity" for peace, Israel's most decorated warrior believed that the guarantee of the peace agreements and their implementation depended on the strength of the Israeli Defense Forces. "The Arab countries must know," he said, "that only a strong and self-confident Israel can bring peace. Here, today, I call upon the leaders of the region to extend their hands to meet our outstretched hand, and toward a 'peace of the brave,' in a region which has known so much war."

While pledging to "bring peace closer on all fronts," Barak said there could be no compromising on the security of Israel, which he stressed, included a "united Jerusalem, the eternal capital of Israel, under our sovereignty."

The Knesset did as Barak asked and adopted the "Basic Guidelines" that set out conditions for peace "through peaceful means." The document stated that the government "views peace as a basic value of life in Israel, whose sources draw on the vision of the Prophets, as expressed in the Declaration of Independence and in the continuing yearning of the Israeli people for peace and security." The foundation for this would be "in the strength of the IDF and on the overall strength of Israel, on the deterrent capabilities of the State."

While committing to continued negotiations with the Palestinians, Arab governments, and the United States, these Basic Guidelines were inflexible concerning "Greater Jerusalem" remaining "united and complete" as part of Israel. Members of all religions would be guaranteed access to the holy places and religious freedom in a city in which Israel would "work toward the development and prosperity of Jerusalem, and continued construction therein for the welfare of all its residents."

They Will Be There and We Will Be Here

In the spring of 2000, Barak once again asked the Knesset to aid in the peace process. This time he wanted the governing body's approval to turn over civilian control of the Jerusalem suburb Abu Dis to the Palestinian Authority. Hardliners who opposed giving administration of any territory to Palestinians were infuriated by this request. On May 15, Barak tried to reassure the protestors. He declared:

> We are in the midst of a diplomatic process whose goal is to strengthen Israel and its security. In any future settlement, Jerusalem will remain united as Israel's eternal capital. They [Palestinians] will be in Abu Dis and we will be in united

Jerusalem. We are committed to moving forward toward a peace agreement that will be 1,000 times better than any alternative. The nature of the reality which will be created here if we do not find the wisdom to reach agreements is clear to all of us. We are charged with an historic and national responsibility to effect a separation in the Land of Israel, they will be, "there" and we will be "here."

He continued:

We have no interest in annexing 30,000 Palestinians to Jerusalem or Israeli sovereignty. Experience has shown us that [transfer] of this kind has served our security well. In 1992, there were 2,400 attacks in Judea and Samaria; in 1999, there were only 140. The entire move strengthens the diplomatic process, strengthens our position in Jerusalem, and strengthens our security.

Despite Barak's assurances, Minister of Interior Natan Sharansky wrote to him about hearing "disturbing news" that "Israel is willing for Arab neighborhoods in eastern Jerusalem to be under the municipal responsibility of the Palestinian Authority," and that Israel "relinquishes physical separation between Jerusalem and the territories under Palestinian control and thus allows the free and unsupervised entrance of people into Jerusalem."

These concerns and complaints of others in the Knesset weakened Barak's position as prime minister at home at the very moment that the president of the United States was preparing to invite Barak and Arafat to meet with him at Camp David in mid-July 2000—a meeting that Bill Clinton hoped would be the crowning achievement of his presidency.

A Christian, a Jew, and a Muslim Went Up a Mountain

"The moment of truth is come and I am prepared for it," Barak said as he departed for the United States on July 10. "The time has now come to put an end to the conflict, and to give our children the opportunity to flourish in peace." Arafat left Gaza from its new international airport with similar expressions of a desire to end more than 40 years of violence. Waiting to welcome them to the mountain retreat of Jimmy Carter's triumph in 1979, President Clinton was eager to play the role of the peacemaker.

Barak arrived with his position on the public record:

◆ Jerusalem would be the unified Jewish capital.

◆ The post-1967 war borders would be amended.

♦ Jewish settlements in Samaria in the West Bank and the Gaza Strip would be under Israeli sovereignty.

♦ No foreign army would be tolerated in the entire area west of the Jordan River.

♦ The problem of Palestinian refugees outside Israeli territory would finally be resolved.

Arafat came with a smile and statesmanlike demeanor that everyone hoped would translate into a breakthrough as dramatic as that provided by Anwar Sadat.

Barak's offer was along lines of the Beilin–Abu Mazen compromise leading to the Oslo accords in 1995. Israel would withdraw from 91 percent of the West Bank and annex the remainder. The Palestinian capital would be Abu Dis. Jerusalem would be under Israeli sovereignty, but with Palestinian administrations in the Christian and Muslim quarters. The Haram would also be under Israeli sovereignty, but with Muslim control and a Palestinian flag, and Jews would be free to pray there.

> **Reverent Remarks**
>
> The government of Israel, and I as prime minister, acted in the course of the Camp David summit out of moral and personal commitment, and supreme national obligation to do everything possible to bring about an end to the conflict, but not at any price, while at the same time, strengthening the state of Israel, and Jerusalem as its capital.
>
> —Ehud Barak, July 25, 2000, heading back to Jerusalem after the failed Camp David summit

Though Barak's proposal was breathtaking in scope and far more compromising than any previous Israeli offers, Arafat rejected it. The sticking point was Jerusalem. "I will not," he said to Clinton, "relinquish Jerusalem and the holy places." Barak would not budge on the Jerusalem issue either. After two weeks of fruitless talking had ended, Clinton announced, "I have concluded with regret that they [Barak and Arafat] will not be able to reach an agreement at this time."

Upon his return to Palestinian Authority headquarters in Ramallah, Arafat received a hero's welcome. He would later tell leaders of Arab nations at a summit (October 21, 2000), "Israel should lift the siege on our cities and people and withdraw from all the Palestinian and Arab territories, including holy Jerusalem, the capital of our independent Palestinian state."

Yasser, He's Our Leader

Hoping to strike an historic peace deal with Arafat, Clinton had chosen for diplomatic reasons to forget Arafat's long record of fomenting terrorism. Under Arafat's leadership and direction, the PLO and its military wing, FATAH, and other terror groups such as Black September, had hijacked airliners and a cruise ship, blown up buses, and massacred Jewish athletes at the 1972 Munich Olympics. While doing all this, he had also created myths about the man who had taken the same name (Arafat) as that of a famous Arab hero.

Part of Arafat's deliberate cultivation of his image as the Palestinian leader was never being seen without a neat black-and-white-checked kafiah flowing from his head and across the right shoulder of an olive drab uniform. Arafat the warrior addressed the United Nations General Assembly with a pistol strapped to his side. One of his biographers described him as "a natural publicist" with an obsessive desire to be the leader of the pack, to get his way, and to justify any means to the desired end. In his mind and in the person he showed to the world, he was the unchallenged Palestinian leader.

> **Reverent Remarks**
>
> Arafat is a brilliant but a hopeless organizer and negotiator. When the peace process began, he refused to delegate, fearing that a successful negotiator could represent a threat to his leadership.
>
> —Gerald Butt, BBC correspondent, in "Arafat: Flawed Symbol of Palestine," November 29, 2000

A Big Man Causes Big Trouble in Jerusalem

While Yasser Arafat was fashioning himself into the living symbol of the Palestinian cause, Israelis had an icon who was the sworn enemy of Arafat. Born Ariel Schneirmann in 1928 in Kfar Malal, Palestine, and nicknamed "Arik," he took the Hebrew name Sharon. Having fought in the wars of 1948, 1956, and 1967, he resigned from the army in 1972, only to be recalled to active duty for the Yom Kippur War. Named defense minister, he commanded troops in destroying PLO bases in a controversial and brutal invasion of Lebanon in 1982.

A bulky figure with a shock of white hair, Sharon was minister without portfolio (1983–84), then minister of trade and industry. As the minister of construction and housing and chairman of a committee on absorbing immigrants from the Soviet Union, he began a controversial program to build 144,000 new apartments in contested areas. Between 1992

> **Reverent Remarks**
>
> More and more people realize that, although it is hard to negotiate with me, maybe I am one of the few with whom they can reach an agreement. I make clear what Israel can and cannot do, and if there is a timetable, it will be implemented. Maybe that is what is needed to move the process forward. And I believe I can do that.
>
> —Ariel Sharon

and 1996, he was a member of the Knesset Foreign Affairs and Defense Committee. In 1998, he was appointed foreign minister and headed talks with the Palestinian Authority.

Following Barak's election as prime minister in May 1999, Sharon became interim Likud party leader, and in September he was elected its chairman while serving as a member of the Foreign Affairs and Defense Committee. With the failure of the Camp David summit, he angrily depicted Barak as a usurper prepared to trade Jerusalem for a peace agreement. He defiantly told the Knesset, "Barak does not have the right to give up Jerusalem, which the people received as a legacy."

To back up his assertions that Jews were entitled to go all parts of the Holy City, on September 28, 2000, Sharon led hundreds of Israeli policemen onto the Haram. The result of a 14-minute tour was outrage among Muslims, Jerusalem's worst rioting in many years, and the start of a second Palestinian uprising (intifada).

The al-Aqsa Intifada

The day following Sharon's visit to the Haram, a large number of unarmed Palestinian demonstrators and numerous Israeli police confronted each other. According to a report by the U.S. State Department, "Palestinians held large demonstrations and threw stones at police in the vicinity of the Western Wall. Police used rubber-coated metal bullets and live ammunition to disperse the demonstrators, killing 4 persons and injuring about 200." Israel claimed police officers were also injured.

"In Jerusalem, where the first clashes erupted last week," wrote Derek Brown of the *Guardian* newspaper of London, there were minor skirmishes as the al-Aqsa Mosque emptied after Friday worship" and Arabs hurled stones at "a dense mass of Israeli police." On October 6, 2000, he informed readers that Prime Minister Barak was "plunging deeper and deeper into crisis as the peace process totters" and that only "a slender thread of hope" remained that a cease-fire might end a week of bloody clashes between Israeli security forces and Palestinians.

> ## Holy Facts!
>
> The *Jerusalem Post* cited an opinion poll taken soon after the eruption of violence. It showed public support for Barak quickly fading in favor of the man he had defeated in the general election, Benjamin Netanyahu. If a snap election were held, the poll indicated, Barak would be defeated. The newspaper suggested that Netanyahu's Likud faction be invited to join a broad-based coalition, arguing that national unity was more important than political advantage.

As the violence of the intifada continued unabated and even started to spread, Arafat made a speech at a meeting of Arab leaders on October 21, 2000, denouncing Sharon for a "premeditated step" meant to desecrate the al-Aqsa Mosque and creating "a new dimension in the Arab-Israeli struggle." Beseeching the heads of the Arab states to support the Palestinians "with strength" and by "all means," he said, "Our people of revolutionary struggle, the people of the glorious intifada, whose waves will only stop with victory, pledge to every Arab, Muslim, Christian, and friend to continue their struggle using all legitimate means to reach victory."

When You Don't Know What to Do, Appoint a Committee

As intifada and Israeli retaliation raged on, President Clinton, leaders of Egypt and Jordan, and representatives of the United Nations and European Union met with Israel and Palestinian Authority leaders to see if they could find some way to restore peace. Confidently calling themselves the "Middle East peace summit," they chose to meet in the Egyptian Red Sea resort town of Sharm el-Sheikh.

The principal result of the 2000 Middle East peace summit was the creation of a fact-finding committee to investigate the causes of the latest trouble between Israelis and Palestinians. Named to head the group was former U.S. Senator George Mitchell, thereby ensuring the findings would be known as "the Mitchell Report." After four months of investigation, it was published in May 2001.

Don't Blame Us, Blame Them

The government of Israel asserted that the immediate catalyst for the violence was the breakdown of the Camp David negotiations, that there was "widespread apprecia-tion" internationally that the Palestinians were at fault, and that the Palestinian Au-thority leadership's intent was "provoking and incurring Palestinian casualties as a means of regaining the diplomatic initiative." Regarding the Palestinian uprising, the Israeli view was that demonstrations had been organized and directed by the Palestin-ian leadership to create sympathy for their cause around the world by provoking Israeli security forces to fire upon demonstrators, especially young ones.

The Palestinian side asserted that Camp David had represented "nothing less than an attempt by Israel to extend the force it exercises on the ground to negotiations," and that the failure of the summit, and attempts to allocate blame on the Palestinians, only added to the tension on the ground." They claimed Israel had responded to the disturbances with excessive and illegal use of deadly force, which reflected Israel's contempt for the lives and safety of Palestinians.

Trying to Sort It All Out

"What began as a series of confrontations between Palestinian demonstrators and Israeli security forces," stated the Mitchell Report, "has since evolved into a wider array of violent actions and responses." It cited exchanges of fire between built-up areas, sniping incidents, terrorist acts, and Israeli reactions. From the Palestinian perspective, the committee found that Israel's characterization of the current crisis as "an armed conflict short of war" was simply a means "to justify its assassination policy, its collective punishment policy, and its use of lethal force."

The committee noted that it had not been provided "persuasive evidence" on which to conclude that there was a deliberate plan by the Palestinian Authority to initiate a campaign of violence, or to conclude that there was a deliberate plan by the government of Israel (GOI) to employ lethal force. Nor had there been anything to show that the Palestinian Authority "made a consistent effort to contain the demonstrations and control the violence once it began"; or that the GOI chose to use nonlethal means to control demonstrations of unarmed Palestinians. "Amid rising anger, fear, and mistrust," the report found, "each side assumed the worst about the other and acted accordingly."

As to the "Sharon visit," to the al-Aqsa Mosque, the committee decided that it was not the cause of the intifada, but was "an internal political act" by Sharon to show contempt for Barak's position at Camp David, and that its timing was poor and the effect foreseeable. "More significant," said the report, were the decision of Israeli police on September 29 to use lethal means against Palestinians, and the failure "of either party to exercise restraint."

Why Did It Happen?

The Mitchell Report noted that the "roots of the current violence extend much deeper than an inconclusive summit meeting at Camp David." Both sides were disillusioned with the behavior of the other "in failing to meet the expectations arising from the peace process" launched in Madrid in 1991 and in Oslo in 1993. The result was each side accusing the other of undermining the spirit of their commitment to resolve differences peacefully.

Both sides saw the lack of full compliance with the agreements reached since the opening of the peace process as evidence of a lack of good faith.

"During the last seven months," said the Mitchell Report on May 20, 2001, "these views have hardened into divergent realities. Each side views the other as having acted in bad faith; as having turned the optimism of Oslo into the suffering and grief of victims and their loved ones. In their statements and actions, each side demonstrates a perspective that fails to recognize any truth in the perspective of the other."

Bill Clinton Gives It Another Try

Two days before Christmas 2000, with less than a month remaining before the forty-second president of the United States turned over the White House to George W. Bush, Bill Clinton decided to have another try at the role of peacemaker. He presented a new plan in an attempt to bridge the chasm between Israelis and Palestinians. Representatives of both sides listened politely to his proposals regarding divisions of land, how to deal with the return of Palestinian refugees, security of Israel, a Palestinian state, and the status of Jerusalem.

His plan rested not only on applying the "general principle" that Arab areas of modern Jerusalem "are Palestinian" and "Jewish ones are Israeli" but to the division of sovereignty in the Old City. He urged the parties to draw a map to "create maximum contiguity for both sides" to ensure that some Jewish and Muslim portions wouldn't be left isolated.

Turning to the Haram/Temple Mount, he expressed his belief that "the gaps are not related to practical administration but to symbolic issues of sovereignty and to finding a way to accord respect to the religious beliefs of both sides." He proposed:

> Palestinian sovereignty over the Haram and Israeli sovereignty over a) the Western Wall and the space sacred to Judaism of which it is a part or b) the Western Wall and the Holy of Holies of which it is part. There will be a firm commitment by both not to excavate beneath the Haram or behind the Wall.

The Palestinian answer on January 2, 2001, was that the Clinton proposals "fail to satisfy the conditions required" for peace. In a point-by-point rejection of all aspects of Clinton's plan, the Palestinians were adamant about Jerusalem being an "open city" with free access to and worship in all holy places and that also guaranteed free movement through the state of Palestine. "Unfortunately," said the Palestinian reply, "the United States proposal makes no reference to this essential concept."

Five days later, a clearly disappointed Clinton said in a speech to the Israel Policy Forum in New York City, "For over three months we have lived through a tragic cycle of violence that has cost hundreds of lives. It has shattered the confidence in the peace process. It has raised questions in some people's minds about whether Palestinians and Israelis could ever really live and work together, support each other's peace and prosperity and security."

As Clinton spoke, the al-Aqsa intifada and Israel's response to it continued. Both are the subject of the following chapter. It's not a story for the squeamish.

The Least You Need to Know

- President Clinton placed hopes for peace on Arafat and Barak.

- The key factor leading to the failure of the Camp David summit was both sides' unwillingness to compromise over Jerusalem.

- Ariel Sharon infuriated Muslims by visiting the sacred Haram.

- Palestinians began the al-Aqsa intifada in September 2000, and violence has raged ever since.

- Palestinians and Israelis rejected a plea for peace made by President Clinton in the waning days of his presidency.

Chapter 18

Slaughter on Ben Yehuda Street

In This Chapter

- ◆ Suicide bombers carry out mass murders in Jerusalem
- ◆ Palestinian terrorist groups join the intifada
- ◆ A spree of murders and suicide bombings
- ◆ Ariel Sharon becomes Israel's prime minister
- ◆ The Israeli Defense Force goes on the offensive

With the outbreak of rioting in September 2000 and the release of Islamic extremist prisoners by the Palestinian Authority, Islamic fundamentalists continued to pursue a path of violence. As the Palestinian Authority expressed a desire to attain a settlement with Israel through the negotiation process, these terrorist groups remained set on undermining the peace process and eventually destroying the Jewish state.

Arafat Takes On the "Warmonger"

Addressing an Arab Summit on October 21, 2000, Yasser Arafat put the blame for the intifada on his archenemy Ariel Sharon. He told an assemblage of Arab kings, presidents, and potentates, "As you know, the main reason behind the convening of this summit was the flagrant acts of aggression inflicted on the Palestinian people. These acts began with the ominous visit of warmonger Ariel Sharon to the area of al-Aqsa Mosque and al-Haram al-Sharif, which triggered these explosive reactions that spilled over into each and every Islamic and Christian village and city."

Declaring that the "provocative crime of Sharon was not committed quite incidentally …" he continued, "What has taken place this time, is a plot agreed upon beforehand and cunningly devised to undermine the peace process, and flare up anew a conflict of religious dimensions which, as you are aware, is very difficult to contain or control its repercussions."

Referring to "horrible, bloody, and barbaric acts" perpetrated by the Israelis, Arafat said:

> Too much noble blood has been shed in this massacre on the Holy Aqsa's area, and more martyrs have fallen, in the footsteps of their predecessors, in defense of their sancties and the honor of their nation. Much Arab dear blood has been already spilled all over every span of Palestine. Since the eruption of the intifada, our unarmed people has been the target of deliberate genocidal crimes and daily barbaric bombing. [The] complete closure of [lands by] the Israeli military machine has isolated the three million Palestinians under a suffocating siege … [This] last wave of turbulence which was triggered by the bloody Israeli aggression on our Palestinian people is a clear-cut evidence, that the absence of a lasting and just peace poses the gravest threat to international stability and security, [that spills into] many geographical areas … Here and now from the highest Arab forum I ascertain, despite all the feelings of frustration and disappointment besetting our endeavor for peace … Our final objective is the liberation of our land and the establishment of our independent state on the blessed soil of Palestine, with Jerusalem as its capital, and the return of the refugees to their homeland.

Why the Renewed Violence and Expressions of Hatred?

When peace had been so close at hand only months earlier, why the sudden outbreak in violence and rabid expressions of hatred? Some historians speculate that the intense political effort following the meetings at Camp David and the Middle East summit at Sharm el-Sheikh brought to the surface the deep issues of historical and religious rights for Palestinians and Israel and concern about the future of both Muslim and Jewish holy sites. It was at this sensitive moment that Ariel Sharon chose to put on his show at the Haram/Temple Mount.

Palestinians responded by falling back on the use of violence as a tool to achieve better concessions than those offered during the political negotiations at Camp David. The Palestinian Authority sought an advantage in what they called "asymmetric confrontation" in order to restore a feeling of nationalism. They declared that the fight for "independence" through an "armed struggle," even at the cost of lives and a high economic price, created the image of a "Palestinian David and an Israeli Goliath" that could be exploited in propaganda aimed at enlisting international support. At the same time, Islamic fundamentalist terror organizations that had no interest in a peace with Israel were working to torpedo the peace process.

Reverent Remarks

On October 13, 2000, the official Palestinian Authority television station broadcast a Friday sermon in the Zayed bin Sultan Aal Nahyan Mosque in Gaza. Dr. Ahmad Abu Halabiya, a member of the Palestinian Authority–appointed "FATWA Council" and former acting rector of the Islamic University in Gaza, declared:

> O brother believers, the criminals, the terrorists are the Jews, who have butchered our children, orphaned them, widowed our women, and desecrated our holy places and sacred sites. They are the terrorists. They are the ones who must be butchered and killed, as Allah the Almighty said: Fight them. Allah will torture them at your hands, and will humiliate them and will help you to overcome them, and will relieve the minds of the believers. Have no mercy on the Jews, no matter where they are, in any country. Fight them, wherever you are. Wherever you meet them, kill them. Wherever you are, kill those Jews and those Americans who are like them. They are all in one trench against the Arabs and the Muslims because they established Israel here, in the beating heart of the Arab world, in Palestine. They created it to be the outpost of their civilization and the vanguard of their army, and to be the sword of the West and the Crusaders, hanging over the necks of the monotheists, the Muslims in these lands. They wanted the Jews to be their spearhead.

Specialists in Urban Terrorism

Two Palestinian groups used terrorism to ensure that the peace process failed. Although in theory they were independent organizations, the Islamic Jihad and

Hamas acted with the implicit consent of the Palestinian Authority, but with the Palestinian Authority reserving the right to regulate terrorist activity if it believed attacks would jeopardize political gains.

Israel had released many members of these organizations from prison as part of the peace process. Once they were free, the Palestinian Authority permitted them to prepare and execute large-scale car-bomb and suicide attacks in Israeli urban areas.

Hamas Hoists the Banner of Allah

While calling itself a social, political, and religious movement and masking its terrorism with activities such as setting up schools and relief programs, *Hamas* declared that its purpose was to "raise the banner of Allah over every inch of Palestine." This meant that the Jews would have to be forced out.

What Does That Mean?

Hamas is an Arabic acronym of *Harakat al-Muqawamah al-Islamiyya,* which translates as "Islamic Resistance Movement." The organization was founded in the 1920s in Egypt to do social work.

Reverent Remarks

The following excerpt of a radio interview with Yasser Arafat is from a program broadcast in the Sooviet Union:

Q: In your opinion, is Hamas a terrorist organization?

Arafat: The Hamas movement is one of many patriotic movements.

Q: Even its military wing?

Arafat: Even its military wing. One should not forget that the movement took an active part in the intifada [of the 1980s].

Legally registered in Israel in 1978, Hamas widened its base of supporters and sympathizers through religious and anti-Israel propaganda in the refugee camps of Gaza and the West Bank. In August 1988 it published the "Islamic Covenant," calling for a struggle against Israel as well as challenging the Palestinian Liberation Organization's (PLO) claim to be the sole legitimate representative of the Palestinian people.

Its military apparatus, Mujahidin, eventually included hit squads called Izz al-Din al-Qassam Battalions to carry out kidnappings and executions of anyone suspected of cooperating with Israel. Another segment of the organization, the Palestinian Holy Fighters, engaged in the preparation of terror attacks. A security section, Jehaz Ama, gathered data on suspected collaborators with Israelis and punished them.

Hamas received strong financial backing from Iran, Saudi Arabia, and other Gulf states. Its network of charity associations served to screen its terror activities.

Islamic Jihad

Based on the militant doctrine of "jihad now," and espousing no political or social agenda, Islamic Jihad obtained strong support financially and in terror training from the Islamic government of Iran. Because the organization's headquarters were in Damascus, the government of Syria also provided aid in financing, training, and expertise in carrying out terrorist attacks.

Founded in 1979 with the Arabic name Harakat al-Jihad al-Islami al-Filastini, it was strongly influenced by the Islamic revolution in Iran and the radicalization and militancy of Egyptian Islamic student groups. It engaged in subversive and terrorist activity in the Israeli-occupied territories in the 1980s and maintained close contact with Iranian Revolutionary Guard units in Lebanon and with Hezballah (a terrorist group based in Lebanon). Until the formation of the Palestinian Authority in 1994, the Islamic Jihad had no connections to Hamas, and the two groups were regarded as rivals in the Gaza Strip. Allied ever since, the organizations often cooperated operationally.

Al-Aqsa Battalions and Other Palestinian Organizations

Formed in 1982 with the support of Yasser Araft's FATAH terror organization, the al-Aqsa Battalions carried out its first terrorist operation in October 1983, killing an Israeli citizen in Hebron. The Islamic Jihad of the Temple (al-Jihad al-Islami-Bait al-Maqdas) began in early 1980 as part of FATAH and carried out an attack in Hebron on April 1, 1980, killing six Israelis as they left a synagogue. It was the organization responsible for lobbing hand grenades onto Israeli soldiers and their families during the graduation ceremony at the Western Wall in Jerusalem on October 15, 1986, that you've read about in Chapter 15.

Effects of the al-Aqsa Intifada

According to Jerusalem Police Commissioner Shlomo Aharonishky, in the first 3 months of the al-Aqsa intifada, Palestinians killed 33 Jews and wounded 513 in a total of 66 attacks. The Palestinian Authority reported that in the last 3 months of 2000 Israeli forces killed 332 Palestinians. The violence also claimed a political victim, as Israeli voters went to the polls to render their judgement on Prime Minister Ehud Barak. While some were disappointed by the failure of the peace talks with Arafat, and many others felt that he had offered Arafat too much, all were outraged by the violence of the intifada and the apparent inability of the government to stop it. The result was a landslide election victory for Ariel Sharon. Ironically, Arafat's rejection of

Barak's proposals and the unleashing of the intifada had brought to power a man who had devoted his entire life to thwarting the creation of a Palestinian state.

In the weeks after Sharon took office, terrorist attacks continued. One of the strangest acts occurred on January 17 when a 16-year-old Israeli youth was lured into a trap by a Palestinian woman and killed. Three days later, two Israelis were abducted while lunching in a restaurant and murdered. In the first two weeks of February 2001, two Israelis were shot to death in their cars on the West Bank, an Israeli soldier was gunned down by a sniper and another while driving, and eight soldiers were run down and killed by a bus driven by a Palestinian. Similar attacks on individuals or upon small groups occurred from March to June, including 5 in a suicide bombing in the town of Netanya carried out by Hamas that wounded 100. On June 1, 21 youths were killed by a Hamas suicide bomber near a Tel Aviv disco. On July 19, an Islamic Jihad suicide bomber killed two Israeli soldiers and wounded 30 civilians at a train station.

Mass Murder in a Pizzeria

On August 9, 2001, while Israelis and tourists were having mid-afternoon snacks in the Sbarro pizzeria at the corner of King George Street and Jaffa Road in the bustling commercial heart of the city, a suicide bomber ignited an explosive filled with nails, screws, and bolts. Fifteen people were killed, including seven children, and 130 were wounded. Hamas and Islamic Jihad claimed responsibility for the massacre.

Bloody August

The killing continued throughout August. On August 25, three IDF soldiers were killed at an outpost. Over the next two days, an Israeli settler was invited into an Arab village and murdered, and another was killed in a roadside ambush. On August 29 the driver of a fuel truck was killed near Nablus. The next day, an Israeli was murdered in a restaurant owned by his Arab friends. On the sixth of September, an IDF officer was slain in an ambush while on his way to a wedding. Three people were blown up by a suicide bomber in Naharia, and a teacher and a school janitor were shot to death in their van on their way to school. And on September 11, 2001, a soldier and a border policeman were killed in an attack at their base. But their deaths were to be barely noted because of terrorist attacks on that day thousands of miles from Israel.

> **Holy Facts!**
>
> When Islamic terrorists belonging to a group known as al-Qaeda hijacked airliners and crashed them into the twin towers of the World Trade Center in New York City and the Pentagon in Washington, D.C., they set off a chain of events that would change the course of an Arab-Israeli conflict. How and why this happened will be discussed in the next chapter.

Human Limbs, Blood, and Wreckage

The violence multiplied on Saturday evening, December 1, 2001. That day, American "Middle East envoy" Anthony Zinni, a retired U.S. Marine general, was in the country on a peace mission on behalf of President George W. Bush and Secretary of State Colin Powell. Zinni had met with Prime Minister Sharon for what the news media called "tough talks" prior to Sharon going to Washington for a meeting with Bush at the White House on Monday.

The Jewish Sabbath ended at sunset that evening, and people—many of them teenagers—gathered on Ben Yehuda Street. Named for Eleazer Ben Yehuda, who'd almost single-handedly revived the Hebrew language, the thoroughfare has been turned into a fashionable pedestrian mall and is the equivalent of the nightlife center in any big city in the United States and Europe.

At 20 minutes till midnight, two suicide bombers, standing about 120 feet apart, set off concealed explosives, sending out not only the blast of detonation, but deadly shrapnel in the form of nails and screws. Hundreds of wounded and stunned survivors fled in panic, screaming and running in all directions as sirens and horns of ambulances and emergency vehicles began to blare. Twenty minutes later, with the air still smelling of explosives and things burning, a car bomb went off about 300 yards away. Experts later explained that the later bomb was intended to kill or wound the emergency response teams. But while the *coup de grace* made a lot of noise and scared and shocked, only one person was injured. When deaths were counted, the toll was 11 teenagers. Injuries: 180.

Twelve hours after the Ben Yehuda Street bombs, in the northern city of Haifa, another blast ripped through a bus, killing 16 passengers and wounding numerous others. Hamas claimed responsibility for both attacks.

Reverent Remarks

A news correspondent described the Ben Yehuda Street scene as "an abattoir of human limbs, blood, and wreckage."

The Middle East Law of Action and Reaction at Work

The deadly cycle of Palestinian terrorism, retaliatory acts by the Israeli government, and loss of innocent lives on both sides of the conflict continued into the new year. In early January 2002, a Palestinian from Tulkarm fired an M-16 assault rifle at a bar mitzvah ceremony in the city of Hadera, killing 6 Israelis and wounding 30. Arafat's FATAH organization said the bar mitzvah murders had been retaliation for death of a FATAH leader in Tulkarm, as part of Israel's policy of targeting FATAH leadership.

A few days later, the Israeli Defense Force decided to take new measures to end the violence. Complaining that Arafat had the power to put an end to Palestinian attacks, but hadn't lifted a finger to do so, the Sharon government sent tanks, armored vehicles, and troops into the West Bank town of Tulkarm in search of terrorists. Of 15 Palestinians detained in the IDF's Tulkarm raid, 11 were on an Israeli list of wanted terrorists. In another IDF sweep in the city of Nablus on the same day, soldiers found and destroyed an explosives laboratory. In that raid, four prominent members of Hamas were killed and four Israelis were wounded.

Holy Facts!

Damage to more than 60 stores on the January 27, 2002, bombing was put at $2.5 million. The cost of bombings and other attacks to the Israeli tourism industry was so great that 55 Israeli hotels decided to sue the Palestinian Authority for hundreds of millions of dollars. The Chamber of Commerce's estimate of economic damage was $35 to $45 billion.

Palestinian payback for the IDF moves into Tulkarm and Nablus began on Monday, January 22. A member of FATAH'S military arm (the al-Aqsa Brigade) dashed from a covered passageway between a clothing shop and a discount drug store on the Jaffa Road. Because it was the peak of Jerusalem's afternoon homeward rush hour, scores of Israelis were waiting at a bus stop. The man began firing with an M-16 rifle into the crowd. Before he was shot dead, he killed 2 and wounded 46, 8 seriously. Then on Friday, a suicide bomber wounded 26 people on a pedestrian mall outside a café in Tel Aviv's central bus station. Later that weekend, a female suicide bomber killed 1 Israeli man and wounded more than 150 on Jaffa Road, nearby the Monday bus stop attack.

Ariel Sharon Orders a Defensive Wall

In an attempt to destroy "the terrorist infrastructure," Sharon instituted Operation Defensive Wall. The policy resulted in arrests of numerous members of terrorist organizations and seizure of guns and other weaponry and equipment. The IDF's news and information office claimed the operation proved that "Nablus constituted the main Palestinian terrorism infrastructure and the headquarters of the terrorist organizations' leadership in the West Bank." The IDF claimed it had found proof of connections among Hamas, Islamic Jihad, and FATAH. While stating that the terrorist infrastructure was "significantly damaged," it warned that the "activists who escaped from Nablus will attempt to return and execute terror attacks as revenge for the IDF operation, and in order to prove that Israel did not manage to eliminate terrorism."

The cost in Israeli lives of Operation Defensive Wall was high. Thirty-five soldiers were killed in action. Israel itself took a propaganda beating in April during a standoff between Israeli forces and FATAH militants who took refuge in the Church of the Nativity in Bethlehem. Although the stalemate would end after 2 weeks with the deportation of 13 militants to Europe and others detained under the supervision of the United States and Britain, daily scenes televised around the world of Israelis surrounding a cherished Christian holy site inflicted severe damage to Israel's national image. Sharon's Operation Defensive Wall took on ugly aspects of a bullying country seeking to crush a defenseless people by brute force.

Holy Facts!

According to figures released by the Palestinian Center for Human Rights, more than 1,500 Palestinians were killed and more than 13,000 were wounded from September 29, 2000 to July 17, 2002, because of Israeli military operations. And a report by the Office of the United Nations Special Coordinator in the Occupied Territories estimated damage done to the West Bank's civilian infrastructure and institutions at $361 million.

An Attempt to Put Yasser Arafat in Isolation

Battered in world opinion, Sharon set his sights on isolating his archenemy Arafat in his headquarters in Ramallah. Seven miles north of Jerusalem on a major crossroads and with a commanding view of its surroundings, the ancient city had become the heart of the Palestinian Authority, containing governing institutions, the offices of the Legislative Council, and the Palestinian West Bank security forces' headquarters. Arafat's offices were located in a cluster of buildings called "the compound."

"Since the beginning of the current conflict," said an Israeli government justification of its assault on Arafat, "Ramallah has stood out as a major center of terrorist activity against Israeli civilians and security personnel. The terrorist infrastructure in the city, and at times in the entire West Bank, are dependent on senior FATAH leadership and senior commanders." Asserting that FATAH had "changed its modus operandi from shooting attacks on roads to suicide bombings in Israeli cities," Israel noted that other terrorist organizations operate from the city, among them the Hamas, which had carried out the major suicide bombings in Jerusalem [the Sbarro pizzeria bombing, the Jerusalem pedestrian mall double-suicide bombing, and the Jaffa Road café attack]. The city of Ramallah was cited as a "relay station" and coordinating point for the suicide attacks in Jerusalem.

In addition to these justifications, Minister of Parliamentary Affairs Dani Naveh issued a report stating that evidence against Arafat was based on intelligence that was gathered in Israel's "campaign to eradicate sources of terror in the area under the control of the Palestinian Authority." Naveh asserted, Yasser Arafat was "personally involved in the planning and execution of terror attacks," encouraged them financially, and "headed the FATAH al-Aqsa Brigade's organization" from his Ramallah "central command post" for terrorist activity and suicide bombing.

The World Watches the Siege of Ramallah

With most of the world watching by television, Israeli tanks and bulldozers rumbled into Ramallah. A report carried on the Cable News Network (CNN) noted, "Several Israeli tanks and armored personnel carriers have been deployed to the compound. Troops could be seen entering through at least seven holes punched in the walls." Viewers saw that the gates of the compound had been destroyed. Heavy gunfire was heard from inside buildings. As searchlights played eerily on their shell-pocked walls, Israeli tanks maneuvered and looked like monsters in the foreground.

Arafat on TV in the Soft Glow of Candlelight

On January 28, 2002, the *Washington Post* reported, "For now, the siege seems only to have inspired Mr. Arafat, who revels in such crises. The 72-year-old warrior has been regaling visitors to his Ramallah compound with tales of his survival" in predicaments of the past. In addition to targeting the Palestinian Authority's infrastructure in Ramallah, IDF bulldozers tore up the runways of the Gaza airport that Bill Clinton had opened with so much fanfare and hopes for a peace breakthrough.

Reverent Remarks

Typical of the international response to the Israeli attack on Ramallah was this statement by the French Foreign Ministry on September 22, 2002: "The military operation under way against the office of the president of the Palestinian Authority is unacceptable. France asks for it to be halted immediately."

Isolating Arafat in his headquarters, Ariel Sharon hoped, would compel the Palestinians to choose a more moderate leadership. Instead, it created an opportunity for Arafat to play the role of martyr. Typical of this strategy was a live interview on CNN. Asked if he would rein in the violence as requested by the United States, he retorted angrily that the Palestinians were suffering from the "terrorist activities of the Israeli occupation." The focus of the crisis, he exclaimed, ought to be "the problem of our people, of our liberty, of our independent Palestinian state."

The CNN report noted that Arafat "was holed up in an office on the second floor of the building with two aides" while two tanks were stationed at the bottom of the stairs. Electricity and phone lines had been cut off. But Arafat had cellular phones that he used to place calls to the leaders of Arab nations and to news organizations around the globe. While he was doing this, the television cameras were showing him in the glow of candlelight in his trademark kafiah and army uniform, with an automatic rifle within reach on his desk.

On the Arab all-news television station al-Jazeera, Arafat said:

> We are not only defending Palestine and Christian and Islamic holy sites, but we are also defending all the free people in the world. We are defending the values and holy sites and the Arab nation and the Palestinian people and all the free and liberated people in the world; let them understand that there will be no one in the Palestinian people who will kneel or surrender or succumb to this aggression and war. To Jerusalem we are going; martyrs in the millions.

He continued:

> What about what he [Sharon] is doing? Isn't occupation terrorism? What about the demolition of Palestinian homes and the killings of children? What about the total siege on Bethlehem and other areas in the West Bank and Gaza Strip?

As the siege of Ramallah continued and Arafat remained defiant, a *Washington Post* editorial opined that the Bush administration "may have little choice but to isolate Mr. Arafat." You will read in the next chapter that this was just what Bush decided to do.

The Least You Need to Know

- Muslim clerics urged Palestinians to kill Jews and Americans.
- Hamas and Islamic Jihad carried out suicide bombings in Jerusalem.
- Israel conducted raids in West Bank towns in an attempt to root out terrorists.
- A surrounded Arafat was seen as a martyr by many people around the world who watched the invasion of Ramallah on television.

Chapter 19

Roadmap to Peace

In This Chapter

- ◆ President Bush refuses to deal with Yasser Arafat
- ◆ Starting down the "roadmap to peace"
- ◆ The Palestinian Authority makes reforms
- ◆ Back-to-back summit meetings in 2003 spark hopes
- ◆ A Jerusalem bus bombing and targeting of Hamas leaders

Eleven days into his eighth month in office, while visiting an elementary school, President George W. Bush was informed of terrorist attacks on the World Trade Center, murdering thousands of people, and that another hijacked plane had hit the Pentagon building, across the Potomac River from Washington, D.C., killing hundreds more.

That night Bush spoke to a stunned, confused, angry, and scared nation from the Oval Office in the White House. Suddenly a wartime commander-in-chief, he declared that he would make no distinction between the terrorists and the countries that harbored them. This declaration was to have a lasting impact on Middle East politics.

Introducing the Bush Doctrine

When Bush traveled up to Capitol Hill on January 29, 2002, for his first state of the union message, his year-old presidency, the nation, and the world were not the same as they had been a year earlier. Referring to the terrorist attacks of September 11, 2001, and a victory in a short war in Afghanistan to depose the Taliban and root out al-Qaeda terrorist training camps, he said that "our war against terror is only beginning." Branding North Korea, Iran, and Iraq an "axis of evil," he warned America's enemies, "I will not wait on events, while danger gathers."

High and Mighty

When the state of Israel was declared on May 14, 1948, George W. Bush was barely two years old. Born on July 6, 1946, in New Haven, Connecticut, where his father was a student at Yale, he grew up in the small town of Midland in the heart of Texas oil country.

Following the Yom Kippur War, "W," as he was called to eliminate confusion between father and son, earned an M.B.A. at Harvard and returned to east Texas to start his own oil-exploration company. After he failed to follow in his father's footsteps by getting elected to Congress, he continued in the oil business.

In the 1980s, Bush organized a group of investors to purchase the Texas Rangers baseball franchise. As the team's managing partner, he was in a high-profile job that not only left him a multimillionaire when the team was sold in 1998, but well known enough to be elected governor and emerge as front-runner for the Republican presidential nomination in 2000. Committing campaign blunders that created the impression he was a lightweight, his political foes and pundits deemed him unready, unworthy, and so uninformed on international issues that he couldn't name world leaders. The declared winner in the contested 2000 election, he was determined as president to downplay foreign affairs and concentrate on domestic issues.

One Thing Leads to Another

After successfully launching an invasion of Iraq to depose Saddam Hussein in early 2003, President Bush found himself pressured to become deeply involved in finding a way for the United States to resolve the Israeli-Palestinian standoff—a conflict that had begun when he was a toddler. In a historic speech on June 24, 2002, he left his audience surprised by looking with favor on the creation of a state of Palestine, but only after the Palestinians rid themselves of the leadership of Yasser Arafat. If they did so, Bush declared, and the Palestinian Authority instituted reforms that moved toward democracy and an end to terrorism, the United States would lean on Israel to pull out of the West Bank and Gaza. In addition, President Bush promised to help negotiate a peace treaty between Israel and Palestine.

The Cowboy from Texas Rides Out to Lasso Arafat

Throughout much of Yasser Arafat's years as head of the PLO and a revered figure among Palestinians, he had been the gun-toting and defiant "indispensable man" with a veto power in all negotiations between Israelis and Arabs. He had signed agreements and shaken hands with prime ministers and presidents. If there were to be a road to peace, he was the gatekeeper. But with the sudden force of a Middle East sandstorm, a Texas cyclone by the name of George W. Bush was informing the Palestinians and the entire world that he was not going to do business with Arafat.

This editorial cartoon of Yasser Arafat inside a rapidly flowing hourglass carried the caption "Time is running out for Arafat."

(Author's collection, courtesy of John Pritchett)

Noting that Israelis "reacted with undisguised glee" at Bush's refusal to negotiate with Arafat, the historian Mitchell G. Bard wrote that the Arab states "were unhappy that the onus had been put on the Palestinians" rather than on the Israelis. The Palestinians were angry and felt "completely betrayed." Although Arafat resisted the move to displace him, Bush was determined that the Palestinians meet his conditions. With a new leadership replacing Arafat, a route to peace and their own state was laid out and waiting.

How to Get from Here to There

The intent of what became known as the "roadmap" was that any settlement negotiated by the two parties would "result in the emergence of an independent, democratic, and viable Palestinian state living side by side in peace and security with Israel and its other neighbors." The bases of the solution were to be the Madrid Conference, the "principle" of Israel giving up land for security and peace, various United Nations resolutions, and peace initiatives that were presented by Prince Abdullah of Saudi Arabia and endorsed by a Beirut Arab League Summit that called for acceptance of Israel as a neighbor living in peace and security.

Reverent Remarks

A two-state solution to the Israeli-Palestinian conflict will only be achieved through an end to violence and terrorism, when the Palestinian people have a leadership acting decisively against terror and willing and able to build a practicing democracy based on tolerance and liberty, and through Israel's readiness to do what is necessary for a democratic Palestinian state to be established, and a clear, unambiguous acceptance by both parties of the goal of a negotiated settlement.

—U.S. State Department, 2002

All of this was to be achieved under the guidance and scrutiny of an international "quartet" consisting of the United States, the United Nations, the European Union, and Russia. The objective of the roadmap was a "final and comprehensive settlement of the Israel-Palestinian conflict by 2005. The plan was laid out in three phases.

Phase I: Ending Terror and Violence, Normalizing Palestinian Life, and Building Palestinian Institutions

By May 2003, there was to be an end of terror and violence, normalization of Palestinian life, and the building of Palestinian institutions—including drafting a Palestinian constitution and free, fair, and open elections. Israel was to take "all necessary steps to help normalize Palestinian life," and withdraw from Palestinian areas occupied since September 28, 2000. At the same time, the Palestinian leadership would issue an "unequivocal statement reiterating Israel's right to exist in peace and security and calling for an immediate and unconditional cease-fire to end armed activity and all acts of violence against Israelis anywhere. Palestinians were required to declare an end to violence and terrorism and undertake visible efforts on the ground to arrest, disrupt, and restrain individuals and groups conducting and planning violent attacks on Israelis anywhere.

For its part, the government of Israel would take no actions undermining trust. There would be no more deportations, attacks on Arab civilians, confiscation and/or demolition of Palestinian homes and property, construction in Arab areas, or anything aimed at the destruction of Palestinian institutions and infrastructure. In addition, the Israeli leadership would issue an "unequivocal statement affirming its commitment to the two-state vision of an independent, viable, sovereign Palestinian state living in peace and security alongside Israel, and an end to violence.

The Israeli government also was to provide the Palestinians assistance with voter registration and movement of candidates and voting officials. It also pledged to reopen a Palestinian chamber of commerce and other closed Palestinian institutions in East Jerusalem based on a commitment that the institutions operate strictly in accordance with prior agreements between the parties.

Regarding Israeli settlements in the West Bank and Gaza, Israel was expected to begin dismantling those it had built since March 2001. Consistent with the Mitchell Report, all such settlement activity was to cease.

Phase II: Transition

According to the roadmap, phase II was to have started "after Palestinian elections and [ended] with [the] possible creation of an independent Palestinian state with provisional borders in 2003." The focus of this phase was to have been the establishment of a viable Palestinian government and raising the standard of living for Palestinians.

Both parties were to continue the goals set out in phase I. At the end of phase II, the quartet would meet to pursue "a comprehensive Middle East peace" between Israel and Syria, and Israel and Lebanon. At this point, the following were to occur: Arab states restore pre-intifada links with Israel and discuss regional issues including water resources, the environment, economic development, refugees, and arms control. This phase was to have been completed by December 2003.

Phase III: Permanent Status Agreement and End of the Israeli Palestinian Conflict

Once again to be determined by the quartet, and taking into account actions of both parties and quartet monitoring, phase III (2004–2005) objectives are further reform and stabilization of Palestinian institutions, sustained and effective Palestinian security performance, and negotiations on a permanent status agreement.

A second conference convened by the quartet would meet in 2004 to endorse an agreement reached on an independent Palestinian state with provisional borders and to formally launch a process leading to a permanent resolution by 2005 on borders, refugees, and settlements. There would also be a negotiated resolution of the status of Jerusalem, taking into account political and religious concerns of both sides, and protection of the religious interests of Jews, Christians, and Muslims worldwide. The city would be the capital of Israel and a sovereign and independent, democratic, and viable Palestine that would live side by side with Israel in peace and security.

An Old Hand in a New Job

On March 19, 2003, Yasser Arafat accepted the fate demanded by President Bush and the roadmap by appointing Palestine's first prime minister. The *New York Times* reported it as "a move that marks the most significant cut" in Arafat's powers since he became the leader of the Palestinian Authority in 1994. The job was a new one, but the man who accepted it was an old hand in the affairs of the Palestinians. As secretary general of the PLO, Mahmoud Abbas, also known as Abu Mazen, was the most senior Palestinian leader after Arafat. In Chapter 16, you met him as a Palestinian negotiator of the Oslo accords.

Born in Safed in British Mandate Palestine in 1935, he is one of the few surviving founder members of FATAH. While exiled in Qatar during the late 1950s, he helped recruit Palestinians who became key figures in the PLO. As co-founder of FATAH with Arafat, he'd accompanied Arafat into exile in Jordan, Lebanon, and Tunisia. He studied law in Egypt before earning a doctorate in Moscow.

Reverent Remarks

In a book titled *The Other Side: The Secret Relationship Between Nazism and Zionism,* Abbas downplayed the number of victims of the Holocaust and accused Jews of collaborating with the Nazis. Denying this in an interview with the Israeli newspaper *Haaretz* in May 2003, he said, "The Holocaust was a terrible, unforgivable crime against the Jewish nation, a crime against humanity that cannot be accepted by humankind. I quoted an argument between historians in which various numbers of casualties were mentioned."

Described in a report by the British Broadcasting Corporation as a figure who "kept to the background, but also built up a network of powerful contacts that included Arab leaders and heads of intelligence services," Abbas was seen as a pragmatist.

Because he'd been an architect of the Oslo peace process, he had accompanied Arafat to the White House in 1993 to sign the accords. In addition to becoming prime minister, he took the job of interior minister. Although not a charismatic figure and with no personal political machine, he was "respected as a statesman both regionally and internationally" who represented continuity to the vast majority of Palestinians.

A Road with Bumps, Potholes, and Dangerous Twists

With a new voice speaking on behalf of Palestinians, the United States formally unveiled the roadmap on April 30, 2003. Both Israel and the Palestinian Authority welcomed it and agreed that "the plan should not be changed." When the Sharon cabinet approved it, it was the first time that an Israeli governing body had endorsed creation of a Palestinian state. At a meeting in Ramallah, the Palestinian Parliament heard Abbas denounce terrorism "by any party and in all its shapes." Praising Israel's move as "an important step forward" and applauding Abbas, the White House let it be known that planning was underway for President Bush to meet with Sharon and Abbas early in June.

> **Reverent Remarks**
>
> I don't know whether we'll succeed, but I'm telling you in the clearest way that I'll make every effort to reach a diplomatic arrangement because I believe that it's important for Israel.
>
> —Ariel Sharon, addressing the Knesset, May 26, 2003

Within hours of Israel's acceptance of the roadmap and Abbas's rejection of the use of terrorism, a Palestinian suicide bomber struck at a seaside pub in Tel Aviv. Eighteen days later, nine people were killed by suicide bombers in two explosions a block apart in Hebron. The blasts came two hours before Sharon and Abbas were scheduled to talk in the first such meeting since the start of the al-Aqsa intifada in September 2000.

Despite demands from some members of the Israeli government that Sharon cancel the conference to protest the bombings, Sharon and Abbas talked until well past midnight, with no result.

At six o'clock that morning, a Palestinian dressed as a religious Jew blew himself to pieces after boarding a number 6 bus in Jerusalem's French Hill section. He killed seven riders. Of the first bus bombing in Jerusalem in six months, correspondent Greg Myre reported to the *New York Times* that the bomb was packed with ball bearings, leaving several of the victims "upright in their seats, with their heads tilted back as if they were sleeping."

The Red Sea Summit

In the first week of June 2003, with the roadmap published and Yasser Arafat having been forced to turn over the negotiations to Abbas, President Bush set out on a state trip that started in Krakow, Poland, and continued on to St. Petersburg, Russia. Next came conferences in Geneva and Evian, France, and a meeting about the roadmap with Egyptian President Mubarak and King Abdullah of Jordan in Sharm el-Sheik, Egypt. His final stop was Aqaba, Jordan, for a summit with Sharon and Abbas on June 4.

When the two prime ministers were photographed talking in the shade of a palm tree with Bush seated between them at what the press called the "Red Sea Summit," observers were quick to note that the American president put himself actually and figuratively into the role of the man in the middle. He had taken on a dilemma that had frustrated occupants of the Oval Office since Harry S. Truman granted recognition of Israel in 1948. At a news conference after half an hour of conversation, the president said, "We have made a good beginning. And I emphasize beginning, because there's a lot of work to do." He recognized "that there are some people who would like to blow up the [peace] process."

A Different Kind of Peace Protest

That evening, thousands of Israelis in the center of Jerusalem vehemently protested the prospect of a Palestinian state. One of their placards proclaimed, "The roadmap to hell is paved with Jewish tombstones." At the same time in the Gaza Strip, militant Palestinian groups vowed not to lay down weapons and denounced the roadmap peace plan as "an American concoction" being forced upon Palestinians.

A Flashback to 1975

On the eve of the summit meeting, newspapers around the world carried a photograph of a smiling Yasser Arafat greeting a man you read about in Chapter 14. Now 68 years old, he had been held prisoner by Israel for 28 years, longer than any other person in the history of Israel. Released with nearly 100 Palestinians by Israel as part of the roadmap, he was Ahmad Jbarah. Israelis who had been around in 1975 knew him as "the fridge bomber" because he had placed a bomb in an old refrigerator in Zion Square, killing 13 people. When Shlomo Bezem, a brother of one of the victims, heard that Jbarah had been set free as part of the roadmap, he said, "His release isn't worth it, even if it brings peace."

Old Habits Are Hard to Break

Just five days after Bush presided over the Sharon-Abbas handshake, the Israeli prime minister okayed the assassination of one the leaders of Hamas. On June 10, an Israeli missile fired from a helicopter came close to killing Abdel Aziz Rantisi. The attempt to eliminate the Hamas leader was part of an Israeli assassination policy that had targeted more than 100 Palestinians in the 32 months of the intifada.

Hamas responded to the assassination attempt with its own brand of murderous violence the next morning on Jerusalem's crowded number 14 bus. Eighteen-year-old Abdel Madi Shabneth, a Palestinian high school student from the city of Hebron and a member of Hamas, got on the bus dressed as a religious Jew. Carrying a suitcase, he boarded it at the Mahane Yehuda Market. Twenty minutes later, sixteen commuters were dead, ripped apart by the blast and shrapnel of Shabeth's bomb. The blast also killed Sharon's plan to fly to Washington for a meeting with President Bush the following Tuesday. "It is clear," said Bush, "there are people in the Middle East who hate peace." Regarding Israel's attempt to kill the Hamas leader, a Bush spokesman reported that the president was "deeply troubled by the strike" and that he was "concerned that [it] will undermine efforts by Palestinian authorities and others to bring an end to terrorist attacks, and does not contribute to the security of Israel."

The target of the missile, Abdel Aziz Rantisi, declared, "Hamas will not put down the gun even if the Israelis assassinate all our leaders. We refuse the roadmap. It is a Zionist conspiracy." An Israeli spokesman, Avi Pazner, responded that Rantisi was "a dangerous terrorist" and one of the main enemies of peace who "had it coming."

Henry Kissinger and Shimon Peres Explain Everything

Former Secretary of State Henry Kissinger offered his opinion of the challenges confronting Israel, the United States, and the Palestinians in a full-page article published in the June 22, 2003 issue of *The New York Post*. Kissinger wrote, "Though every moment of hope in the Middle East seems to come at the price of a spasm of violence, it is important to retain perspective. The most recent bloodletting was triggered not by frustration with the peace process; rather by the determination of terrorist Hamas to frustrate the momentum given to it by President Bush's visit to the Middle East." Kissinger was all too familiar with the need for perspective, having served as the top U.S. diplomat during the Yom Kippur War.

Expressing doubt that the roadmap's objective of attaining peace by 2005 was attainable, he found it "unimaginable that a new Palestinian prime minister [Abbas] precariously extracted from Arafat will be in a position to renounce the right of [refugees] to return to their place of origin" and make other concessions, or that Israel would make a deal that didn't end terrorism. It was necessary, he continued, that the United States "convince the Arab world that terrorism is not a strategy but a dead end."

Although former Israeli Prime Minister Shimon Peres saw Israeli and Palestinian leaders "at a hopeful juncture," he also warned about the threat from terrorists. He wrote in a newspaper column, "The Palestinians are trying to put an end to the terrorist activities through negotiations. However, should the promoters of terror, who represent a minority, feel that any agreement depends on words alone, they may choose to stick to the rifle rather than decide on their destiny at the polls. In their mind, a minority with rifles is better than an elected majority."

Hamas Finds Itself in the Spotlight

A serious dilemma facing those who had drawn the roadmap was its requirement that the Palestinian Authority disarm and dismantle Hamas, which Israel and the United States had labeled a terrorist organization but Palestinians regarded as a self-defense militia and a provider of vital educational and social services to an economically deprived people. The dual nature of Hamas was noted in an analysis by Middle East correspondent Conat Urquhart. Under the headline "It's More Than a Militia" in the New York newspaper *Newsday*, he wrote:

> In the 16 years in which it has moved from obscurity to center stage, Hamas has built a powerful place in Palestinian society, especially in the seething slums of Gaza. Less noted abroad than its suicide bombings against Israeli civilians is a welfare network of schools, clinics, orphanages, and charities that has helped it become, by at least one poll published [in 2002], the most popular Palestinian political group.

Yet President Bush made it clear that America's policy required the destruction of Hamas as a condition of the roadmap. "The free world," he told an Oval Office news conference in mid-June 2003, "must deal harshly with Hamas and the killers."

Whether the roadmap would lead to peace between Israelis and Palestinians or be recorded as another failed attempt to get Arabs and Israelis to live in peace was an open question. In a part of the world where something that occurred 1,000 years ago was as fresh in the memories of Jews and Arabs as what happened yesterday, it would be answered only with the passage of time.

A First Visit to the White House Rose Garden

On July 25, 2003, Palestinian Prime Minister Abbas found himself admitted to a place that President George W. Bush had closed to Yasser Arafat. Standing in the Rose Garden of the White House, he basked in the glow of Bush's praise. "To break through old hatreds and barriers to peace, the Middle East needs leaders of vision and courage and a determination to serve the interest of their people," said the president. "Mr. Abbas is the first Palestinian prime minister, and he is proving to be such a leader."

Abbas replied:

> We remain committed to the roadmap and we are implementing our security and reform obligations. Security for all Palestinians and Israelis is an essential element in progress, and we will achieve security based on the rule of law. We have succeeded significantly, where Israel, with its military might, has failed in reducing violence, and we will continue. A transformation in the human conditions on the ground must occur. As you have said many times, Mr. President, attacks on the dignity of the Palestinians must end. Palestinians must be able to move, go to their jobs and schools, and conduct a normal life. Palestinians must not be afraid for their lives, property, or livelihood. Some steps have been taken by Israel so far, but these steps remain hesitant. The new era of peace requires the courageous logic of peace, not the suspicious logic of conflict.

Reverent Remarks

This is the time of possibility in the Middle East. And the people of the region are counting on the leaders to seize opportunities for peace and progress. Too many years and lives have been squandered by resentment and violence. The Palestinian people, like people everywhere, deserve freedom. They deserve an honest government and they deserve peace.

—President George W. Bush, July 25, 2003

Sharon Makes His Eighth White House Visit

A week after Abbas's first visit to the White House, Ariel Sharon stood at the same spot in the Rose Garden and informed everyone listening that he was there for the eighth time. As he had done with Abbas, President Bush praised his guest for "the positive steps" that Israel had taken "to further the cause of peace." Noting that Sharon and Abbas were holding regular meetings, he said, "Much hard work remains to be done by Israelis and Palestinians, and by their neighbors. If we are ever to reach our common goal of two states living side by side in peace and security, leaders must assume responsibility."

Reverent Remarks

The United States of America will continue to act in the interest of peace. We will continue to be a firm warrior against terrorism wherever it is found. We will encourage all parties to keep their promises and monitor the progress that is made. We will also help the parties find solutions to legitimate concerns. As we head down the road to peace, my commitment to the security of Israel is unshakable, as is the enduring friendship of our countries."

—President George W. Bush to Israeli Prime Minister Ariel Sharon, the White House, July 31, 2003.

Sharon replied:

> We are currently at an important juncture in our relations with our Palestinian neighbors ... We are thankful for every hour of increased quiet and less terrorism, and for every drop of blood that is spared. At the same time, we are concerned that this welcome quiet will be shattered any minute as a result of the continued existence of terror organizations which the Palestinian Authority is doing nothing to eliminate or dismantle ... I wish to move forward with a political process with our Palestinian neighbors. And the right way to do that is only after a complete cessation of terror, violence, and incitement, full dismantlement of terror organizations, and completion of the reform process in the Palestinian Authority ... If calm prevails and we witness the dismantlement of terror organizations, Israel will be able to take additional steps.

Less than three months later, suicide bombings resumed, Israel retaliated, Abbas resigned, and Arafat was back in complete control with overwhelming support of Palestinians. With threats from Israel to exile Arafat, and calls from some Israelis to kill him, observers pronounced the roadmap another failure. After thousands of years, in the Holy City of three religions that traced their roots to the patriarch Abraham, eternal peace seemed as unattainable as ever.

The Least You Need to Know

- ◆ President Bush at first gave the Middle East scant attention.
- ◆ The "Bush Doctrine" was aimed at crushing world terrorism.

- The United States refused to negotiate with Arafat.

- Terrorism by Hamas threatened a renewal of the peace process.

- A "roadmap" provided hope for peace at last.

Part 5

A Tale of Four Cities

In these final four chapters, we'll explore the daily lives and problems of the present residents of the vibrant and modern international metropolis. You'll also read about the influence of ultra-orthodox Jews on Israeli politics, how residents of the city deal with terrorism, and the Israeli government's controversial policy of displacing Arabs and taking over their homes and businesses.

Chapter 20

Life as a Jew in Jerusalem

In This Chapter

- ◆ Rubbing elbows with history and the Bible
- ◆ Tensions between the religious and the secular
- ◆ Living day by day in the shadow of terrorism
- ◆ Efforts to make Jerusalem a totally Jewish city

The Jerusalem of Jews is filled with reminders of their history found in the Bible, Israel's wars for independence and survival as a state, and the latest terrorist atrocities. It's a city in which those who believe in strict adherence to orthodox tenets of Judaism clash with the realities of modern politics and demands of a larger secular society. In addition to exploring these themes, this chapter also looks at the effects of terrorism on the daily lives of Jerusalem's Jews and an Israeli government policy of Jewish territorial expansion through the displacement of the city's Arab population.

Who Holds the Legal Deed to Jerusalem?

The old saying "Possession is nine tenths of the law" is a reality today in Jerusalem. Jews are in control of the city that they claim was given to them by God, and many of them don't want to share it. But the Arabs offer a compelling case that prior to Israel's takeover of Jerusalem in 1967, the only period in which Jews had possession of the city was roughly 400 years between King David's conquest and the invasion by the Babylonians, during which Solomon's Temple was destroyed and Jews were forced into exile. After the Babylonians, it was under the control of the Persians, Greeks, Romans, Byzantine Christians, the Crusaders, Arabs, Egyptians, Ottomans, and the British, with the Jewish residents mostly confined to the Jewish Quarter of the Old City.

> **Holy Facts!**
>
> The last Jewish house of worship on the Temple Mount was destroyed by the Romans in A.D. 70. Since the late seventh century, the Temple Mount has been the site of the Muslim Dome of the Rock.

Arabs point out that for centuries before creation of the state of Israel in 1948, they and the Jews of Jerusalem had lived side by side in peace. What changed everything, they said, was the Zionist movement's manipulation of the collective guilt of the Western world over the Holocaust to demand that Jews be given a homeland in Palestine. This belief helps explain why bitter Arab rhetoric often scorns the state of Israel as "the Zionist entity."

As far back as March 1946, more than a year before the state of Israel was declared, the Anglo-American Committee of Inquiry on the future of Palestine heard complaints about "Zionists and the support given to them by certain [Western] powers." The Arabs took note of the "entry of incessant waves of immigrants" that "prevents normal economic and social development and causes constant dislocation of the country's life." The statement went on to predict, "It is bound to arouse continuous political unrest and prevent the establishment of political stability on which the prosperity and health of the country depend. The unrest is likely to increase in frequency and violence as the Jews come nearer to being the majority and the Arabs the minority."

An Integral Part of Jewish History

Israeli policy concerning Jerusalem was stated by David Ben-Gurion, Israel's first prime minister, on December 12, 1949. He declared that …

> Jewish Jerusalem is an organic, inseparable part of the state of Israel, just as it is an integral part of Jewish history and belief. Jerusalem is the heart of the state of Israel. We are proud of the fact that Jerusalem is also sacred to other religions, and will gladly provide access to their holy places and enable them to worship as

and where they please ... Twice in the history of our nation were we driven out of Jerusalem, only after being defeated in bitter wars by the larger, stronger forces of Babylon and Rome. Our links with Jerusalem today are no less deep than in the days of Nebuchadnezzar and Titus Flavius, and when Jerusalem was attacked after the fourteenth of May 1948, our valiant youngsters risked their lives for our sacred capital no less than our forefathers did in the time of the first and second temples. A nation that, for two thousand and five hundred years, has faithfully adhered to the vow made by the first exiles by the waters of Babylon not to forget Jerusalem, will never agree to be separated from Jerusalem. Jewish Jerusalem will never accept alien rule after thousands of its youngsters liberated their historic homeland for the third time, redeeming Jerusalem from de-struction and vandalism ... Had we not been able to withstand the aggressors ... Jewish Jerusalem would have been wiped off the face of the earth, [and] the Jewish population would have been eradicated and the state of Israel would not have been.

> **Reverent Remarks**
>
> Jerusalem has a thousand faces, and each one of us has his own Jerusalem.
>
> —Yitzhak Rabin, Washington, D.C., October 1975

A Counting of Heads

If Jews ultimately outnumbering Arabs is the goal of Zionism, how well has it suc-ceeded? Assessing the situation in his book *Divided Jerusalem*, historian Bernard Wasserstein found that when Israel took over Arab East Jerusalem in 1967 the popu-lation of the city was 267,800, with 74 percent Jewish and 26 percent non-Jewish. But by December 2000, in a population of 658,000, the number of Jews had declined to 68 percent and that of others had grown to 32 percent. "Thus, after three decades," Wasserstein noted, "the population of the city had more than doubled but the Jewish population of the total had shrunk." This was attributed to the Arab birthrate being higher than that of the Jews.

Washington Post foreign service correspondent Lee Hockstader, in an article dated August 16, 1998, noted that the population tilt was taking place despite decades of Israeli efforts to limit the growth of the Palestinians' population, but that they had not been able to stop them from having babies.

Populations of Jews and Arabs by Percentage

Year	Jerusalem		Israel	
	Jews	Arabs	Jews	Arabs
1967	74.2	25.8	85.9	14.1
1996	70	30	80.5	19.5

Source: Jerusalem Institute for Israel

How Jewish Must Jerusalem's Jews Be?

In a city in which two thirds of its 600,000 residents are Jews, the ultra-orthodox are a small proportion. In all of Israel, they constitute less than 10 percent of the population. But they are different statistically from most of their fellow Israelis in their birthrate. Although the overall number of births in the country has been declining, the ultra-orthodox have been steadfast in obeying God's decree that they be "fruitful and multiply." According to a 1994 survey, 52 percent of Jewish children under the age 10 in Jerusalem were ultra-orthodox. In 2003, they constituted more than half of the six-year-olds starting school.

No longer confined by their own choice to the section of the city called Mea Shearim, the strict adherents to Judaic law have become an increasingly significant portion of the populations of northern sections of the city. Their rise in numbers has been important not only in terms of the demographics of Jerusalem, but in the governance of the city. When a conservative candidate, Ehud Olmert, opposed the re-election of Teddy Kolleck as mayor in 1993, he formed an alliance with the ultra-orthodox that provided his margin of victory. Chief among their goals is a more religiously observant Jerusalem, with fewer theaters, places of entertainment, and nonkosher restaurants.

Adamantly against sharing the city with Palestinians, the ultra-orthodox also refuse to recognize the legitimacy of the government of Israel. Insisting that Israel can be established and governed only by God, they refuse to pay taxes and serve in the army. Ironically, because most of them are poor, many rely on social programs of the very government they don't accept. All of this has resulted in resentment among the secular Jews who recognize that the only way they will ever live in peace and security is by negotiating with the Palestinians.

The growing power of Jerusalem's ultra-orthodox was demonstrated in April 2003, with the election of an ultra-orthodox rabbi to be the greater city's third Jewish mayor. Fifty-one years old, with twelve children, Uri Lupolianksi was described by the *New York Times* as a man with "a quick smile and an agenda focused more on potholes than suicide bombers" and "in sharp contrast to his high-profile predecessors, Teddy Kollek and Ehud Olmert, who rarely missed opportunities to inject themselves into the middle of a political fracas."

But critics of the new mayor faulted him for remaining silent about the Israeli government's policy of claiming larger and larger portions of land in East Jerusalem for Jews, along with the creation of Jewish settlements in the West Bank, that began in the 1990s and greatly accelerated when Ariel Sharon became prime minister in March 2001.

God Says that This Land Is My Land

As of May 2003, nearly a quarter of a million Jewish settlers were living in 150 communities on formerly Palestinian land in the West Bank. Jews who moved onto the land claimed it was theirs because God had promised it to them. Pointing to the doubling of the settler population in a decade, Palestinians asserted that the purpose of the Israeli policy was to seize so much land that the Palestinians would be unable to create a viable state. In addition to these "authorized" settlements, Jews built "outposts" that Palestinians said were for the purpose of filling in "gaps" between existing settlements, with the hope that they would merge into one large community.

According to a report of the Foundation for Middle East Peace, Israeli West Bank settlements as of 2000 totaled 130. There were 16 in the Gaza Strip and 1 in East Jerusalem. The report documented the following growth in settler population:

> **Reverent Remarks**
>
> When we have settled the land, all the Arabs will be able to do about it will be to scurry around like drugged cockroaches in a bottle.
>
> —Raphael Eitan, IDF chief of staff, *The New York Times*, April 4, 1983

Israeli's Settlement Population in Occupied Territories

Year	West Bank and Gaza Strip	East Jerusalem
1972	1,500	6,900
1992	109,784	141,000
2000	213,672	170,400

The report estimated that 100,000 Israelis, comprising 50 percent of the settler population, resided in eight settlements. The average population in the remaining 140 settlements was 714. In September 1993, there were 32,750 dwelling units in the West Bank and Gaza Strip settlements. Between 1993 and July 2000, construction was begun on 17,190 units.

Reverent Remarks

The settlement of the land of Israel is the essence of Zionism. Without settlement, we will not fulfill Zionism. It's that simple.

—Former Prime Minister Yitzhak Shamir, February 21, 1997

The *New York Times* reported on May 26, 2003, "During the 1990s, the settler population grew close to 10 percent a year. Since the current round of violence began in September 2000, the increase has slowed to about 5 percent annually, according to official figures. Still, that amounted to an additional 10,000 settlers each year." Most of them oppose a Palestinian state. Settlers in outposts that are vulnerable to terrorist attacks see themselves as "rugged pioneers." How the Palestinians feel is the subject of the next chapter.

The Transformation of Jerusalem into an Israeli City

You've read earlier that when the Israeli Defense Force took over all of Jerusalem in the Six-Day War they found that the Jewish Quarter of the Old City was a mess. This was not just because of the fighting to take it in June 1967. It was also the result of what had happened during and after the 1948 war, when the quarter was under Muslim control. Synagogues were vandalized, made into warehouses and stables, or left abandoned. The Jewish cemetery on Mount Herzl had been despoiled. The Western Wall was obscured in a narrow dead-end alleyway surrounded by overshadowing buildings.

With the area of the Western Wall cleared, the Israeli government commenced rebuilding the remainder of the Jewish Quarter, resulting in the reconstruction or refurbishing of historic sites dating to the Roman era.

Attention was also paid to the Jerusalem outside the Old City. The Israeli government established an association for development and renovation of West Jerusalem as the capital of Israel. The Israelis continued to renovate and develop the Old City and surrounding areas despite objections voiced by the international community and protests from Arabs that Israeli annexation of the city was illegal.

It's at this time that the United Nations Security Council took a stand by issuing Resolution 242. The resolution called on Israel to withdrawal its armed forces "from territories occupied in the recent conflict." Since its adoption on November 22, 1967, Resolution 242 has been the basis of all the negotiations, summit conferences, "talks," back-channel dealings, and pressures on Israel in the search for settlement of the Arab-Israeli conflict and guaranteeing the territorial inviolability and political independence of every state in the area. The resolution was described by Golda Meir in her autobiography as "a device" for forcing an Israeli withdrawal from "all these territories in a way and at a time that was not acceptable to us."

Reverent Remarks

When we came back to a unified city after the Six-Day War, we were attacked, we drove them away, the city became one. We didn't touch any of the holy places. We gave freedom of access and freedom of prayer, of course, and free-dom of education to every one of the many groups in the city.

—Former Mayor of Jerusalem Teddy Kolleck

Escalation, Comprehensiveness, and Mobilization

If the terrorism that has plagued Israel is a war, it was declared in July 1968 by the Palestinian National Council. In adopting a national charter, it asserted, "Armed struggle is the only way to liberate Palestine." The "nucleus" of a "popular liberation war" was to be "commando action." This would require "escalation, comprehensive-ness, and organization and involvement in the armed Palestinian revolution." Arabs had a "national duty" to "repel the Zionist and imperialist aggression" aimed at the "elimination of Zionism in Palestine."

Six months later (December 1968), Yasser Arafat's group, FATAH. set out its "objective of the war against Israel" in what it said was its "doctrine." It said that "armed violence will necessarily assume diverse forms in addition to the liquidation of the armed forces of the Zion-ist occupying state; namely, it should turn to the destruction of the factors sustaining the Zionist society in all their forms: industrial, agricultural, and financial."

Reverent Remarks

The Jewish state is an aber-rant mistaken phenomenon in our nation's history and therefore there is no alternative but to wipe out the existential trace of this artificial phenomenon.

—FATAH Doctrine, December 1968

The Bloody Toll Reaped by Suicide Bombers in Israel (2000–2003)

Date	Place	Number Killed
Jan. 1, 2000	Netanya	0
March 1, 2000	Mei Ami	1
March 4, 2000	Netanya	3
March 28, 2000	Deh Hemed	2
April 22, 2001	Kfar Saba	1
May 18, 2001	Netanya shopping mall	5
June 1, 2001	Tel Aviv nightclub	21
June 22, 2001	Dugit in Gaza Strip	2
July 16, 2001	Binyamina train station	2
Aug. 9, 2001	Sbarro pizzeria, Jerusalem	15
Aug. 12, 2001	Kiryat Motzkin	21
Sept. 9, 2001	Nahariya train station	3
Oct. 7, 2001	Kibbutz Shluhot	1
Nov. 29, 2001	Gan Shmuel bus	3
Dec. 1, 2001	Ben Yehuda pedestrian mall, Jerusalem	11
Dec. 2, 2001	Bus in Haifa	15
Jan. 27, 2002	Jaffa Street, Jerusalem	1
Feb. 16, 2002	Karnei Shomron, West Bank	2
Feb. 18, 2002	Maale Adumim	1
March 2, 2002	Mea Shearim, Jerusalem	11
March 5, 2002	Bus in Afula	1
March 9, 2002	Moment Café, Jerusalem	11
March 20, 2002	Bus in Kfar Musmus	7
March 21, 2002	King George Street, Jerusalem	3
March 27, 2002	Hotel in Netanya	29
March 29, 2002	Kiryat Yovel supermarket, Jerusalem	2
March 30, 2002	Coffee shop, Tel Aviv	1
March 31, 2002	Restaurant, Haifa	15
April 1, 2002	Car in Jerusalem	1
April 10, 2002	Bus in Haifa	8
April 12, 2002	Market, Jerusalem	6
May 7, 2002	Pool hall, Rishon Letzion	15

Date	Place	Number Killed
May 19, 2002	Market, Netanya	3
May 22, 2002	Park, Rishon Letzion	2
May 27, 2002	Ice-cream parlor, Petach Tikvah	2
June 5, 2002	Bus near Megiddo Junction	17
June 11, 2002	Restaurant, Herzliya	1
June 18, 2002	Patt Junction, Jerusalem	19
June 19, 2002	French Hill, Jerusalem	7
July 17, 2002	Tel Aviv Neve Shaanan	4
August 4, 2002	Meron Junc	8
Sept. 18, 2002	Umm el-Fahm	1
Sept. 19, 2002	Tel Aviv bus bombing	5
Oct. 10, 2002	Bnei Brak bus bombing	1
Oct. 21, 2002	Karkur Junction car bombing against bus	14
Oct. 27, 2002	Gas station at Ariel Junction	2
Nov. 4, 2002	Kfar Saba mall	2
Nov. 21, 2002	Jerusalem bus bombing	11
Jan. 5, 2003	Neve Shaanan Tel Aviv	23
March 5, 2003	Haifa bus	15
April 24, 2003	Kfar Saba train station	1
April 30, 2003	Tel Aviv seafront	2
May 17, 2003	Hebron	2
May 18, 2003	French Hill, Jerusalem	7
May 19, 2003	Afula mall	3
June 12, 2003	Jerusalem bus	17

Learning to Live with Terrorism

Following a suicide bombing of a Jerusalem bus in which 17 riders were killed on June 12, 2003, an Associated Press report noted that 6 out of 10 people interviewed on the street had been injured themselves or knew someone who had been hurt or killed in terrorist attacks since the start of the al-Aqsa intifada in December 2000.

In addition to thousands of Israeli deaths and injuries in more than three decades of violence, the "diverse forms" of violence adopted as a Palestinian strategy have inflicted psychological wounds.

Living Daily with the Luck of Life

Many Israelis have, sadly, accepted that terrorism is a part of everyday life. In a typical response to the situation, West Jerusalem café owner Yehuda Asian told a British Broadcasting Corporation interviewer, "I am philosophical. If a suicide bomber comes, he comes. It's just the luck of life. When a stranger comes in, people look, but what can you do? We have a guard, but I don't really believe that he will save us if a suicide bomber comes. The terrorist might get past the guard, or shoot him."

"In Israel," noted an Associated Press report, "the word of a bombing overloads cellular phone networks, as panicked friends and relatives check on each other. The sound of more than one ambulance racing down a street, or even a car backfiring, can also stir panic. Some Israelis, a few bus drivers in particular, have survived multiple attacks."

Holy Facts!

Because it's Jewish tradition that a funeral be held on the day after a death, the grim and gruesome task of recovering remains at the scene of a bombing primarily falls to the ultra-orthodox. After an attack, they painstakingly scour the location carrying plastic bags in search of intact corpses and body parts.

For the Jerusalem manager of Magen David Adom—Israel's version of the Red Cross—treating the victims of terrorism has become "a greater and greater part" of the emergency service's work. "On arrival at the scene of a bomb attack," he explained, "I have to make sure, as far as possible, that our medical crews are safe. It's a worry that there might be a second explosion. The second task, the most difficult, is to determine first who of the victims are salvageable, who are the people we have to work hard on to perform life-saving procedures, and who we should not put a lot of effort into treating them because it's clear that we won't be able to save them."

The Least You Need to Know

◆ The Jews' claim to Jerusalem is Biblical and historical.

◆ Jerusalem's Jewish population is slowly declining.

◆ The ultra-orthodox Jews, who oppose the establishment of a Palestinian state, wield growing political power in Israel.

◆ Israel implemented a "settlement" policy to displace Palestinians from their land.

◆ Many Israelis have accepted terrorism as a reality of daily life.

Chapter 21

Life as a Muslim in Jerusalem

In This Chapter

◆ Why Palestinians say that Jerusalem is a Muslim city

◆ Israeli restrictions on Arab residents since 1967

◆ Economic and social effects of the city's division

◆ Israel takes over an important Palestinian symbol

◆ Refugees demand a right to return

In this chapter, we'll further explore the Muslim response to the Jewish claim to Jerusalem. We will also put ourselves in the shoes of Palestinians living under strict Israeli travel restrictions to see what their lives are like.

Seeing Jerusalem's History Through Arab Eyes

You read in the previous chapter how the Jews cite the Bible and their interpretation of history to justify their claim to Jerusalem. The Arab answer is that the religious and historical basis for the creation of the state of Israel in 1948 was a distortion of the facts by European Zionists. The Palestinians also point out that the 1947 UN–mandated division of Palestine called for Jerusalem to be a "corpus separatum" under international supervision. But the Israeli-Arab war of 1948 led to the division of the city into an eastern part under the rule of Transjordan and a western part under the rule of Israel.

When the IDF troops captured East Jerusalem from the Jordanian army in 1967, the government of Israel extended its jurisdiction and borders into the Arab part of the city. Palestinian inhabitants were issued identity cards and subjected to Israeli laws. Although the Israeli government promised the Arabs that they would receive the same social welfare benefits as Israelis, Arabs have claimed that "discriminatory measures" increased over time and that their status as residents was increasingly called into question. For instance, Arabs claim that Israel often revoked Arabs' residency status, leaving Arabs with no way of proving that Jerusalem was the "center of their existence." Once that happened, they found themselves labeled "foreigners" and threatened with expulsion.

What All This Meant to Jerusalem's Arabs

For Palestinians the Israeli "occupation" of East Jerusalem meant discriminatory housing and planning policies, revocation of East Jerusalem residency rights, and restrictions on travel through the closing of roads. By imposing these restraints in 1967, noted a report by a Palestinian human rights group, Israelis introduced a five-point policy to alter the population ratio of Arab East Jerusalem. These steps included …

- Expanding municipal boundaries to include Palestinian land, but excluding Palestinian population.

- Expropriating Palestinian land for Israeli construction and limiting Palestinian construction.

- Excluding Palestinians from the process of municipal planning.

- Keeping Palestinian land as "green areas," effectively saving it for Israeli developments.

- Denying Arabs permits to build and demolishing Palestinian homes to make way for future confiscation and Israeli settlement.

Municipal boundaries of Jerusalem were expanded from an area of 27,000 acres to include an additional 3,750 acres. "Although these boundaries were expanded to confiscate as much Palestinian land as possible," the human rights organization noted, "they avoided highly populated areas so as to avoid including Palestinians." With approximately 80,000 Palestinians excluded from these areas, the government encouraged the building of settlements on the confiscated lands.

In this process approximately half of the city of East Jerusalem was set aside for Jewish settlements and construction, with another 47 percent labeled as "green areas" on which building was prohibited. Much of the small portion of remaining land available to Palestinians was already built on.

For Palestinians to renovate or build a home, they were required to obtain a permit from the Israeli authorities. Failure to do so could lead to total or partial demolition of the structure. These permits were nearly impossible to obtain, and the process could be very expensive, leaving many people with no choice but to build illegally, whereas Jewish builders obtained permits easily. The Israeli government demolished hundreds of so-called unlicensed homes. Making matters even worse, the government confiscated and demolished many Israeli homes to create a network of bypass roads connecting Israeli settlements on Palestinian land.

> **Holy Facts!**
>
> At the same time, during the first year of the second intifada, the IDF demolished at least 360 Palestinian homes in the Gaza Strip. Since October 2000, more than 200 houses have been demolished in the West Bank.

This development of Israeli settlements was a "highly secretive process" in which the Israeli government had no public meetings where public protest could be expressed. Those who stood to lose land or houses were usually informed after the process had been approved.

> **Reverent Remarks**
>
> All the Jewish settlements in the occupied territories are illegal and, therefore, cannot continue.
> —Malcolm Rifkind, British foreign secretary, November 3, 1996

Determining a Palestinian's Residency Status

Following the 1967 annexation of East Jerusalem, Israel conducted a census and granted Israeli identity cards to East Jerusalem residents who were counted. This gave them "permanent resident" status. Those who were absent when the census was taken lost the right to return to their homes. Their families were required to submit a request for "family unification" so they could live together in the city. Although Israel declared that East Jerusalem residents could apply for Israeli citizenship, most declined. Arabs live in constant fear that the Israeli government will arbitrarily deport any Palestinian by revoking the identity card and permanent residency status.

Limiting Freedom of Movement and Travel

The Israeli government first implemented its policy of military "closure" in the West Bank at the beginning of the 1991 Gulf War. Imposed several times over the ensuing

> **Reverent Remarks**
>
> Palestinians living in the city of Jerusalem, their home for thousands of years, are subjected to premeditated, deliberate, preplanned, discriminatory policies designed to gradually eliminate their presence in the Holy City.
>
> —Statement of an East Jerusalem resident posted on the Internet, June 2003

years, the closures kept more and more Palestinians from entering Israel. To cross into Israel, Palestinians need a special permit that is usually reserved for work or school; however, in some cases, usually in response to terrorist attacks, the government denies access to all West Bank Palestinians—even if they work in Israel. A policy of permanent closure, imposed in 1993, cut off East Jerusalem residents from those in the West Bank.

The closures create economic and cultural hardships by preventing Palestinians from working in Israel and worshipping at their holy sites in the Old City. The closure policy also has reduced the contact between the West Bank and the Gaza Strip. To pass through Israel to visit a family in Gaza, West Bank residents must apply for a permit. The permit process is lengthy, bureaucratic, and arbitrary. Few Palestinians succeed in obtaining the permit.

The Personal and Economic Costs to Palestinians

Palestinians claim that under Israeli "occupation" the standard of living steadily decreased for those living in East Jerusalem. One report noted, "Forced evictions, demolitions, and general insecurity have had a negative impact on individuals, families, and communities. The socioeconomic effects of Israeli occupation have led to a decreased level of education as children drop out of school early to help the family (average 15 years); and the health of residents, especially children, is negatively effected. The population density for Palestinian residents is nearly twice that of Israeli residents, further contributing to a decline of health and living conditions."

A Changing Economic Base Hurts Palestinians

During the period of the British Mandate (1917–1947), the economy of Jerusalem expanded significantly. Because the city developed as an administrative center, improvements were made in the water system, transportation, and communications. The result was more religious pilgrims as well as Jewish immigrants. With little to offer in the way of exportable natural resources, the economy of the city was largely dependent on the growing tourist trade.

Following the 1948 war, the economy of Israeli West Jerusalem expanded, while at the same time the government of Jordan downplayed East Jerusalem in favor of its own capital city, Amman. As a result, the economy of East Jerusalem turned sluggish or even stagnant. Although it experienced a slight rebound after 1967 and the Israeli annexation, the overall Palestinian economy, and East Jerusalem in particular, remained subordinate to the larger Jewish Israeli economy.

Holy Facts!

When Israel imposes military closures on the West Bank and Gaza in response to terrorist attacks, Palestinians who are not Jerusalem residents are barred from entering the city unless they obtain a permit. This cuts off East Jerusalem from the West Bank and contributes to higher unemployment. In response to the frequent closures, some retailers have shifted their businesses to Palestinian areas in the West Bank. Although a new business district in East Jerusalem developed in cramped space along Salahadin Street, it competes with a shopping district along Jaffa Street in Jerusalem. Consequently, Jerusalem has developed two economies, Jewish and Palestinian.

A study prepared by the economic department of the Jerusalem chamber of commerce found that Israeli measures to isolate Jerusalem have negatively affected tourism and other commercial sectors in the city. In 16 businesses operating in Jerusalem in the fields of industry, services, tourism, transportation, banks, contracting, and commerce, jobs declined 37 percent, daily work hours dropped by 50 percent, and production was down almost 90 percent. These changes were attributed to difficulties in the marketing of products, problems getting raw material, workers not able to get to their factories, and unfair competition from imports of Chinese and Turkish goods that were cheaper.

The chamber of commerce also reported that banks had reduced financial support for the industrial sector by more than 25 percent since the outbreak of the first intifada. It noted that factories have suffered a liquidity problem that makes it difficult for them to continue production. They also have difficulty getting products to the markets as a result of the Israeli closures.

The commerce sector has also suffered from the Israeli measures, with some businesses experiencing a decline of up to 90 percent. The worst hit are souvenir shops. Least affected are supermarkets. Employment in commerce has declined by 12 percent, while daily work hours have declined by 27 percent. The chamber of commerce attributed the decline to difficulty in distributing products to the markets because of the closures. And the city's electricity supplier, the Jerusalem District Electricity Company, has reported having between 80 and 100 million Israeli shekels ($20–25 million) in uncollected bills from subscribers who don't have money to pay them.

Terrorism Scares Away the Tourists

Tourism is a pillar of Jerusalem's economy, and the combination of Palestinian terrorism and Israel's retaliation, which has kept visitors away in droves, has hit both Palestinian and Jewish economies hard. The effects have been most severe in the Old City, however. Christian pilgrims have shied away and Israel's travel restrictions have barred most Muslims from entering even if they wanted to.

> **Holy Facts!** _____
>
> The chamber of commerce study found that 3 out of 13 companies working in tourist transportation were forced to shut down their business. Many tour buses were put up for sale. The number of people working in tourism dropped by half.

The East Jerusalem tourist industry was crippled even more during the first intifada. Hotel occupancy in East Jerusalem fell to almost zero and several hotels were forced to close. Despite the Oslo accords, Palestinian tourist guides had a difficult time getting licenses from Israel. The difficult permit process made it hard for Palestinians to build hotels so that they could expand the tourism trade. With the outbreak of the second intifada in December 2000 and the Israeli military responses, few travelers have been willing to risk going to the Holy City.

The House that Became a Symbol of Palestinian Pride

Like Americans who cherish the White House as a symbol of national identity, Palestinians adopted an old and elegant former home and hotel in the Sheikh Jarrah district of East Jerusalem to signify their national hopes and aspirations.

Built by Ismail Musa al-Husseini in 1897, the Orient House had been used to host diplomatic functions, including a tea party for Germany's Kaiser Wilhelm when he visited Jerusalem in 1898. King Abdallah, King Ali, and Prince Zaid accepted condolences at the Orient House when their father, Sharif Hussein Ben Ali (Sharif of Mecca), was laid to rest at the Haram al-Sharif in 1930. Emperor Haile Selassie of Ethiopia and Empress Minan of Abyssinia (Ethiopia) also found it a haven when Italians invaded their country in 1936.

When Ismail Musa al-Husseini died in 1945, he left the house to his son Ibrahim. Following the 1948 war, Ibrahim allowed it to be used as the temporary headquarters of the United Nations Conciliation Committee. It was then opened to the public as a hotel known as The New Orient House Hotel. After the 1967 Six-Day War and the deterioration of the political and economic conditions, tourist traffic dwindled. The owners decided to close the building and return it to use as a private residence.

Finding the maintenance of such a large building difficult, they rented the top floor to an international refugee agency. The building soon suffered from neglect, but in 1983 the Arab Studies Society rented a section of the building for offices, archives, and a press facility. During the first intifada, the Arab Studies Society emerged as a body to promote Palestinian political interests.

According to the Palestinians, several attempts were made by the Israelis "to shut off and suspend services provided by the Orient House," including breaking into it in 1988, thereby "depriving Palestinians of their only source of support and representation in the city." Following the Oslo accords, the Orient House reopened on October 26, 1992. In the view of its leadership, the Orient House was playing "a vital role" in the peace process as the "official Palestinian political address in Jerusalem."

Israelis saw the presence of the Orient House quite differently. "The appearance of the Palestinian office in the heart of the Israeli capital," wrote historian Bernard Wasserstein, "aroused an uproar on the Israeli right." Mayor Olmert denounced the Orient House as a violation of Israeli law and a "provocation." But in a letter to Norwegian Foreign Minister Johan Jurgen Holst at the time of the Oslo agreement, Israeli Foreign Minister Shimon Peres had pledged that Israel wouldn't interfere with Palestinian institutions of East Jerusalem. He wrote that the "interests and well-being of the Palestinians of East Jerusalem are of great importance and will be preserved." He also promised that Israel wouldn't "hamper their activity" and "the fulfillment of this important mission is to be encouraged."

On April 11, 1999, Prime Minter Benjamin Netanyahu's cabinet put out an order for the closure of the Orient House. It cited as its reason "a series of provocations" by the Palestinian Authority at the Orient House, including summoning "Gaza-based representatives of Arab countries to Jerusalem on Israel's Independence Day." The statement added that orders would also be issued against "persons working on behalf of the PA at the Orient House in contravention of the law and the political agreements."

Although the decision seemed to spell the end of the Orient House, an Israeli court ordered that nothing be done until after a pending Israeli election. When the voters chose to replace Netanyahu's right-wing government with a less militant one formed by Ehud Barak, the order to shut down the Orient House languished, as Barak pursued a peace settlement that culminated in the Barak-Arafat-Clinton meeting at Camp David (see Chapter 17). As you've read, those talks failed, Sharon paid his controversial visit to the Haram/Temple Mount, the al-Aqsa intifada was launched, and Sharon replaced Barak as prime minister.

Suspecting that the Orient House was involved in the Sbarro pizzeria suicide bombing, Israeli security forces barged into the house at two in the morning on August 10, 2001, took down the Palestinian flag, and raised the Israeli flag. The government claimed that searches uncovered documents, tapes, computers, and "considerable material from various periods" that pointed to "the direct link between Orient House, the PA, and PA Chairman Yasser Arafat," and that Palestinian Authority officials carried out activities in the Jerusalem area in "complete contravention of the agreements that have been signed with them."

Among the seized material, said the Israelis, "were operational documents" that described activity by the Palestinian security services in Jerusalem, including lists of names of East Jerusalem residents with whom the Palestinian security services had dealings, and records regarding employment of Orient House security guards in the framework of the Palestinian security services." The documents also showed that "part of the financing transferred by the PA was designated for the reconstruction and rehabilitation of structures and properties of residents of eastern Jerusalem, including the Old City, and featured the direct involvement of Yasser Arafat" to "prevent the transfer of real estate to Jews." Israel alleged that these and other materials proved that the Orient House was deeply involved with Arafat, and through him with terrorist groups.

On August 13, 2001, Dr. Nasser al-Kidwa, Ambassador and Permanent Observer of Palestine to the United Nations, complained to the world body that the "decision of the Israeli government of Mr. Ariel Sharon to take such a step" in regard to Palestinian institutions" was a dangerous escalation in Israel's "bloody military campaign being waged against the Palestinian people since last September." He said it was an assault on their "national dignity" and violated Palestinian rights in Jerusalem."

Tales of the Displaced

Jerusalem historian Mitchell Bard calculated that by the middle of 2000, the number of Palestinian refugees had risen to nearly 4 million. This was five or six times the number who'd left Palestine in 1948. Though the popular image is of refugees in squalid camps," Bard pointed out, less than one third of the Palestinians were in 59 camps established by the United Nations. During the years that Israel controlled the Gaza Strip, they attempted to shift the Palestinians into permanent housing, but militant Palestinian groups opposed such moves because bitter inhabitants of the camps provided a steady supply of volunteers, including suicide bombers, for the various terrorist groups. The refugees were also viewed as an advantage to Arab states, who held them up as examples of Jewish "oppression."

According to one Palestinian official, keeping more than 400,000 refugees in camps was a "political decision" made to influence the "final-status" talks with Israel. The Palestinian Authority held that an agreement to end the half century of conflict would have to include a "right of return" for all Palestinians. In an opinion poll conducted in the refugee camps to the north of the West Bank, the sweeping majority of those questioned insisted on returning to the lands of the forefathers. Conducted by a group called Tadamon (Solidarity) Institution for Human Rights, the poll found that 95.4 percent demanded on the right of return.

Eighty-seven percent refused resettlement in Jewish settlements in the West Bank instead of their 1948 homeland. More than three fourths said that no one was authorized to surrender their right of return, and 84 percent said they still hoped to return to their original cities, towns, and villages. This stance put the refugees at odds with Israel's policy of rejecting a right of return.

> **Reverent Remarks**
>
> We will not accept under any circumstances the right of return to Israel. We will not do it at any price.
>
> —Prime Minister Ehud Barak, 2001

The Roadmap to Peace Goes Slow on the Right of Return

Under the roadmap to peace devised by the United States and the other members of the "quartet" (the United Nations, the European Union, and Russia), which was accepted by Israel and the Palestinian Authority in June 2003, the last stage of the plan includes a "just, fair, and realistic solution" to the refugee issue, and a negotiated resolution on the status of Jerusalem that "takes into account the political and religious concerns of both sides, and protects the religious interests of Jews, Christians, and Muslims worldwide."

The hope is that by following the roadmap the Palestinians and Israelis will fulfill "the vision of two states, Israel and sovereign, independent, democratic and viable Palestine, living side by side in peace and security." Both Mahmoud Abbas for the Palestinians and Ariel Sharon for Israel have stated that no changes should be made in the plan.

The Israel Government Decides on a Go-Slow Policy

That the roadmap to peace will not be as easy to follow as the quartet hoped became clear on May 8, 2003. Despite Sharon saying that no changes should be made, the prime minister declared in an interview on Israel Radio that the right of return "is a recipe for the destruction of Israel." Because it would mean a flood of Arabs into Israel, he said, "We will not accept such a thing."

When the roadmap was presented to the Israeli cabinet on May 25, 2003, 11 ministers were in favor of acceptance, 7 opposed, and 4 abstained, including former Prime Minister Netanyahu. When a second vote overwhelmingly rejected the right of return, Sharon stated that Israel's policy would be to take some steps in the plan's demand for Israel to start withdrawals of IDF forces in Gaza and Bethlehem and deal with its settlements and outposts. But he pledged to work to change the roadmap on the issue of the right of refugees to return. The result was that the roadmap was left intact with no certainty that Israel would succeed in its goal of preventing the "flood of Arabs into Israel" that Sharon feared would follow acceptance of the right of return. But Sharon made clear that he was complying because of pressure from the United States government not to take any detours from the roadmap. In an interview with the newspaper *Yediot Ahronot* on May 25, he explained, "The decision I made is based on the recognition that the moment has come to cut, the moment has arrived to say 'yes' to the Americans. The moment has arrived to divide this tract of land between us and the Palestinians."

> **Reverent Remarks**
>
> Israel accepted a plan that could lead to the establishment of a Palestinian state. Nonetheless, it still insists on its right to defensible borders, and that any Palestinian state will not be a source of any future threat.
>
> —Dore Gold, an adviser to Sharon, May 25, 2003

A month later, Israeli forces withdrew from northern Gaza and Sharon pledged to dismantle some illegal Jewish settlements in the West Bank. Of these steps, the man who had spent his life fighting Palestinians and vowing that they would never have their own state told his cabinet, "If we are united and we act quietly, we can, in my opinion, achieve security and, with God's help, peace."

The Least You Need to Know

- ◆ Palestinians claim a historical right to Jerusalem.

- ◆ Israel imposed residency and travel restrictions on Palestinians living in the West Bank and Gaza.

- ◆ East Jerusalem suffered severe economic hardships due to the violence of the intifada and Israeli restrictions on building and travel.

- ◆ Israelis raided and closed the Palestinian Authority's Jerusalem headquarters.

- ◆ Israel opposes the right of return of Arab refugees.

Chapter 22

Life as a Christian in Jerusalem

In This Chapter

♦ The rise and decline of Christian power in Jerusalem

♦ Christians in the Palestinian liberation movement

♦ Christians join Muslims to protest Israeli restrictions

♦ A historic visit by Pope John Paul II

♦ How American Christians see the Israeli-Arab conflict

Although Christians shaped the history and physical development of the Holy City since the era of the Byzantine Empire, the end of the British Mandate and the 1948 war brought a sharp decline in Jerusalem's Christian population. Most Christians who remained in the city felt that they were oppressed by Israel's policies after the 1967 takeover and became even more resentful as restrictions on citizenship and travel were imposed on all Palestinians, including Christian Palestinians.

The City of Christ, Catholics, and Crusaders

Since the crucifixion of Jesus of Nazareth by Roman decree on a rocky hill called Golgotha on the outskirts of Jerusalem, Christians had succeeded so well in making Jerusalem the heart of their religion that in a 1922 British census, they constituted 51 percent of the population. Year after year, thousands of pilgrims came to follow the Via Dolorosa to the Church of the Holy Sepulchre, pray at the Garden Tomb, climb the Mount of Olives, and visit the Garden of Gethsemane to ponder Jesus' prayerful agony on the night before his trials and crucifixion. Christian archaeologists had explored and dug around to unearth and identify not only sites related to Jesus, but also those important to the Jews.

Whereas the Muslims had the Haram and Jews venerated the Western Wall, the Christians had numerous churches in the Old City and vestiges of the Crusades to symbolize their presence. Permanent residents were well educated and mostly members of the mercantile class who lived primarily in the western section of the city.

> **Reverent Remarks**
>
> Perhaps the most significant change in Jerusalem over the past century has been the decline in numbers and influence of Christianity in the city.
> —Jerusalem historian Bernard Wasserstein, in *Divided Jerusalem*

During the years of Islamic rule of the city, Christians had continued to live and worship there. But in 1948, according to historian Sami Hadawi, more than half of them were expelled from their homes by Israelis, creating the largest single numeric decline of Christians in Palestine's in history. Hadawi's study concluded that a higher proportion of Christians became refugees (37 percent) than Muslims (17 percent).

Declaring that Christians had become "an insignificant part of the population" of Jerusalem, Canon Riah Abu El Assal, archdeacon of the diocese of Jerusalem, noted that since the Israeli annexation in 1967, the number of Christians dropped from 28,000 to 7,000. Had the 18 percent Christian population of the 1922 to 1947 period remained, noted Don Wagner, associate professor of Religion and Middle Eastern Studies, and executive director of the Center for Middle Eastern Studies at North Park University, "Palestinian Christians would have numbered close to 300,000 by the early 1990s."

The Shrinking Body of Christians

Throughout Israel, the number of Palestinian Christians grew to approximately 160,000 by 1993, compared to a Muslim population of 650,000. However, by the

second intifada, the emigration patterns
continued to the extent that Christians
were an estimated 1.6 percent of the
Palestinian population in the West Bank,
Gaza, and Jerusalem. Scholars estimate
that if these rates continued over the next
generation, the Palestinian Christian population

Holy Facts!

The median age of Christians
in Jerusalem is 32, whereas the
average age of the rest of the
population is 16.

will be on the verge of extinction within a generation. Some call it the "museum-
ification" of Christian Palestine and Israel. Some predict that there will be only "a
small number of elderly Christians left to show churches to western tourists, but the
churches will be empty, having no local community to worship and inhabit them."

Fears of Jerusalem Becoming a Christian Theme Park

After visiting Jerusalem in 1992, Great Britain's Archbishop of Canterbury, Dr.
George Carey, said his fear was that the Holy City and the Church of the Nativity
in nearby Bethlehem were in danger of becoming "a kind of Walt Disney Christian
theme park." He was referring to the seasonal tide of tourists who traveled to Israel
in the Christmas and Easter seasons. But with the calling of the second intifada, even
the number of sightseeing Christians declined dramatically.

Christians and the Intifadas

During both intifadas, the number of Christian pilgrims dwindled. "Before the troubles began," noted one observer, "Easter brought so many tourists to Jerusalem that
many had to be turned away from the crowded site. This year [2000], the few visitors
who made the journey to Jerusalem found they could walk right in to the ornate interior of the church. This has triggered a debate among some community leaders about
the future of the sites themselves, in an area where there are fewer and fewer Christians and the major faiths are Judaism and Islam." The Reverend Jerome Murphy-
O'Connor, a scholar and Roman Catholic priest at Ecole Biblique in Jerusalem,
worried that if the local Christians left, holy places would be "museums, and people
like me, foreigners, would be the curators."

In 2000, the smaller Christian presence was painfully evident on Good Friday. Only
several hundred Christians in small groups of Italians, Germans, Swedish, South
American, Filipino, and English pilgrims walked the Via Dolorosa in the annual ceremony to retrace Jesus' steps toward crucifixion. "This is nothing like it used to be
when thousands used to come from all over the world," said Father Simon, a Franciscan monk. Yousef Abu Ghannam, whose family operated a souvenir concession and

held the key for the Mosque of the Ascension on the Mount of Olives reported, "We used to get 700 to 800 people a day [before the intifada]. Now we're lucky to get 150. People are afraid." Another observer noted that the few visitors who braved Jerusalem encountered a metropolis that was "edgy and turbulent." While the city's churches, mosques, and synagogues provided tranquillity to pilgrims, travel in the area was so potentially dangerous that the U.S. State Department put out a warning advising Americans against visiting Jerusalem.

The situation was so worrisome that in January 1999 several American bishops wrote to Israel's ambassador to Washington complaining of "confiscation of East Jerusalem identity cards from Palestinians and the attendant denial of residency rights in Jerusalem." The clerics declared the strictures "detrimental to the continued presence and witness of the Christian churches in Jerusalem." They added, "The churches in the Holy City of Jerusalem are not composed only of stones, but more importantly are communities of faithful, worshipping believers. Any further diminution of their numbers or weakening of their vitality is a matter of great concern to the churches everywhere. We call upon the government of Israel to safeguard their rights, to rescind these deleterious policies, to restore identity cards that have been confiscated, and to refrain from further confiscation."

Then, on the evening of the 2000 Camp David summit, several Christian leaders sent a letter to President Bill Clinton, Israeli Prime Minister Ehud Brak, and Palestinian Authority President Yasser Arafat. Signed by Diodoros I, Jerusalem's Greek Orthodox patriarch; Michel Sabbah, the Latin (Catholic) patriarch; and Armenian patriarch Torkom Manoogian II, it said:

> We appeal to you as foremost political leaders and negotiators to ensure that the Christian communities within the walls of the Old City are not separated from each other … We regard the Christian and Armenian quarters of the Old City as inseparable and contiguous entities that are firmly united by the same faith. Furthermore, we trust that your negotiations will also secure that any arrangement for Jerusalem will ensure that the fundamental freedoms for worship and access by all Christians to their holy sanctuaries and to their headquarters within the Old City are not impeded in any way whatsoever.

On July 23, 2000, the United States submitted a proposal, based on an Israeli plan, to grant the Palestinians full sovereignty in the Muslim and Christian quarters, including Christian holy sites, but leaving the Jewish and Armenian quarters under Israeli control. In response to this, Arafat told President Clinton, "I will not agree to any Israeli sovereign presence in Jerusalem, neither in the Armenian Quarter, nor in the al-Aqsa Mosque, neither on the Via Dolorosa, nor in the Church of the Holy Sepulcher."

Three years later, the question of who will attain administration of the Christian Quarter remains unresolved.

The Dilemma of Christianity in Palestine

From the start of the Arab-Israeli conflict following creation of a Jewish state, the primary concerns of Christians were sanctity of the holy places in Jerusalem and unrestricted access to them. Consequently, the Roman Catholic Church decided that the way to ensure this was to give its support to the United Nations plan to internationalize the city. When Israel rejected the proposal and then took possession of the Old City in 1967, relations with the Vatican became strained and remained so. As you've just read, the imposition of residency and travel restrictions on Palestinians, including those who were Christian, drew a rebuke from America's Roman Catholic, Orthodox, and Armenian bishops.

While relations between the Jewish state and its small Christian community remained contentious, Palestinian liberation leaders recognized the region's Christians as potential allies in their struggle against a "Zionist entity" that "oppressed" anyone who wasn't Jewish. In courting friendship with Christians, no one was more publicly enthusiastic than Yasser Arafat. To demonstrate that Christians would have nothing to fear in the creation of a Palestinian state, he made a point of attending the Christmas Eve services at Bethlehem's Church of the Nativity. Christians also held important positions in Palestinian liberation organizations.

A Christian Palestinian Revolutionary

Whereas most Americans believe that only Muslims have been waging war against Israel, one of the movement's most important figures was a Christian. Born in 1926 in Lydda, George Habash and his family were driven from their home in 1948. Graduated in 1951 with a medical degree from American University in Beirut, Lebanon, he soon left the profession for a lifelong struggle to liberate Palestine. He co-founded the Arab Nationalist Movement in 1952. Operating in Amman, Jordan, he was actively engaged in its management with the purpose of unifying the entire Arab world to confront Israel. Although Habash and Yasser Arafat presented a public show of unity, they often disagreed privately on policy. While Arafat formed FATAH to wage violent revolution, Habash felt it essential that Arab unity and the liberation of Palestine be achieved through a conventional war. He saw a link between "Arab nationalism and local activism." But that dream went up in the smoke of the Six-Day War.

Confronted with the impotence of the Arab "confrontation states," Habash concluded that guerrilla warfare was "a necessity" and formed the Popular Front for the Liberation of Palestine (PFLP). Its inaugural statement declared that "the only language which the enemy understands is that of revolutionary violence." The PFLP's "historic task" was to open "a fierce struggle" against the enemy, "turning the occupied territories into an inferno whose fires consume the usurpers."

Based in the Gaza Strip, the Front chose as a tactic the hijacking not just of Israeli civil aircraft but also American, British, and Swiss airliners. PFLP justified a machine gun attack on an El Al airliner at Athens airport on the ground that the airline was an integral part of the enemy war machine. "When we hijack a plane," Habash explained to the German publication *Der Stern* in 1970, "it has more effect than if we killed a hundred Israelis in battle. For decades world public opinion has been neither for nor against the Palestinians. It simply ignored us. At least the world is talking about us now." After the Yom Kippur War, he insisted that there must be "no deviation from revolution until victory."

> **Reverent Remarks**
>
> With the Popular Front among the 20 Palestinian groups rejecting the Oslo accords, Habash blamed Christians in the United States for rushing to sanction the creation of a Jewish state, as well as for the continued oppression of Palestinians. He said, "The Israelis could not have done what they did without the support of American Christians. He said they were responsible for "those sitting in [refugee] camps" that were "little better" than Nazi concentration camps for Jews.

A Christian Woman Makes the Palestinian Case on American TV

Second only to Yasser Arafat in familiarity to Americans who saw the numerous confrontations between Israel and Palestinians on television, Hanan Ashrawi was born into an Anglican Christian family in 1946 in Ramallah, on the West Bank. Her father was a founder of the Palestine Liberation Organization. With Bachelor's and Master's degrees in literature from the Department of English at the American University of Beirut and a doctorate in Medieval and Comparative Literature from the University of Virginia, Charlottesville, she returned to the West Bank in 1973 to establish the Department of English at Birzeit University.

Appointed spokeswoman of the Palestinian delegation at the Middle East Peace Conference in Madrid, Ashrawi headed the Preparatory Committee of the Palestinian

Independent Commission for Citizens' Rights in Jerusalem, and was the founder and commissioner general of that committee until 1995. In 1996 she was elected to the Palestinian Legislative Council, Jerusalem District, and served as the Palestinian authority minister of higher education and research in Arafat's first government. In 1998, she founded the Palestinian Initiative for the Promotion of Global Dialogue and Democracy and served as its secretary general.

A frequent guest on American TV news programs, she was an articulate advocate of the Palestinian cause. In an interview in the October 8, 1993, issue of *Commonweal* magazine, in which she was asked how being an Anglican Christian affected her Palestinian identity, she answered:

> I keep reminding people that Christianity started in Palestine. It's a Middle Eastern religion, and we are extensions of the earliest community in Palestine. We have been there for centuries. Part of our own self-definition as Palestinians is that we are the original Christians and that we also have centuries of Muslim history. This society, which is so complex, has developed in ways in which mutual tolerance grew organic! I do not even know who is Christian and who is Muslim among my friends. We were together as part of Palestinian authenticity, Palestinian nationality. So Palestinian Christians are not a minority. We are Palestinians and we happened to be Christians, and this is part of our heritage and our authenticity.

Reverent Remarks

They [Israelis] are targeting the very existence of the Palestinian people, destroying our institutions and breaking our spirit. But no army has defeated a nation and no colonial occupation can last for ever.

—Hanan Ashrawi

The Vatican Amends Its Policy on Jerusalem

On April 20, 1984, Pope John Paul II declared, "For the Jewish people who live in the state of Israel and who preserve in that land such precious testimonies to their history and their faith, we must ask for the desired security and the due tranquillity that are the prerogative of every nation." Two years later, he visited the Great Synagogue in Rome and said, "With Judaism, we have a relationship that we do not have with other religions. You are our dearly beloved brothers; in a certain way, indeed, it could be said that you are our elder brothers." The statements had the effect of recognizing the state of Israel and reversing the Church's desire for an internationalized Jerusalem.

Muslims Plan a Christian Birthday Party

At a conference sponsored by the European Commission in Brussels, Belgium, for the purpose of raising funds for the "Bethlehem 2000 Project" to mark the 2000th anniversary of the birth of Christ in Bethlehem, Jerusalem's Latin patriarch, Vicar Bishop Hanna Bathish, said that while the 2000 celebrations would be mainly Christian, they were also to be for all mankind, including the believers in Islam. "We know very well that our brothers, the Moslems, venerate so much Jesus Christ who is mentioned often in the Holy Koran in different ways about many things," he said. Noting that Muslims living in Bethlehem and elsewhere had a major interest in making the celebrations a success, he asserted, "We simply cannot live separated or divided. Not only we cannot but also we do not want to live in isolation. We want to be all together and we want to live side by side."

Arafat Sends an Invitation

Hoping to bolster the importance of the Bethlehem celebration, Yasser Arafat invited Pope John Paul II to attend. The pontiff's acceptance was announced by Vatican Secretary of State Cardinal Angelo Sodano. He said the Pope had expressed "great happiness for this call" and hoped that the Bethlehem 2000 project would be successful. John Paul II issued a statement saying, "We always head to Bethlehem, considering it the place where Jesus was born."

Then, on Tuesday, February 15, 2000, Yasser Arafat paid his ninth visit to the Vatican. The purpose was a meeting with John Paul II and the signing of a document in which the Roman Catholic Church obtained guarantees of religious freedom and the legal status of Christian churches. It recognized "inalienable national legitimate rights and aspirations of the Palestinian people" and declared that any "unilateral decisions and actions altering the specific character and status of Jerusalem are morally and legally unacceptable."

Israel immediately expressed its "great displeasure" with the declaration in Rome for including "Jerusalem and other issues which are the subjects of Israeli-Palestinian negotiations on permanent status." It went on to call the Vatican-PLO agreement "a regrettable intervention" in Israeli-Palestinian talks.

A Papal Apology to Jews

With plans being formulated for the historic papal visit to the Holy Land, Pope John Paul II recognized the centuries of "sins" by Christianity against Jews. On March 12, 2000, he said, "Let us pray that, in recalling the sufferings endured by the people of

Israel throughout history, Christians will acknowledge the sins committed by not a few of their number against the people of the Covenant and the blessings, and in this way will purify their hearts. God of our fathers, you chose Abraham and his descendants to bring your name to the Nations. We are deeply saddened by the behavior of those who in the course of history have caused these children of yours to suffer, and asking your forgiveness we wish to commit ourselves to genuine brotherhood with the people of the Covenant. We ask this through Christ our Lord."

Analysts of the Vatican's recognition of Palestinian rights and Pope John Paul II's acknowledgment of centuries of Christianity's offenses against Jews agree that the dramatic events reflected a desire of the Roman Catholic Church to be a part of any solution of the problem of the status of Jerusalem. Having backed off its earlier demand that it be neither Jewish nor Muslim, but under some kind of international administration, the position of the Vatican as expressed by Cardinal John O'Connor of New York was that the Church had "no particular interest" in who controlled the city. It wanted only to ensure "equal rights for everyone" with freedom of access to the holy places.

Hopeful Reflections upon History

Writing about the pope's arrival in Israel on March 2, 2000, journalist Uri Dan recalled earlier times. He noted:

> [T]he very fact that the government of Israel, the Jewish state, welcomes the pope in the airport bearing the name of Ben-Gurion, the state's founder, demonstrates to the entire world that the organized wall of hate has fallen between the Catholic Church and the Jewish people in its land—the Promised Land. How much would Theodor Herzl, the greatest prophet in the last 2,000 years, have been ready to pay to see with his own eyes this pope in Hebrew Jerusalem? He, Herzl, only 100 years ago, pleaded in vain in the Vatican to help him to realize his dream of establishing the Jewish state. It arose without the aid of the Vatican, of course. It thus fell to the current pope to open a new and exciting chapter in Jewish-Christian relations for the third millennium.

In remarks at the airport, John Paul II also had history on his mind when he said:

> The establishment of diplomatic relations between us in 1994, set a seal on efforts to open an era of dialogue on questions of common interest concerning religious freedom, relations between church and state and, more generally, relations between Christians and Jews. On another level, world opinion follows with close attention the peace process which finds all the peoples of the region

involved in the difficult search for a lasting peace with justice for all. With new-found openness towards one another, Christians and Jews together must make courageous efforts to remove all forms of prejudice.

Reverent Remarks _____

My journey therefore is a pilgrimage, in a spirit of humble gratitude and hope, to the origins of our religious history. It is a tribute to the three religious traditions which coexist in this land …. I pray that my visit will serve to encourage an increase of interreligious dialogue that will lead Jews, Christians and Muslims to seek in their respective beliefs, and in the universal brotherhood that unites all the members of the human family, the motivation and the perseverance to work for the peace and justice which the peoples of the Holy Land do not yet have, and for which they yearn so deeply.

—Pope John Paul II, Ben-Gurion Airport, March 21, 2000

On the second day of the historic papal pilgrimage, thousands of Muslims and officials of the Palestinian Autonomous Territories gathered at Bethlehem's airport heard John Paul II ask:

> How can I fail to pray that the divine gift of peace will become more and more a reality for all who live in this land, uniquely marked by God's interventions? Peace for the Palestinian people! Peace for all the peoples of the region! No one can ignore how much the Palestinian people have had to suffer in recent decades. Your torment is before the eyes of the world. And it has gone on too long.

The welcome ceremony was followed by mass in Manger Square, a visit to the Dheisheh Refugee Camp, and a meeting with Arafat.

At Yad Vashem the following day (the last day of the journey), John Paul II paid homage "to the millions of Jewish people who, stripped of everything, especially of their human dignity, were murdered in the Holocaust." He spoke of "the echo of the heart-rending laments of so many. Men, women and children cry out to us from the depths of the horror that they knew. How can we fail to heed their cry? No one can forget or ignore what happened. No one can diminish its scale." Declaring that Jews and Christians "share an immense spiritual patrimony, flowing from God's self-revelation," he said:

> As Bishop of Rome and successor of the Apostle Peter, I assure the Jewish people that the Catholic Church, motivated by the Gospel law of truth and love and by no political considerations, is deeply saddened by the hatred, acts of persecution and displays of anti-Semitism directed against the Jews by Christians at any time and in any place.

Tragically, the goodwill and peace between Jews and Muslims for which the Pope had prayed at the end his "Jubilee Year" visit to the Holy City remained elusive. In September, Ariel Sharon made his provocative visit to the Haram, triggering violent protests that continued for more than two years as the al-Aqsa intifada, a campaign of suicide bombings, and Israeli military and political retaliation.

Christian Fundamentalists, the Holy Land, and Jerusalem

The Washington-based Holy Land Foundation has attributed the departure of Christians from Jerusalem to the freedom of all Palestinians being "severely compromised" by policies imposed by Israel. The Christian organization feared that if the exodus continued "it is possible they could disappear in the very land where Christ founded his church."

A contrary view held by many American Christian fundamentalists was voiced by the founder of the Christian Coalition, religious broadcaster Pat Robertson. On his *700 Club* television program and his website, he denounced the sponsors of the "roadmap to peace" as "enemies of Israel." He warned, "If the United States takes a role in ripping half of Jerusalem away from Israel and giving it to Yasser Arafat and a group of terrorists, we are going to see the wrath of God fall on [the United States]."

But other Christian leaders are in favor of the roadmap. Members of the General Assembly of the Presbyterian Church (United States) voted in favor of the roadmap. They criticized Israel for its "arbitrary arrests, detention, humiliation, torture, and harassment" of the Palestinians. And the National Council of Churches general secretary, Bob Edgar, declared, "Everyone knows that [Israel needs] to move back to the 1966 boundary lines."

The Least You Need to Know

- In 1922 Christians were 51 percent of Jerusalem's population. Today, they make up only 1.6 percent.
- Christians fled Jerusalem to avoid wars, terrorism, and harsh Israeli policies.
- Some Christians joined the Palestinian resistance movement.
- The Vatican reversed its policy against a divided Jerusalem.
- Pope John Paul II made a historic Holy Land pilgrimage in March 2000.

Chapter 23

Life in an International City

In This Chapter

- ◆ Some nations choose not to move embassies to Jerusalem
- ◆ The makeup of Jerusalem's population
- ◆ Tourism and terrorism
- ◆ Entertainment in the Holy City

Imagine what might have happened more than 200 years ago, when the capital of the United States was moved from Philadelphia to the rough new city of Washington, D.C., if the nations of the world had decided to keep their ambassadors in the comforts of the City of Brotherly Love. Picture President John Adams or his secretary of state, Thomas Jefferson, wanting to consult with the ambassador of Great Britain, France, or Spain. They would have to wait days for the summons to be delivered, and days more for the ambassador to arrive in Washington. That's exactly what happened when Israel declared Jerusalem its capital in 1967. Few nations relocated their embassies from Tel Aviv to Jerusalem.

Now put yourself in the shoes of Israel's Prime Minister Levi Eshkol in 1967, and all of his successors, who've dealt with the refusal of the United States, Great Britain, and other nations to switch their embassies from Tel Aviv to Jerusalem. While the travel time from the Mediterranean coast to the Holy City is about an hour by car, the decision to keep the world's most important diplomats from setting up shop in Jerusalem has undercut the legitimacy of the Israeli declaration that the city was rightfully theirs. Despite efforts by influential Jewish groups in the United States, as well as campaign pledges by presidential candidates of both parties to move the U.S. embassy to Jerusalem, it was still in Tel Aviv in 2003, with no sign that it would be relocated before Israel and the Palestinians settle their half-century dispute over the status of the city.

Four Decades of Changing Identity

You've read that after Israel took over Jerusalem in the Six-Day War in 1967 it launched a vast reclamation, restoration, and building program with the purpose of making Jerusalem not only a worthy capital, but also a modern international city. This physical transformation was followed by a policy of displacement of Palestinians and a program of confiscating Palestinian property in East Jerusalem and establishing new settlements in parts of the West Bank. To justify these actions, Israel cited a need for security against Palestinian attacks and terrorism and their belief that the city and all of Israel had been given to them by God.

Reverent Remarks

Israel's claim to Jerusalem is based on the words of God in this Bible passage: "Since the day I brought My people out of Egypt, I have not chosen a city in any tribe of Israel to have a temple built for My Name to be there, nor have I chosen anyone to be the leader of My people Israel. But now I have chosen Jerusalem for My Name to be there, and I have chosen David to rule My people Israel." (II Chronicles 6:5–6)

Although Jews had been the majority of the population of pre-1967 Jerusalem and Palestine, immigration from the Soviet Union and Soviet bloc nations of eastern Europe, along with that from other countries, contributed to a dramatic increase in Jewish residents. In 2002, two thirds of Jerusalem's 683,000 population were Jewish. With 18,000 babies born in that year, Jerusalem's birthrate was 13 percent of that of all of Israel.

A City of the Young and Old

A recent Israeli government study of Jerusalem's demographic and social characteristics found that young people constituted a high proportion of Jerusalem's population.

This was attributed to a high percentage of large families among the orthodox Jewish and the non-Jewish. This large number of children, the study noted, had "important implications" with regard to the public services provided for infants, children, and teenagers, as well as in the areas of education and health services.

In 1995, about 44 percent of Jerusalem's total population was under age 19, of whom approximately 13 percent were under age 4. While senior citizens constituted 8 percent of the population, in the non-Jewish sector, 52 percent was 19 years of age or younger. In the orthodox Jewish neighborhoods, over 50 percent of the population was between the ages of 0 and 19. In orthodox and non-Jewish neighborhoods combined, the population of the under-20 age group exceeded 20 percent, whereas the city average was around 13 percent.

A City of Senior Citizens

The elderly were most heavily concentrated in the center of the city, where they were as much as 20 percent of the population. This percentage declined away from the city center and was lowest in peripheral neighborhoods. There was an increase in those aged 65 or over among the Jewish population of Jerusalem. Whereas this group constituted 8.5 percent of the city's Jewish population in the mid-1980s, it rose to over 9 percent in 1991 to nearly 10 percent in 1995.

The increase in the number of senior citizens was attributed to new immigrants, a relatively high proportion of whom were seniors, and a migration among the younger population. As the rate of nonworking young and elderly increased, so did the economic burden on the working young. According to Israel's National Insurance Institute, the dependency rate in Jerusalem was as high as 99.4 per 100. (The national average was 87.7.) Statistically this meant that every person of working age in the city had dependents, either children or elderly. The ratio of children to people of working age in Jerusalem was 80.5 per 100. This was significantly higher than either the national ratio or the ratio of Israel's two other leading cities, Tel Aviv and Haifa.

A Place of Big Families

A study in the mid-1990s found that Jerusalem had a particularly high percentage of large families. The 1994 Statistical Yearbook of Jerusalem noted the average number of persons per household was 3.9, but 3.5 among the Jewish population and 5.3 among the non-Jewish population. About 23 percent of Jerusalem households had 6 or more members, while 38 percent had only 1 or 2 persons. Two studies of the ultra-orthodox neighborhoods, conducted by the Division for Strategic Planning and

Research between July 1992 and July 1993, found that the average size of families in those neighborhoods reached 7 to 7.3 persons per household. This meant that Jerusalem's educational system had to cater to a very large number of school-aged children (155,000) in 3 distinct sectors of the population (Jewish, including 95,000 nonorthodox and modern orthodox; ultra-orthodox (60,000), and Arab (23,000).

The Lifeblood of Jerusalem

Israeli Prime Minister Golda Meir once joked that she was angry with Moses because the leader of the Exodus of the Hebrews from bondage in Egypt had taken the Jews to settle on the only territory in the Middle East that didn't have oil deposits. Despite the lack of petroleum to fuel the economy, Israel in 2003 enjoyed a bigger economy than oil-rich Saudi Arabia, with the value of all goods and services valued at $100 billion a year.

Israel's economy is based on other natural resources, from copper and salt to potash and phosphates from the Dead Sea area. Others products include rubber, plastics and chemicals, and citrus fruits and vegetables that grow abundantly in former deserts made arable by irrigation. The manufacture of clothing and other household goods provides jobs for more than 46,000 people. Other exports include cut and polished diamonds, electronics, lasers, image-processing equipment, and fiber optics.

But all these industries combined were once rivaled by Israel's travel industry, with more than 2,000,000 tourists visiting the country every year, accounting for more than $3.2 billion in 2000.

In 2000, a travel guide advised prospective tourists to Jerusalem and the Holy Land that despite occasional alarming headlines about terrorism and rioting, violence "hardly ever affects visitors." Then came the second intifada.

As bursts of terrorism and Israel's violent responses scared away tourists, a booming economy that had registered a meteoric growth rate of 6.4 percent in 2000 dropped by half, to its lowest growth rate since 1953. Travel restrictions imposed on Palestinian workers contributed to a drop in production in the business sector that had shot up 8.5 percent in 2000 to a decline of 2.2 percent in 2001. The gross national product fell by 3 percent. Investment in the Israeli economy dipped 11 percent.

A significant portion of this falling off was in tourism, which was down 47 percent in the months after the start of the intifada. In 2001 the number of visitors was 1.2 million (down 51 percent), with the worried tourist industry predicting that fewer than 1 million tourists would come in 2002 and that by the end of 2002, Israel would have lost 4 million tourists at a cost of $4 billion.

In an effort to bring foreigners back, the Jerusalem Municipality advertised that Jerusalem was "not just a journey back in time." It extolled "a vibrant modern city" with lively shopping malls and cultural activities, music, theater, and significant museums. It highlighted entertainment opportunities, pubs, restaurants, and night clubs with an ambience of their own in recently renovated [Old City] quarters. It also offered the enticement of the human element of "Jews, Arabs, religious and nonreligious, rabbis and priests, ecumenical students and yeshiva students, diplomats and tourists, government employees and art students, nuns and girls in mini skirts."

This Israeli rose-colored-glasses view of Jerusalem was countered by warnings such as this statement about eating out in Jerusalem by one travel guide in 2003: "Security guards are now part of the dining scene, and by law, every restaurant has to have one at the door." It noted also that a security tax of 2 to 5 new Israel shekels per person would be added to the bill.

The guide went on to describe the "Trendy Emek Refa'im Road in the German Colony" as "home to the most stylish cafés in the city," catering to "a yuppie crowd" and "serving up the best sushi in town." In the Nahalat Shiva section, pricier restaurants competed with one another not only in food prices, but also for the best-dressed clientele. "The Ben Yehuda pedestrian promenade and adjoining Yoel Solomon Street," the travel guide continued, were "packed with inexpensive to moderate cafes and restaurants serving local, Italian, Mexican, and American fare." This was true, but it wasn't far from Ben Yehuda Street, where a Sbarro pizzeria had been the target of a suicide bomber.

Catering to a World of Tastes

In keeping with the Israeli government's design to make Jerusalem an international city, its many restaurants offer a global array of dining options. Among the many choices are, of course, *kosher* and Arab food, as well as eastern European, Italian, French, and Japanese fare.

Jerusalem also has a large number of fast-food restaurants, which serve up traditional treats such as kebabs, falafel (deep-fried mashed chick peas), shawarama (grilled pressed lamb or turkey), challah (sweet, braided bread made for holy days and the Sabbath), pitta iraquit (Jewish pita), and bourekas (baked pastry filled with goat's cheese, potato, and spinach).

What Does That Mean?

Kosher restaurants obey Judaism's dietary laws. One that serves meat won't offer dairy products, and vice versa.

And just because Israelis tend not to drink much alcohol, it doesn't mean that there's no night life. Restaurants and clubs along Ben Yehuda Street offer tables where patrons can see and be seen, although on Saturday nights it tends to be dominated by teenagers. More intimate places are in Rivlin Street and nearby Salomon Street as well in the Russian Compound. Pubs and bars offer live music and dancing.

In a Holy City You Get to Celebrate Plenty of Holy Days

Being the capital of a Jewish state, Islam's third most venerated site, and the most important city in Christendom, Jerusalem has more holidays a year when business stops or slows down than any other city. It's also a place with three calendars. The Hebrew and Islamic years are based on cycles of the moon, but Islam does not make adjustments with a quadrennial leap year. The Christian calendar is solar.

Key Jewish, Muslim, and Christian holy days are as follows:

Jewish:

> Tu Be Sheavt: Feast of the Trees (January/February)
>
> Purim: Festival of Queen Esther (February/March)

Pesach/Passover: Feast of Unleavened Bread (March/April)

Lag BeOmer: Marks the 33rd day of the year 1 B.C. when no deaths occurred during an epidemic (Spring)

Shavuot: Feast of Weeks (May/June)

Tish B'av: Mourning for the second temple (July/August)

Rosh Hashanah: New Year (September/October)

Yom Kippur: Day of Atonement (September/October)

Sukkot: Feast of Tabernacles; Exodus (September/October)

Simhat Torah: Rejoicing for the Law (September/October)

Hanukkah: Festival of Light (November/December)

Holy Facts!

The Hebrew year dates from the Jews' traditional year of the Creation (3761 B.C.). Islam counts time from the year Muhammad moved from Mecca to Medina (622 A.D.). The Christian calendar is based on the traditionally accepted year of the birth of Jesus.

Holy Facts!

Israeli state holidays are Holocaust Memorial Day (May), Memorial Day for the fallen in Israel's wars (May), and Israeli Independence Day (May).

Muslim (dates vary):

> Maulid: Muhammad's birthday

> Beginning of Ramadan: Ninth month of the calendar

> Lailat al-Kadr: The twenty-sixth day of Ramadan, celebrating the giving of the Koran

> Id al-Fitr: Last three days of Ramadan

> Id al-Adha: Sacrificial celebration

Christian:

> New Year: (January 1 for Western churches; January 14 for Eastern)

> Easter: (March/April)

> Christmas: (Western: December 25; Eastern: January 6)

Celebrating Easter in Jerusalem

No religious holiday in Jerusalem better demonstrates the meaning of *ecumenism* than Easter. In the days leading up to it, Israelis welcome and protect the Christian visitors who boost the city's and Israel's economy, and Muslims respect Christians in keeping with Islam's veneration of Jesus as a prophet. (They also profit from their visits.) As the atmosphere of Easter starts to assert itself, notes Bethlehem University professor of sociology Bernard Sabella, the stands of Arab merchants who sell souvenir items are on every street corner and in front of the souvenir shops in the Christian Quarter leading to the Church of the Holy Sepulchre. Candles of all sizes and designs are offered for sale, and local children, on Easter vacation from school, employ their freshly learned foreign words and phrases to entice pilgrims to buy souvenirs.

> **What Does That Mean?**
>
> Ecumenism is the practice of promoting cooperating and understanding among people of different faiths.

Just as Jews thronged to the second temple each year, Christian pilgrims have flooded into the Old City of Jerusalem from all over the world to commemorate Easter. The week starts with Palm Sunday. Symbolizing Jesus' entry into the city a week before the crucifixion, Christians walk from Bethphage, a village on the eastern slopes of the Mount of Olives, to the Church of St. Anne inside St. Stephen's Gate in the Old City. At the end of this procession as the palms are shaken and the Latin patriarch enters the church, Christian and Muslim boy scout troops from all parts of Palestine circle the Old City walls in colorful uniforms and wave flags as a band plays popular nationalistic tunes.

On Good Friday, thousands of pilgrims walk the Via Dolorosa, mourning the death of Jesus. Saturday is "Sabt an-Nour" (Holy Fire Saturday and Saturday of Light). The resurrection of Christ is commemorated in the ceremony of "Holy Fire" in the Holy Sepulchre. Hundreds of Cypriot, Greek, and Copts have slept overnight by the tomb in order to be among the first to receive the holy fire. Locals start joining them in the early morning as the church, the square, and rooftops become packed with crowds carrying candles and glass lanterns.

Holy Facts!

Protestants who come to Jerusalem to celebrate Easter mark the resurrection at the Garden Tomb.

Around noontime, the Greek Orthodox patriarch and his entourage proceed from his residence to the Holy Sepulchre by a staircase leading from the roof. Christian youths in one of the squares of the Christian Quarter proceed through the narrow alleys to the church shouting religious slogans. Members of old Arab Orthodox families take part by carrying embroidered banners and flags.

At the end of the procession, the patriarch is led into the chapel of the tomb. The crowd falls silent in anticipation of the appearance of Holy Light. Around 1:30 P.M., the "Light" appears and is quickly passed from one bundle of candles to another, or to lanterns, and the light spreads through the church and outside.

Home Base for Sightseeing in the Holy Land

No matter what religion a tourist observes, or if a visitor to Jerusalem is interested only in its history, there are numerous attractions of interest. Among places of interest are the following, arranged geographically in an arc from the south, eastward, and to the north.

- ◆ **Bethlehem.** In the traditional birthplace of Jesus, a few miles south of Jerusalem, it's always Christmas. The key attraction is the Church of the Nativity, where tradition places the grotto where Jesus was born and visited by three gift-bearing wise men. Surrounding shops—mostly owned by Arabs—sell Christmas cards year-round, as well as an assortment of Christian scenes and icons. Nearby is Bait Sahur. Known as "Shepherds' Fields," it's a mainly Christian village with a number of churches; it is thought to be the place where the angels appeared to inform shepherds of Jesus' birth.

♦ **Hebron.** About 15 miles south of Jerusalem, Hebron is sacred to Jews as Israel's capital before David shifted it to Jerusalem, and to Jews, Muslims, and Christians as the traditional burial site of Abraham and his wife Sarah.

♦ **Jericho.** About 20 miles northeast of Jerusalem, here Joshua is said to have brought down Jericho's walls by marching his men round and round it to the blare of trumpets. Herod the Great had his winter palace here. Nearby is the Monastery of the Temptation where Christian tradition holds that Jesus fasted for 40 days in the wilderness while resisting temptations by Satan.

Holy Facts! _____

Because religious and historical sites east, south, and north of the city are in the Palestinian West Bank, the travel restrictions imposed by Israel during the intifada have limited access to them, while areas to the west and along the Mediterranean are in Israel, with the exception of the Gaza Strip.

♦ **Cumran.** A city on the Dead Sea dating from the time of Jesus and founded by a group called the Essenes, Cumran is where the Dead Sea Scrolls were found in caves in 1947.

Holy Facts! _____

The Dead Sea is the lowest point on earth, about an hour's drive from Jerusalem.

♦ **Massada.** Originally a mountaintop fortress built by Herod the Great, the Massada was held by Zealot rebels against a Roman siege in the 66 A.D. war in which the second temple was destroyed. Rather than surrender or be killed by the Romans, the Jews killed themselves.

♦ **Tiberias.** Overlooking the Sea of Galilee and dating to the Roman times, it was and is a resort.

♦ **Meggido.** An archaeological site containing ruins of a fortress and stables built by King Solomon, the Meggido was one of the most-fought-over sites in the ancient world because it stood on vital trade routes.

What Does That Mean?

It's from **Meggido** that we get the word Armageddon, meaning the final battle between God and Satan's forces of evil.

♦ **Nazareth.** The town where Jesus grew up and site of the Church of the Annunciation, marking the place where an angel told the Virgin Mary that she would bear the Son of God.

♦ **Ramallah.** Just north of Jerusalem and a Palestinian unofficial capital and head-quarters of Yasser Arafat, it was frequently put under siege by the Israelis during the intifada. Famous for good restaurants and fine food, it's a symbol of Palestinian history, culture, and national pride.

Can Anyone Settle the Dispute Over Jerusalem?

Now that you've reached the end of the long story of Jerusalem, you're probably scratching your head and asking yourself whether it will ever live in peace. What you've read isn't exactly encouraging. In thousands of years since someone chose to settle on a hilltop with nothing to recommend it except that no one else was living there, it's been earth's most treasured and embattled place. For a reason known but to the God of three faiths, it became a city of eternal hope for Jews, birthplace of Christianity, and a sacred site of Muslims. Despite the centuries of conquests and destruction, the rise and fall of empires, desecrations, deportations, revolts, suppressions and oppression, wars, and terrorism, it's retained the name "the Holy City."

Jerusalem's political future has been placed in doubt again because of claims placed upon it by Israelis and Palestinians. With the rest of the world urging them to fashion a way to live side by side amicably, the people of three great faiths carry on life amid the walls, stones, streets, alleys, churches, synagogues, and mosques of the Old City, wondering—along with the rest of the world—if tomorrow will bring the city lasting peace.

The Least You Need to Know

♦ The United States and many other countries don't recognize Jerusalem as Israel's capital.

♦ Jerusalem's economy relies heavily on tourism.

♦ Fears of terrorism and violence have scared visitors away from Jerusalem since the fall of 2000.

♦ Israel has made Jerusalem a modern international city.

A Chronology of Jerusalem

Jewish Jerusalem (B.C.)

Date	Event
1000	King David takes Jerusalem from the Jebusites.
964	Solomon begins building the temple.
586	Nebuchadnezzar of Babylon destroys the temple and city.
539	King Cyrus lets Jews return and rebuild the temple.
332	Alexander the Great conquers Jerusalem.
313	King Ptolemy of Egypt takes the city.
169	Antiochus of Syria desecrates the temple, leading to the revolt of the Hasmoneans.
63	Pompey claims the city for the Roman Empire.
37	Herod the Great begins his rule.
19	Construction of the second temple (actually the third) commences.
4	Death of Herod.

Christian Jerusalem (A.D.)

Date	Event
4 B.C.–A.D.30	Birth and lifetime of Jesus.
30–64	Christianity is in its infancy.
	Paul carries Christianity to the Gentiles.
66–73	The First Jewish Revolt; destruction of the temple.
132–135	The Second Jewish Revolt is defeated.
135	Roman Emperor Hadrian names the rebuilt city Aelia Capitolina; Christianity's first Jerusalem church (upper room).
303	Violent persecution of Christians by Diocletian.
312–313	Emperor Constantine embraces Christianity.
326	Emperor Constantine's mother Helena finds Golgotha; Christianity flourishes in Jerusalem.
362	Christians rejoice at Jews' failure to rebuild the temple.
380–614	Christian Byzantine Empire.
614	Persians take Jerusalem, aided by Jews.
629	Emperor Heraclius recaptures the city, exiles Jews.

Islamic Jerusalem

Date	Event
570–632	Birth and life of the Prophet Mohammad.
636	Islamic conquest of Jerusalem.
638	Jews allowed to return to Jerusalem.
691	Dome of the Rock built on the Temple Mount.
750–1258	Abbasid Dynasty.
1096	Crusades begin:
	I. 1096–1099
	II. 1147–1149
1171	Saladin recaptures Jerusalem from Crusaders.
1188	Crusades resume:
	III. 1188–1192
	IV. 1202–1204
	V. 1217–1221

Date	Event
	VI. 1228–1229
	VII. 1248–1250
1291–1516	Mameluke rule.
1520–1566	Suleiman the Magnificent rules.
1566–1917	Ottoman Empire
	Jewish immigration from Europe begins.
	Theodor Herzl's Zionist *The Jewish State* (1896) published.
	First Zionist Congress convened (Switzerland, 1897).

British Mandate

Date	Events
1917	Beginning of British rule.
1922	Britain given Palestinian mandate by League of Nations.
1929	Muslim Brotherhood founded in Egypt.
1933	Hitler takes power in Germany.
1933–1939	Jewish flight from Nazis.
1939	British White Paper on limiting immigration.
1939–1945	World War II; the Holocaust; Israeli-Palestinian struggles.
1947	United Nations proposes Jewish and Palestinian states; British withdraw; Israel declares independence (May 14); Five Arab states attack Israel (May 15).
1948	First Israel-Arab war; Jerusalem divided.
1949	First Israeli parliament (Knesset) elected.
1956	Israel, France, Britain defeat Egypt in Sinai War.
1963	Founding of Palestine Liberation Organization.
1967	Six-Day War; Israel takes all of Jerusalem; United Nations adopts Resolution 242 calling for two states.
1973	Yom Kippur War.
1977	Egyptian President Anwar Sadat visits Jerusalem.
1978	Camp David accords.
1979	Israeli-Egyptian peace treaty.
1981	Sadat assassinated.

continues

British Mandate (continued)

Date	Events
1987	First intifada; widespread violence and terrorism.
1989	Mass migration of Soviet Jews begins.
1991	First Gulf War; Iraq fires Scud missiles at Israel; Madrid Peace Conference; Oslo accords.
1993	Formation of Palestinian Authority.
1994	Yasser Arafat, Shimon Peres, and Yitzhak Rabin awarded Nobel Peace Prize.
1995	Palestinian Council elected; Rabin assassinated.
1998	Israel celebrates fiftieth anniversary.
2000	Camp David summit (Arafat, Ehud Barak, Bill Clinton) ends in failure; Ariel Sharon visits Temple Mount; Palestinians riot; wave of terrorism scares away tourists and severely damages Jerusalem's economy.
2000–2003	Al-Aqsa intifada; suicide bombings; Israel imposes restrictions on Palestinians, isolates Arafat; Mahmoud Abbas (Abu Mazen) elected prime minister of Palestinian Authority.
2003	United States proposes "roadmap to peace"; cease-fire declared; Israel begins limited withdrawals from Gaza and Bethlehem; whether the roadmap succeeds remains an open question.

Mayors of Jerusalem

Term	Mayor
1899–1907	Yussef Diya'audin Din al-Khalidi (Pasha)
1907–1909	Faidi al-Alami
1909–1917	Selim Effendi al-Husseini
1917–1918	Aref al-Dajani
1918–1920	Musa Qassem al-Husseini
1920–1934	Regheb Nashashibi
1934–1937	Hussein Fakhri al-Khalidi
1938–1944	Mustafa al-Khalidi
1944–1945	Daniel Auster
1948–May 1948	Municipal Committee
Aug. 1948–Jan. 1949	Military governor

Term	Mayor
Jan. 1949–1950	Daniel Auster
1950–1952	Shlomo Zalman Shragai
1952–1955	Yitzhak Kariv
1955–Nov. 1, 1959	Gershon Agron
Nov. 1959–1965	Mordechai Ish-Shalom
1965–1993	Yeddy Kollek
1993–2003	Ehud Olmert
2003–	Uri Lupoliansk

Mayors of East Jerusalem

Term	Mayor
1948–1950	Anwar al-Khatib
1950–1951	Aref al-Aref
1951–1952	Hanna Atallah
1952–1955	Omar Wa'ari
1955–1957	Municipal Committee
1957–1967	Ruhi al-Khatib
1967–1999	Faisal Abdul Qader al-Husseini

Prime Ministers of Israel

Term	Prime Minister
1948–1954	David Ben-Gurion
1954–1955	Moshe Sharett
1955–1963	David Ben-Gurion
1963–1969	Levi Eshkol
1969–1974	Golda Meir
1974–1977	Yitzhak Rabin
1977–1983	Menachem Begin
1983–1984	Yitzhak Shamir
1984–1986	Shimon Peres

continues

Prime Ministers of Israel (continued)

Term	Prime Minister
1986–1992	Yitzhak Shamir
1992–1995	Yitzhak Rabin
1995–1996	Shimon Peres
1996–1999	Benjamin Netanyahu
1999–2001	Ehud Barak
2001–	Ariel Sharon

Prime Ministers of the Palestinian Authority

Term	Prime Minister
Mar.–Sept. 2003	Mahmoud Abbas
Nominated Sept. 2003	Ahmed Qurei

Glossary

Abraham   Biblical patriarch of Jews and Muslims.

al-Aqsa   Mosque on Haram al-Sharif/Temple Mount; name given to a Palestinian uprising in 2000 (see *intifada*).

Al-Quds   Arab/Islamic name for Jerusalem.

Balfour Declaration   British pledge of a Jewish state made in 1910.

caliph   Islamic ruler.

Calvary   A rocky hill outside of Jerusalem where Romans crucified criminals; it is here that Jesus was crucified. Also known as Golgotha, it's within the Church of the Holy Sepulchre.

Canaan   Biblical region now known as Israel/Palestine.

Cardo   Excavated ancient Roman street in Jerusalem.

Constantine   Byzantine Emperor, converted to Christianity.

crusaders   Christian armies formed to seize control of Jerusalem from Muslims.

Diaspora   Jews exiled by Babylon; Jews living outside Israel.

Dome of the Rock   Islamic shrine in Jerusalem; also known as "the Noble Sanctuary," built between 688 and 691.

Garden Tomb   Protestant alternative site of the tomb of Jesus, located outside the Old City wall.

Golgotha   See *Calvary.*

Hagannah   Post-World War II Israeli liberation organization.

Hamas   Palestinian opposition group providing social services in Gaza while waging terrorism against Israel.

Haram al-Sharif   Meaning "noble sanctuary," the name that Muslims have given to the site of the Dome of the Rock (Jews call the same site the Temple Mount). Both religions identify this area on Mount Moriah as the site where Abraham offered up his son in sacrifice.

Holy Sepulchre   Traditional tomb of Jesus located in the Church of the Holy Sepulchre.

intifada   Arabic for "shaking off"; Palestinian uprisings in 1987 and 2000 ("al-Aqsa.")

Irgun   Violent anti-British Jewish group that worked to oust the British in the period preceding Israeli sovereignty.

Islam   The name of the Muslim religion; Arab for "surrender."

Islamic Jihad   Palestinian terrorist group.

Jebusites   People defeated by King David when he took Jerusalem.

kloitzel   Small, disorganized synagogue.

madrasas   Islamic schools.

Martyrium   First church located on the site of Golgotha.

minaret   Tower of mosque from which the call to prayer is made.

Mount Moriah   The hill on which Jerusalem was built.

Mufti   Islamic municipal ruler.

Muslims   People who accept the Islamic way of life.

Old City   Ancient, walled Jerusalem.

piulist   A hard-headed disputant in rabbinical arguments.

Quartet   How the four parties—the United States, the United Nations, European Union, and Russia—that are proponents of the "Roadmap to Peace" are referred to.

Rushalimum   The first known name for Jerusalem.

second temple   Solomon's temple, destroyed by Romans in 70 A.D.

Sephardic/Sephardim   Jewish exiles from the Spanish Inquisition.

shofar   Hollowed-out ram's horn sounded on Jewish high holy days.

souk   Also "souq." A market bazaar.

Stern Gang   Jewish terrorist group, off-shoot of the Irgun.

synagogue   Jewish house of worship; Greek for "convocation."

Talmud   Book of interpretation of Hebraic law.

Temple Mount   Site of the Jews' first and second temples and present site of the Dome of the Rock and al-Aqsa Mosque.

ultra-orthodox   Jews who strictly follow Hebraic law and believe only the Messiah can rebuild the temple.

Via Dolorosa   Old City Street believed to be the route Jesus walked to the crucifixion marked with "stations of the cross."

Western Wall   Only visible remains of the second temple; Judaism's holiest site. (Also called the Wailing Wall.)

Yad Vashem   Holocaust memorial in Jerusalem.

Yerushalayim   Israeli name for Jerusalem.

Yiddish   Eastern European Jewish language, from the Hebrew word "yehudi," meaning "Judean."

Zealots   Jewish rebels in Roman times.

Zion   The land of Israel.

Zionists   Proponents of a Jewish state in Palestine.

Appendix

C

Further Reading

Armstrong, Karen. *Jerusalem: One City, Three Faiths.* New York: Knopf, 1996.

Atkinson, Rich. *Crusade.* New York: Houghton Mifflin Co., 1993.

Bard, Mitchell G. *The Complete Idiot's Guide to the Middle East Conflict.* Indianapolis: Alpha Books, 2002.

Becker, Jillian. *The PLO.* New York: St. Martin's Press, 1984.

Begin, Menachem. *The Revolt.* New York: EP Dutton, 1978.

Churchill, Randolph S., and Winston S. *The Six-Day War.* New York: Penguin, 1967.

Eban, Abba. *My Country: The Story of the Modern Middle East.* New York: Random House, 1972.

Gilbert, Martin. *Jerusalem in the Twentieth Century.* New York: John Wiley & Sons, Inc., 1996.

Hourani, Albert. *A History of the Arab People.* New York: Warner Books, 1992.

Josephus, Flavius. *The Complete Works of Josephus*. New York: Holt, Rinehart and Winston, 1974.

Kollek, Teddy. *Jerusalem*. Washington, D.C.: Washington Institute for Near East Policy, 1990.

Laqueur, Walter, and Barry Rubin, editors. *The Israel-Arab Reader*. New York: Penguin Putnam, 1969.

Lewis, Bernard. *Islam and the West*. New York: Oxford University Press, 1994.

McDowall, Neville. *Palestine and Israel: The Uprising and Beyond*. California: University of California Press, 1990.

Meir, Golda. *My Life*. New York: G.P. Putnam's Sons, 1975.

Netanyanhu, Benjamin. *A Place Among the Nations: Israel and the World*. New York: Warner Books, 1998.

O'Brien, Connor Cruise. *The Siege: The Saga of Israel and Zionism*. New York: Touchstone Books, 1986.

Onma, Nick, and Ferdie MacDonald, editors. *Jerusalem and the Holy Land*. London: Dorling Kindersley Publishing, Inc., 2000.

Prag, Kay. *Israel and the Palestinian Territories*. London: A & C Black Publishers Limited, 2002.

Sachar, Howard. *A History of Israel: From the Rise of Zionism to Our Time*. New York: Alfred A. Knopf, 1998.

Siegel, Richard, and Carl Rheins, editors. *The Jewish Almanac*. New York: Bantam, 1980.

Wasserstein, Bernard. *Divided Jerusalem*. New Haven: Yale University Press, 2002.

Index

F

G

J

P

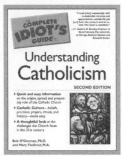

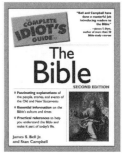

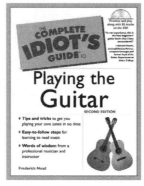

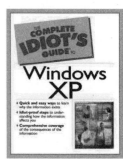